ADAM,
THE ALTAIC RING
&
"THE CHILDREN OF THE SUN"

by
James R. Granger, Jr.

URAEUS PUBLISHING, INC.
Washington, D.C.

Library of Congress Cataloging-in-Publication Data

Granger, James R., 1944-
 Adam, the Altaic ring &"the children of the sun."

   Bibliography: p.
   Includes index.
     1. Race--Miscellanea. 2. Bible. O.T. --Criticism,
interpretation, etc.--Miscellanea. 3. Civilization--Miscellanea. 4.
History--Philosophy--Miscellanea.
   I. Title II. Title Adam, the Altaic ring, and
"the children of the sun."
BF1999.G684   1987   909   87-51202
ISBN 0-945023-00-6 (PBK.)

+---+
| OTHER BOOKS BY JAMES R. GRANGER, JR |
| -MO' |
| -WHERE DID THOSE DUDES COME FROM? |
| -A BLACK MAN'S BIBLE |
+---+

ADAM, THE ALTAIC RING & "THE CHILDREN OF THE SUN"
by
James R. Granger, Jr.

Copyright 1987
by
Uraeus Publishing, Inc.
P.O. Box 50058
Washington, D.C. 20091

DEDICATION

This book is dedicated to all the parents and teachers
who teach children to look up unfamiliar words in a dictionary,
to the children who learn the lesson and to the beautiful
future that those children will inherit.

FOREWORD
SOMEBODY(?) SPEAKS WITH FORKED TONGUE

Information Please
Excerpts from the press briefing conducted by White House spokesman Martin Fitzwater yesterday...

Q: ...What is the policy [on press relations regarding the Persian Gulf]?

Fitzwater: The political judgment at this point is that in this case, we are not prepared to confirm the incident [a U.S. plane reportedly fired two missiles at an Iranian aircraft] or to discuss it or to release any information about it...

Q: Hasn't it been confirmed on background at the Pentagon?

Fitzwater: I don't know whether it has. I know that [Defense Secretary Caspar W.] Weinberger refused to confirm it on the record this morning, and I cannot do anything different...

Q: Can you say that the president approved or in any way was involved in the discussions [about] the handling of this information? When was he informed as to this incident, whether he believes it is a non-incident?

Fitzwater: I have no idea about the information discussions. The president was informed soon after the incident happened.

Q: Which incident?

Fitzwater: ...The incident that I'm not confirming.

—*The Washington Post,* 8/12/87, p. A20.

..."We've got to call a spade a spade and a perverted human being a perverted human being."...

—U.S. Sen. Jesse Helms, (R.-N.C.) 1987

ADAM,
THE ALTAIC RING
&
"THE CHILDREN OF THE SUN"

TABLE OF CONTENTS

CHARTS AND ILLUSTRATIONS

INTRODUCTION

Approximately 6,000 years ago, *circa* 4000 B.C., a cataclysm occurred that changed the social history of this planet and continues to affect the course of humanity. What happened? How did it happen? Why did it happen? These are questions, each of which represents a puzzle with many pieces. Some pieces, because of the very nature of our natural history, might never be found. However, it is this author's opinion that, through the work of many scholars, it is now possible to tell a story that needs telling. This book is a synthesis, with some original input, of the historical record. The focus is on the time period since the previously mentioned cataclysmic event. However, it is necessary to look at the period immediately prior to that event in order to measure the impact of the cataclysm. Therefore we will be looking at civilizations dating back to 10,000 B.C., but we will focus on the events after 4000 B.C.

The reader should understand that the author is an American black man. With that understanding, the reader might be assisted in assessing any prejudices evident in the interpretations of the historical events chronicled in the subsequent chapters of this book. There is no doubt in my mind that some will find my interpretations, shall we say, "unorthodox." I agree with that assessment.

However, "unorthodox" does not necessarily mean untrue. All advances come from the "unorthodox." If somebody hadn't been "unorthodox," no progress would have ever taken place.

Some will consider this book in the light of serious history. Others might view it in a different light. To those in the latter category, I simply say, "Find the errors." If you do that, then everybody will benefit. This book is intended as serious history.

Organization and Conventions:

There are six substantive chapters after this introduction. The first chapter sets the natural history backdrop to the subsequently discussed cultural and social histories. The rationale for selecting the natural history backdrop from the many available theories is presented.

Chapter 2 examines the environment, social conditions and culture in Africa prior to the aforementioned cataclysmic event. Chapter 3 examines the same aspects of Indo-European society. Chapter 4 traces the ethnic migrations of various groups of humanity.

Chapters 5 and 6 are extrapolations on the historical patterns identified in Chapters 2 through 4. Chapter 7 is a summary of the findings.

Many sources are used to document the assertions offered in this work. One key resource is the Judeo-Christian *Bible,* which is used as a historical tool. The reader might find it helpful to keep a version of that book handy. The essential references are presented within this book, but supplementary material is incorporated by reference for simplicity and economy.

This book is written in an engaged style. Humor is injected from time to time. The reader should not construe these elements as representing a lack of seriousness on the part of the author. The author believes that learning should be fun. The objective of these elements is to hold interest while informing: An unread message is no message.

Megahistory:

This book is written at the megahistory level. What is megahistory?

> ... "the history of the world is the history, not of individuals, but of groups, not of nations, but of races, and he who ignores or seeks to override the race idea in human history ignores and overrides the central idea in all history. What, then, is a race? It is a vast family of human beings, generally of common blood and language, always of common history, traditions and impulses, who are both voluntarily and involuntarily striving together for the accomplishment of certain more or less vividly conceived ideals of life." ...
>
> W.E.B. Du Bois, 1897.
> Quoted in *W.E.B. Du Bois Speaks,* edited
> by Dr. Philip S. Foner, Pathfinder Press,
> New York, 1970, p. 75.

The above excerpt gives the reader the definition of megahistory, and, *en passant,* illustrates the method of presenting direct references in this book. Excerpts from other works are reduced and indented from the text. The referenced source documents are shown at the end of each excerpt. The page number in the references refer to the pages in the original works on which the excerpts begin. Quotation marks are not used, unless the excerpt involves someone speaking. The intention is not to deceive. To these eyes, the reduction and indentation mark the excerpts more clearly than quotation marks. The intention is to avoid the cumbersome convention of quotes within quotes, and sometimes within quotes. The convention of indented excerpts also avoids those nasty little rascals called footnotes. All of the data on the reference material is presented in the flow of the document, and the reader does not have to relocate the spot where he or she was diverted to the footnote. Unorthodox, yes. But I hope that you find the conventions followed in this book allow ideas to flow while maintaining strict accountability for authorship.

The Limitations of "Norms:"

During World War II, Englishmen found their normal social boundaries disrupted by the necessities of war. It became necessary to go to areas in England that were not necessarily in one's normal circle. It became necessary to speak to and work beside people with whom, in less trying times, one did not necessarily come in contact.

Londoners found that sometimes translators were required to speak to their own countrymen, who lived only a few miles from London, because of the differences in English dialects. The Londoners and their country relations both spoke English; but there is English, and there is English. Anybody who has been to England recently could have heard differences in "English," without even leaving London. "Henry," in BBC English, is quite a bit different from "Enery" in Cockney, East End English. English is spoken in such distant places as Sydney, Australia; Mobile, Alabama and Kingston, Jamaica. All of these languages are different, and yet all retain common themes. All are called "English."

In subsequent chapters, cultures of large groups of people will be examined. Descriptions such as "black culture" and "European culture" will be used. As it is with "English," these descriptions represent themes and do not represent an accurate description of any group within the culture. The descriptions certainly do not describe individuals.

However, to view the historical record over such a long period of time, it is necessary that we accept the limitations of "norms" for the sake of economy and focus. Rather than submit to the tyranny of qualifying statements, it is this author's opinion that it is preferable to specify the limitations of "norms" at the outset. Do not fall into the trap of, "Sister Sukie isn't like that, and therefore the [an] assertion is wrong!" Sister Sukie's peculiarities are not relevant to a discussion about the similarities among millions of Sister Sukies.

4

The Responsibility of Historians:

It is often said that, "He who wins the war gets to write the history books." That is undeniably a true statement, but it isn't the whole truth. The empires that have won the wars and justified their conquests with politicized history books have sown the seeds of their own destruction. How? They taught their children false premises about themselves and about others. If one starts with false premises, one necessarily ends with false policy. It's *The Law of Truth or Consequences*. Some think that "Truth or Consequences" is just a game. They are wrong. It is the fundamental natural law of survival.

The history presented in this book is the truth as I see it. If I am in error, one needs only to provide a convincing case against my arguments. Name calling is not productive for anybody, unless "the shoe fits." If the shoe fits any of us, we just have to "wear it." The consequence of not wearing the shoe that fits is to doom our children to have somebody else write a politicized history about them:

...."All empires must fall."...

Ricardo, a Salvadoran guerrilla leader.
quoted in *The Washington Post,* 11/7/85, p. A35.

Many variations on Ricardo's wisdom are apparent from the historical record: "One Reb is worth ten Yankees!" "Slavs and Jews are subhuman!" The more the temporary victors deluded themselves with false premises, the shorter the time span of their empires. How long did the "Thousand-year Reich" last? Answer: Twelve years!

The historical patterns, as perceived by this author, are traced to current times in the last three chapters of this book. However, to take advantage of poignant moments in the historical record and to build to the conclusions, relationships to today's events are identified periodically throughout the walk through history. Bear with them. Their purpose will become apparent, if you read this book in sequence. You cannot skip around and understand the flow of history. History is a river, not a punctuated series of glacial lakes.

If you persevere, you will find out the answers to such questions as why women, plants and animals were created twice in the *Book of Genesis.* You will find out the symbolism of the Sphinx. The real nature of Noah's ark will also be identified for your consideration. I hope that this book engenders discussion. Readers are not asked to accept what is written in this book as fact. Instead, readers are asked to consider what is written here, read the referenced works and anything else that is germane, think, and then follow the advice of the brilliant teacher, Jesus:

... "Why do you not judge for yourselves what is right?"

Luke 12:57

The question was, and is, rhetorical.

It is now time to look at the possible natural history backdrops to the play, of many acts, called megahistory.

Chapter 1

THE NATURAL HISTORY

The physical environment is the backdrop for all history. Dinosaurs lived and died in particular environments. Humanity has lived through ice ages and climates much warmer than today's. Roaches seem to have seen it all. However, nobody can objectively deny that the physical environment plays a strong role in the waxing and waning of species, including the human species.

Recognizing the fundamental role of environment on social history, any serious history that deals with periods of time which transcend environmental changes must establish an environmental backdrop. As it is a fundamental precept in this book that more than one significant environmental change has occurred during the period of interest (since *circa* 10,000 B.C.), a natural history backdrop must be established for the social and cultural discussions. This chapter examines the rationale for selecting the natural history backdrop to the play called megahistory.

For simplicity and brevity, only three possible theories of natural history will be examined. The excluded theories of natural history are essentially permutations of these primary theories. The pros and cons associated with the primary theories are generally applicable to the permutations. The three theories of natural history that will be examined are (1) The Literal Biblical Theory, (2) The Newton-Darwin Theory and (3) The Velikovsky Theory.

The Literal Biblical Theory:

The first five books of the Judeo-Christian *Bible* are called the *Pentateuch,* or the *Books of Moses.* Most biblical scholars agree that these books were written (or at least conceived in present form) in the 15th century B.C. However, the *Pentateuch* includes a history of the Hebrew people back to "the Creation," allegedly the creation of the universe by the god of Israel.

The geneologies and the longevities of the Hebrew patriarchs who are described in the *Pentateuch* provide, if literally interpreted, a means for dating "the Creation." The date of "the Creation," so calculated by many biblical scholars, is 4000 B.C., plus or minus a few years due to calendar variations and minor calculation differences.

If one accepts the Mosaic dating of "the Creation" literally, many problems immediately present themselves. It is known that people and civilizations existed before 4000 B.C. We know that other life forms existed on this planet before man. Scientists have dated the earth at several billion years old. Indeed, the Israeli government has dated the city of Jericho at 8000 B.C. This dating exceeds the time available from a literal interpretation of the Mosaic chronology by 4,000 years.

European cultures have adopted four primary methods of dealing with this apparent conflict between their secular and religious information. One method, the purely secular approach, is to reject the *Pentateuch*. Another method, the fundamentalist approach, is to reject secular science. A third means of reconciliation is figurative interpretation of the *Books of Moses*. The fourth method of reconciliation is the most common: Don't think; watch soap operas.

Since this author doesn't believe that the early Jews or any other people would simply write to be writing, and certain events in the *Books of Moses* can be traced to events documented by secular science, complete rejection of the *Books of Moses* is not indicated. A figurative interpretation still yields certain problems. Notably, the *Books of Moses* provide an incomplete history of the planet as indicated by secular sources, other theologies and mother wit. There is not a single dinosaur or ice age mentioned in the *Books of Moses*.

Conclusion? "The Creation," as described in *Genesis,* is apparently a significant event, but not literally the beginning of time. The *Books of Moses* provide a historical tool for assessing some developments since the significant event that occurred approximately 6,000 years ago.

The Newton-Darwin Theory:

During the 19th century A.D., Charles Darwin shocked the Judeo-Christian world with his publication of *The Origin of Species By Means of Natural Selection or the Preservation of Favored Races in the Struggle for Life.* The full title of Darwin's work is not usually rendered in Newspeak. In any case, Mr. Darwin had the temerity to suggest in that book that species evolve by a process of "random mutations" and "natural selection," or "survival of the fittest."

According to Darwin, the various species of plant and animal life produce random mutations from time to time (agent unknown—the żeitgeist maybe), and the mutated lifeforms—over time—become different species from their unmutated parent forms. The mutants and their unmutated parent forms become incapable of procreation with one another. When these mutations are blessed with survival equipment (longer teeth, etc.) that is superior to the parents' equipment, the mutations gradually replace the parent forms because they are more "fit" to win the competition for food and procreation rights. New, more "fit" species are thus created—according to Mr. Darwin.

The environment implicit in Darwin's theory was essentially static over long periods of time. In Darwin's 19th century, the earth and other heavenly bodies were moving merrily along their prescribed orbits as dictated *solely* by the mechanics of Sir Isaac Newton. Wasn't it always so? Any changes in climate had taken place in the eons of the murky past. Sufficient time was *assumed* for the "random mutations" to take place and the slow replacement of the less "fit" species by the more "fit."

Darwin's theory had many problems. First, it was in conflict with the Judeo-Christian scriptures. The pre-Darwin Judeo-Christian conflicts with secular science (remember Galileo?) were again unleashed. Darwin's theory was, in fact, in direct contradiction to some real substance of the literally interpreted scriptures. God could not have created all the animals of the earth in a single day, if the animals were still evolving. God could not have created man separate from the animals, if man descended from the apes. "The Scopes Monkey Trial" and the so-called "Scopes II" case are manifestations of the theological/secular conflict that has plagued European society since at least the time of Socrates.

The conflict with Judeo-Christian theology was not the only problem encountered by Mr. Darwin. His theory was internally inconsistent. The static environment over long periods of time (that was *assumed*) implied a peaceful solar system. No perturbations in the heavens could have affected earth because there were no environmental changes to speak of—Darwin's mutations were *random*. If there were no celestial disturbances, how did the ice ages (of which Darwin knew) evolve? What was the agent of change? If the agent was terrestial, when did it go away? Newton's mechanics certainly apply to the terrestial plane. Nothing physical happens without a force.

The physical evidence also contradicted the prerequisite long periods of tranquility. Darwin himself observed that the western coastline of South America appears to have been elevated in recent times. Darwin was perplexed because there was physical evidence that whole species of apparently "fit" plants and animals became extinct quite suddenly, not over long periods of time as he had postulated. Mammoths were found in Siberia with tropical plants in their mouths and stomachs. The mammoths had died and been frozen so suddenly that their flesh was eatable, and was eaten, in the 19th century A.D. Darwin could not explain why mammoths became extinct and elephants survived, mammoths being every bit as "fit" as elephants for survival.

To this day, there is no documentation of a single species producing a survivable random mutation that is incapable of procreation with its unmutated parent form. Quite frankly, it would be difficult for such a thing to happen. For Darwin's theory to work, either all mutations (to new species) would have to be hermaphrodites capable of reproducing by themselves, or male and female mutations of the same species would have to "randomly" mutate in close enough proximity to get on with the business of propogating the new, more "fit" species. The mutated males and females would also have to "randomly" mutate in close enough genetic proximity to procreate. Mutations happening without an agent present some problems for *real* scientists also. People who accept Darwin have forgotten Newton.

Conclusion? Darwin's theory found a degree of acceptance for reasons that exclude anything that can be objectively described as "scientific." The political reasons for the acceptance of Darwin's theory and other pseudo-science will be examined later in this book, but we are still without a credible and comprehensive natural history. Enter Velikovsky.

The Velikovsky Theory:

With a single hypothesis, Immanuel Velikovsky unlocked the key to understanding the earth's past. That hypothesis was that electromagnetism plays a role in the movements and orientations of all heavenly bodies, including, of course, the earth.

Today, over thirty-five years after Velikovsky published *Worlds in Collision* in 1950, the idea that electromagnetism plays a role, indeed a significant role, in the movements and orientations of heavenly bodies seems trite. But in 1950, the mechanics of Newton reigned alone with only a few quiet challenges. The accepted dogma of 1950 was that Newton's laws of gravitation and inertia were sufficient to explain all celestial movements. Electromagnetism played *no role*. In 1950, one had to have faith in Velikovsky's hypothesis and his logic built on that hypothesis. The requirement for faith was soon eliminated. Empirical data eliminated the requirement. In 1955, radio emissions (electromagnetic force) from Jupiter were announced. In 1957, the Van Allen radiation belts around the earth were discovered. Space probes confirmed the high temperature on Venus that Velikovsky had predicted, contrary to the accepted dogma of 1950. The Mariner 2 probe identified the retrograde and earth-synchronous rotation of Venus, phenomena that are, at best, difficult to explain with exclusively Newtonian theories on the origin and behavior of the solar system. Whole galaxies have been observed colliding. Again, that is very difficult to explain using only Newton's laws. Radio emissions from pulsars are common knowledge today. For a more comprehensive look at these issues read *Worlds in Collision* and *Velikovsky Reconsidered,* but are we to believe that these forces have no role in the universe?

To accept *only* Newton, one has to reject Newton. Electromagnetism is force, and force mandates a reaction. But Newton didn't know about electromagnetism, and galaxies colliding suggest that Sir Isaac's mechanics alone are insufficient to explain the movements and orientations of celestial bodies.

Prior to 1950, several scientists, including Enrico Fermi, had postulated theories about the presence of electromagnetic forces in space. Velikovsky's generally rejected contribution was to synthesize such information and to relate the physical science to the recorded history on earth. For that significant contribution, we now see Immanuel Velikovsky as a recognized giant in our children's textbooks. Right?

Try to find the name in your child's science or history book. Why isn't it there? Merit rules in the United States, doesn't it? Velikovsky was proven right on the essentials of his theory, wasn't he?

If there was ever a classic example of the mythical nature of the American society of "merit," the Velikovsky affair was it. Velikovsky's publisher was threatened with a boycott by "authorities" on the accepted dogma. Fortunately, Velikovsky's publisher had the courage to print anyway, and Velikovsky's books have gone through many printings. His name is still absent from most American textbooks, however. What did the "authorities" hope to accomplish with their threatened boycott?

These wizards, like the great and wonderful Oz, were anxious, for many reasons, to protect their auras of infalliblity and other perceived personal advantages. Science? Society? The future? Their own children? All were of little consequence. The wizards didn't want to entertain Velikovsky's ideas on their "merits" or lack thereof. Velikovsky was given the modern hemlock. He was ignored and "trashed."

>...What the Velikovsky affair made crystal clear...is that the theories of science may be held not only for the truth they embody, but because of the vested interests they represent for those who hold them...
>
>Editorial, *The Daily Princetonian,* 2/64.

What did Velikovsky's theory imply that was so dangerous? For openers, one has to understand what Velikovsky wrote, and readers of this book are strongly urged to read *Worlds in Collision* and *Earth in Upheaval.* The books do not lend themselves to summarization. Out of necessity, an attempt will be made here, but there is no substitute for reading the original works. They are available in any good library or bookstore.

Building on the then hypothesis that electromagnetism plays a significant role in the behavior of all heavenly bodies, Velikovsky was able to provide documentation of worldwide cataclysms in recorded history through analysis of the written and oral histories of people around the world (*Worlds in Collision*); and analysis of empirical data and scientific theories (*Earth in Upheaval*).

Rather than the long periods of calm that Darwin *assumed,* Velikovsky *documented,* in detail, two worldwide cataclysms in recent history: one in the 15th century B.C. ("the plagues of *Exodus*") and one beginning in the 8th century B.C. ("the commotion of Uzziah" and the celestial prodigies described in *The Iliad*). These cataclysms were brought about by the near collision of the earth with other large celestial bodies and electromagnetic disturbances associated with the near contacts. In some cases, small fragments of the celestial bodies actually fell on the earth. In some cases, the earth was turned over, with the north and south poles exchanging places. The cataclysms were frequently accompanied by poisonous and/or choking gasses such as evidently killed the Siberian mammoths, many Egyptians—and many Hebrews:

>...The rabbinical tradition, contradicting the spirit of the Scriptural narrative, states that during the plague of darkness the vast majority of the

Israelites perished and that only a small fraction of the original Israelite population of Egypt was spared to leave Egypt. Forty-nine out of fifty Israelites are said to have perished in this plague.*...

*Targum Yerushalmi, *Exodus Mekhilta d'rabbi Simon ben Jokai* 10:23; (1905), p. 38.

Immanuel Velikovsky, *Worlds in Collision,*
Pocket Books, New York, 1977, p. 74.
Originally published in 1950.

...and there was a thick darkness in all the land of Egypt three days...

Exodus 11:22

"A *thick* darkness???"

An earlier cataclysm ("the Deluge" or "the flood of Noah") was mentioned, but details of that cataclysm and earlier cataclysms alluded to by Velikovsky were evidently edited out of the published versions of Velikovsky's books. To my knowledge, details of those earlier cataclysms were never published.

But what was so dangerous? Certainly Galileo, Darwin and many other scientists and pseudo-scientists had run afoul of the Judeo-Christian dogma. Velikovsky was just one more in a long line. But Velikovsky threatened secular as well as theological privileges.

If 98% (forty-nine out of fifty) of the Hebrews died in the so-called "plague of darkness," then selection by God could not really be all that attractive.

Ordinary pain? The popular Christian rendition of the scriptures had already taken the mantle of the select from the Hebrews anyway. What was the big deal? The big deal was that the Christian world had never denied the original divine selection of the Hebrews. Christians asserted only that the divine selection had changed. Christians (narrowly defined gentiles of the Hebrew literature) became the select and enjoyed the amazing or mysterious grace of God:

...Pope John Paul II, in an anniversary pronouncement, terms Augustine the "common father of our Christian civilization."...Augustine...taught salvation by God's mysterious grace, not by good works...

Time, 9/29/86, p. 76.

If there were never any "chosen people," the mantle of the select could not be transferred. Although there is evidence which suggests that Velikovsky went to some lengths to protect "vested interests" himself (the point will be examined later in this book), what he did write was a clear and present danger to "vested interests." In the East Wing of European civilization, Velikovsky would have been exiled and/or summarily shot. The West Wing has used that brutishness as a propaganda tool, and the West Wing's techniques are at first more delicate—but don't tread too long, witness Dr. King's murder.

The West Wing's lies are much more artistic. They have been used to control populations from Singapore to Lagos to Wilkes-Barre to Watts, but they are still lies, requiring "chosen people," "master races" and/or "mysterious grace."

Captive black, brown—and white—audiences around the world are reminded constantly of the divine authorization for exploitation. Holy Mother Church, not only said little or nothing on the issues, but played a key role. Many priests (Catholic and Protestant) in Africa and the Americas were slavers and shared in the booty:

> ...The Portuguese Christianization of the Kongo created something more than chaos. It was a revolting mess, no matter from what angle it is viewed. To begin with, priests were not only among the leading slave traders, but they also owned ships to carry the "black cargoes" to distant lands. Priests also had their harems of black slave girls, some having as many as twenty each. They were called "house servants" by these "holy fathers."...
>
> Chancellor Williams, *The Destruction of Black Civilization*, Third World Press, Chicago, 1976, p. 269.

If divine sanction failed to rationalize exploitation, there was always the rationale of "white supremacy." It was in the nature of things. "Social" Darwinism (racism) preceded "scientific" Darwinism by many centuries, but privilege under any banner requires "chosen people" or "master races" who, like James Bond, are taught and licensed to kill—with or without divine sanction. Velikovsky's challenge to "scientific" Darwinism was a clear and present danger to "social" Darwinism such as illustrated in the ideas of the following prominent European philosophers:

> ...to have their taste of blood like puppies...
>
> Plato (on why children should be taken to war)

> ...The strong men, the masters, regain the pure conscience of a beast of prey; monsters filled with joy, they can return from a fearful succession of murder, arson, rape and torture with the same joy in their hearts, the same contentment in their souls, as if they had indulged in some students' rag. When a man is capable of commanding, when he is by nature a "master,"

when he is violent in act and gesture, of what importance are treaties to him? ...

   Friedrich Whilhelm Nietzsche

...Man must rise or fall, He must win and rule or lose and serve, be the anvil or the hammer...

   Johann Wolfgang von Goethe

"Diplomats" in European societies are trained on such perverted nonsense, and, consequently, they have no chance of bringing peace. They have no chance because they cannot (or will not) see that beasts of prey, like lions, hunt to eat and otherwise try to avoid fighting. Lions try to frighten their enemies and fight tenaciously usually only when they are hungry, or their boundaries of respect are crossed. Lions also have the mother wit to fight (physically) when they can win or when their survival is threatened and flight is not possible. Two or three wild dogs can, and do, run off lions.

Therefore, there is nothing to suggest that lions *enjoy* killing, only eating. I wonder if the above philosophers knew that lionesses do most of the hunting? Did Richard-the-Lionhearted know? Did anyone (including Herr Nietzsche) ever see a lion, a beast of prey, "jump bad" with a vegetarian elephant? Until such time as that phenomenon is documented as a normal event, treaties will have no value to diplomats trained on Plato, Nietzsche, Goethe *et al*:

...Instead [former CIA director, William J.] Casey is said to have embraced and defended a paramilitary program pursuing the vague, protracted goal of pressuring the Sandinistas.

"It was nickel and dime," said one diplomat, speaking of the program as a whole and voicing a complaint that seems almost universal among those who worked with it. If it was going to be done, "it should have been serious from the beginning. We should have put $100 million into it at the start, not $19 million," the first amount Reagan authorized in 1981. "We should have pushed hard instead of drawing it out. But it was hubris; we were going to knock off these little brown people on the cheap."...

   The Washington Post, 12/16/84, p. A26.

"Almost universal?" The "diplomats" referenced in the preceding excerpt evidently do not remember the hundreds of thousands, perhaps millions, of dollars spent to kill each Viet Cong (to uncertain end). They certainly haven't been trained on Du Bois:

..."So soon as the prejudiced are forced into this inevitable dilemma, then the real bitterness and indefensibleness of their attitude is apt to be revealed;

they say bluntly that they do not care what 'Niggers,' 'Dagos,' 'Chinks,' or 'Japs' may be capable of—they do not like them and they propose to keep such folk in a place of permanent inferiority to the white race—by peaceful policy if possible, but brute force if necessary. And when a group, a nation or a world assumes this attitude, it is handling dynamite. *There is in this world no such force as the force of a man determined to rise.* The human soul cannot be permanently chained."...

> W.E.B. Du Bois, 1910.
> Quoted in *W.E.B. Du Bois Speaks,* edited
> by Dr. Philip S. Foner, Pathfinder Press,
> New York, 1970, p. 217.

Given the dynamics of European civilization and the personal interests of the wizards of accepted dogma, Velikovsky was given the modern hemlock. Darwin, whose theory has never been validated by empirical evidence, is much better known to American schoolchildren. The children are, of course, being taught ignorant.

Some readers might now be thinking, "Here is a black author, letting his personal prejudices govern scientific thought." To that idea I will respond with a polite "Maybe," and disdain the much more satisfying alternative responses available. However, I have to accept and extrapolate on Velikovsky's theory until such time as somebody disproves the essence of his theory on real merit.

Velikovsky's theory, with its history of war in the heavens and severe impacts on earth, is meritorious from this view because (among other reasons):

1.) Velikovsky's natural history coincides with social histories available from many sources,
2.) The geological evidence (such as the recently raised coastline of South America) is consistent with the theory,
3.) The wholesale extinction of "fit" species is explained,
4.) The evidence of electromagnetic influences in the celestial arena is consistent with the theory, and
5.) An agent for mutations (radiation) is provided—no hermaphrodites or "random" mutations of opposite sexes in the same geographic and genetic locale are required.

Censorship does *not* constitute merit:

...Conventional chronology says that King Tut died about 1350 B.C.; Velikovsky's reconstruction of ancient history has Tutankhamen entombed no earlier than 850 B.C. Five hundred years difference. In order to settle the issue Velikovsky tried for ten years to have some pieces of King Tut's treasure released for C14 dating. Finally, in 1971, a few pieces of wood and reed mat were analyzed by the University of Pennsylvania radiocarbon laboratory; the results indicated that the reed for the mats had been picked in 846 B.C.

Needless to say, The University of Pennsylvania did not make public this astounding result...

> Michael Bradley, *The Black Discovery of America,* Personal Library, Toronto, 1981, p. 46.

What is the tuition at the University of Pennsylvania? Isn't it an Ivy League school? One of America's best? Is "doublethink" *ever* indicated?

> ...And if all others accepted the lie which the Party imposed—if all records told the same tale—then the lie passed into history and became truth. "Who controls the past," ran the party slogan, "controls the future: who controls the present controls the past." And yet the past though of its nature alterable, never had been altered. Whatever was true now was true from everlasting to everlasting. It was quite simple. All that was needed was an unending series of victories over your own memory. "Reality control," they called it; in Newspeak, "doublethink.".. .

> George Orwell, *1984,* New American Library, New York, p. 32. Originally published in 1949.

In order to avoid "doublethink," the following cataclysms will be assumed as the natural history backdrop to the subsequently examined social history:

Cataclysms in Recorded History	
Dates	Description
c. 4000 B.C.	"The Creation"
24th century B.C.	"The flood of Noah" or "the Deluge"
15th century B.C.	"The plagues of Exodus"
8th century B.C.	"The commotion of Uzziah"

The last three cataclysms listed above are either examined in detail or mentioned in *Worlds in Collision* and/or *Earth in Upheaval* by Immanuel Velikovsky. Again, the reader is encouraged to read the original works. The applicable definition of the word "cataclysm" should be kept in mind at all times:

CATACLYSM: A sudden and violent physical action producing changes in the earth's surface.

Now, do I accept Velikovsky's theory in all details? Absolutely not! I have some serious problems with his social history, that will be examined later, and a few problems with the details of Velikovsky's natural history. I do, however, accept the following salient points from his natural history:

1.) The earth has had a cataclysmic natural history.
2.) The most recent cataclysms occurred in historical times.
3.) The agents causing the cataclysms were of celestial origin.

Do I deny that mutations take place? Absolutely not! I just deny that they happen without an agent and/or in long static environments as Darwin hypothesized and Carl Sagan *et al* evidently agree. Moreover, most so-called "mutations" do not involve changes in genetic codes. Instead, they are manifestations of the waxing of physical traits carried by *existing* codes in response to the environment. Even Darwin acknowledged that this type of "mutation," sometimes called an "acquired mutation," is the most common.

It is now time to do the impossible: examine a civilization before Adam.

Chapter 2

"THE CHILDREN OF THE SUN"

As previously indicated there is a great deal of evidence of people
and cultures existing on this planet before Adam, before *circa* 4000
B.C. One such culture existed in *Bilud as Sudan,* the land of the
blacks. In this abbreviated look at the civilization that existed before
Adam in *Bilud as Sudan,* three books will provide the bulk of the
background material: (1) *The Destruction of Black Civilization* by
Chancellor Williams, (2) *The Black Man of the Nile and His Family*
by Yosef Ben-Jochannan, and (3) *The Black Discovery of America*
by Michael Bradley. Like Velikovsky's books, these books do not
lend themselves to summarization. The reader is therefore encouraged
to read the original works.

Where and Who:

Where was *Bilud as Sudan* in 4000 B.C.? Before Adam, *Bilud as
Sudan* included the whole continent of Africa, the Arabian penin-
sula, which was at that time probably connected to the mainland of
Africa at its southern end, and the Middle East. There is significant
evidence that black people, racially black people, inhabited a much
wider swath of territory stretching across southern Asia to the islands
of the Pacific and around the world. However, little is known, at
least to this author, about the cultures in those areas before Adam,
and this discussion will focus on the culture of the black people in
what is known today as Africa and the Middle East. Even that
smaller territory might put a credibility strain on minds poisoned by
"the double-whammy of black history." "What double-whammy?"
Wham 1 is: "You never accomplished anything!" Wham 2 is: "If
you did accomplish something, you are nevertheless cursed by God
for oppressing *HIS* chosen people." Both whams, as will be shown,
are lies.

Sure, some will concede Africa as the original homeland of black
people; but the Middle East...never! However, it is known from
surviving records and legends that the Middle East was originally part
of *Bilud as Sudan.* The earliest known civilization in that area, later
known as Sumer, was a black civilization:

...."What became of the Black People of Sumer?" the traveller asked the old man, "for ancient records show that the people of Sumer were Black. What happened to them?" "Ah," the old man sighed. "They lost their history, so they died..."

> A Sumer Legend, quoted in *The Destruction of Black Civilization* by Chancellor Williams.

Legends of any people about themselves can be self-serving, but there is other evidence about the original residents of the Middle East, *at least* as far from Africa as the Fertile Crescent. The Judeo-Christian *Bible* is certainly one such source:

> ...A river flowed out of Eden to water the garden, and there it divided and became four rivers. The name of the first is Pishon; it is the one that flows around the whole land of Hav'ilah where there is gold; and the gold of that land is good; bdellium and onyx stone are there. The name of the second river is Gihon; it is the one that flows around the whole land of Cush. And the name of the the third river is the Tigris, which flows east of [or eastward toward] Assyria. And the name of the fourth river is the Euphrates.

> *Genesis* 2:10-14

The first and second rivers are not definitely known and probably now diverted or buried. We will address the issue of the first two rivers of *Genesis* later in this book. What *is* known is that the two known rivers were within the land of Cush:

CUSH OR KUSH: A legendary region of northeastern Africa where the biblical descendants of Cush settled; often identified with Ethiopia.

This author cannot think of any kind of a cataclysm that would cause riverbeds to jump over one another. Therefore, it may be concluded that the perspective of the author(s) of *Genesis* is from (what is today) the north or northeast. The Tigris is river number 3; the Euphrates is river number 4. Look at the map on the next page.

The name "Hav'ilah" should be remembered for future reference.

Am I the only one who interprets *Genesis* this way? Let's be ecumenical in our evidence and look at an interpretation from a European Christian of the previous excerpt from *Genesis:*

> ...It may be inferred from this passage and from the geographical notices in *Genesis* 10.6-12 that there was a primieval Cush in Central Asia, and a later Cush (called Ethiopia) in Africa...

Explanatory notes to *Genesis* 2:13 by Rev.
John Brown, Late Minister of the Gospel at
Haddington and Professor of Divinity to the
Associate Synod, *Brown's Self-Interpreting
Bible,* John E. Potter and Company, Phila.,
1873, p. 4

The word "primieval" is a bit strong, but it will be accepted here as
meaning "before Adam." If the unknown second river bounded the
land of Cush, and Cush derived its name from Cushites (black people), one must conclude that the Fertile Crescent, at least, was occupied by black people at the time of Adam. The third and fourth
rivers (the Tigris and Euphrates) define the Fertile Crescent.

THE FERTILE CRESCENT

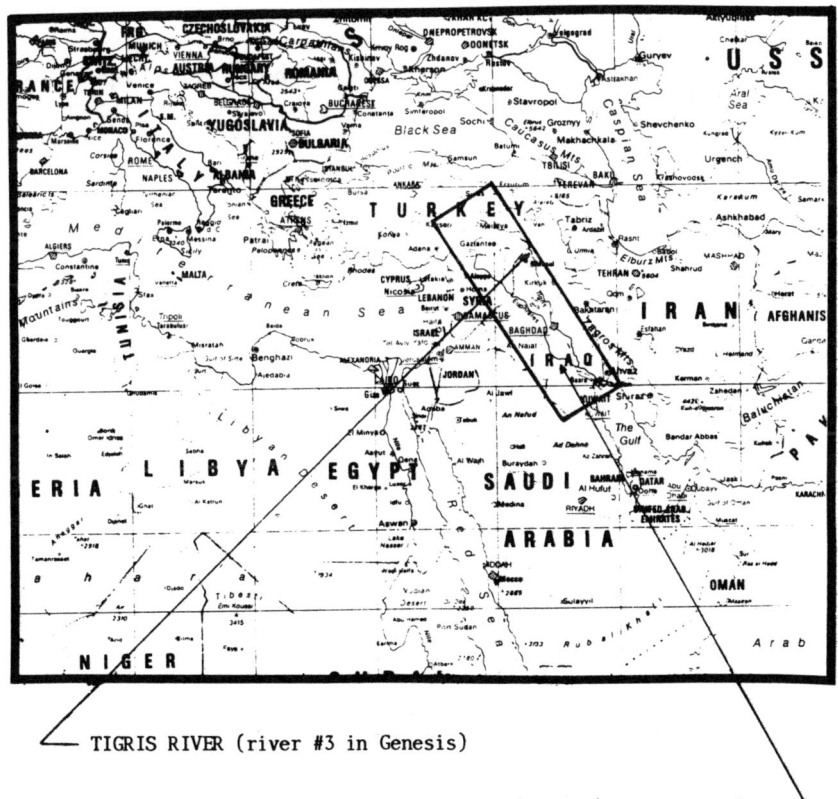

TIGRIS RIVER (river #3 in Genesis)

EUPHRATES RIVER (river #4 in Genesis)

As an extra bonus, we have the implicit admission from Rev. Brown that Adam was not the first human being. If he was, how could there have been "a primieval Cush in Asia?" It is interesting to note that Rev. Brown listed 4004 B.C. as the beginning of time in another section of the above referenced *Bible*. What kind of tortured intellect could engage in such "doublethink?" This man was not some country bumpkin without an education. He was a professor of divinity. We're not talking the Middle Ages here either. We're talking the 19th century A.D., about one hundred years before the University of Pennsylvania had their publicity campaign on the validation of Velikovsky's dating of King Tut. Alas, the same "doublethink" exists today. A *version* of the *Bible* printed in the 1980s lists a period of unspecified length called the "primordial" era before Adam's time, *circa* 4000 B.C. The concept of time before creation is, to say the least, a strained reconciliation of Judeo-Christian dogma with reality.

Velikovsky pointed out that the earth was, in historical times, warmer on average than it is today. This higher mean temperature was due to two reasons: (1) The earth was closer to the sun before its recent encounters with other celestial bodies; and (2) The angle of the earth's orbit around the sun was much less severe than today. Seasons were evidently less marked than is the case today.

Documentation of the implied calendar changes and the locus of the sun relative to the horizon is available in abundance in Velikovsky's work and will not be repeated here. But here is a teaser offered in the hope that the reader will be motivated to read the original work:

> ...Prior to the last series of cataclysms [prior to the 8th century B.C.], when, as we assume, the globe spun on an axis pointed in a different direction in space, with its poles at a different location, on a different orbit, the year could not have been the same as it has been since.
>
> Numerous evidences are preserved which prove that prior to the year of 365 1/4 days, the year was only 360 days long. Nor was that year of 360 days primordial; it was an transition form between a year of still fewer days and the present years...
>
> Immanuel Velikovsky, *Worlds in Collision,*
> Pocket Books, New York, 1977, p. 74.
> Originally published in 1950.

Given the previously described solar orientation of the earth before Adam, it is probably fair to assume that the torrid regions of the planet were larger than they are today. "You disagree?" What would you assume, given that the earth was closer to the sun?

In that hot environment, black people were equipped to function in the most torrid environments. They were black—and proud. They looked at their black skins as a gift from God, protection from the sun. Indeed, they called themselves "the children of the sun," and any objective historian will find that appellation in the early monuments in Africa. Some, including some black historians, have pointed to that self-description as "racism." Everyone is entitled to his or her opinion, but these eyes see no racism in the description. The description cannot be racism, if racism is bigotry based on race. The description cannot be racism, because it isn't bigoted. That which is true cannot, by definition, be bigotry. *It is undeniably true* that people with darker complexions are less prone to malignant melanomas and other skin disorders caused by exposure to the sun. It is undeniably true that nobody, but God, chooses one's complexion. Of course, one doesn't need a medical opinion. One only needs to visit a beach on a hot summer day and look around.

The description was (is) simply a statement of pride. In the holistic, traditional African pattern of thought, it expressed the appropriateness of a people to their native land. I suspect that as Europeans destroy more and more of the earth's ozone layer, the accusations of racism on this point will abate.

It should also be pointed out that "the children of the sun" didn't deny that others had gifts appropriate to their native environments. The gifts of others will be examined later in this book. If today's experience is any indication, the statement was seldom, if ever, used in a haughty way. John Gunther, in his book *Inside Africa,* described Africans as offering polite condolences to visiting Europeans for their pale, sun-sensitive skins.

How did "the children of the sun" cope in an area that is hot today and was hotter before Adam? Very well, thank you. The Sahara (Arabic for "wasteland") region *was hotter* than today before Adam, *but it was not arid.* The area included a large lake called The Albion Sea, Lake Triton. This lake, and rivers since buried by the tectonic changes during "the plagues of *Exodus,*" generously fed the area with water well after Adam—approximately 2,500 years after Adam.

The Sahara was then capable of significant food production, and food was produced utilizing agricultural science that dates back to perhaps 10,000 B.C., and perhaps before that date. The Sahara region was, in fact, the cradle of African civilization. In that area, the foundations for the more famous, and much later, achievements of "Egypt" were born:

...If West Africans hold that their origins were in the northeast, and Egyptians remember theirs as being in the southwest, it seems reasonable to suppose that the epicenter of cultural beginnings was somewhere in the Sahara, perhaps not far from the mountains of Tassili...

> Michael Bradley, *The Black Discovery of America*, Personal Books, Toronto, 1981, p. 21.

The shifting sands of the Sahara periodically reveal its secrets, and from time to time artifacts and cities are revealed. As Velikovsky and Michael Bradley, a white Canadian soul brother, pointed out, the initial artifacts were passed off as the work of Phoenicians, the ubiquitous Phoenicians. "Egyptian" markings in abundance stamped "lie" to that "doublethink," but there is no concerted archeological effort to unearth the evidence. The black governments in the area are too poor and too busy trying to feed their people, fend the corruptions of the superpowers and protect against the excesses of the "Arabs." The Arabs have no interest in unearthing evidence that they are new arrivals. Europeans have to maintain the double-whammy.

In view of the historical record, I would be quite happy to see the Sahara finds remain in the sand until such time as real scientists, *sans* politics, are prepared to unearth them. Was that a bad pun, or what?

Chancellor Williams noted, in his previously referenced book, that structures similar to the structures along the Nile had recently, in 1976, been unearthed in the region of Chad. His conclusion was that "Egyptian" influence had extended westward rather than the other way around. But Williams also chronicled histories of tribes in Central Africa whose tradition is that they have been there since the beginning of time. Since the available literature is replete with the northeast to southwest references in the oral traditions described by Michael Bradley, I have to go with his interpretation until such time as the cities of the Sahara are unearthed and scientifically dated, although I would pick northern Chad or Niger as the site of the origin of African civilization.

In addition, the Nok culture of West Africa has been dated as at least 5,000 years old (3000 B.C.). Cultural similarities to the Saharan culture have been noted.

Some, including Chancellor Williams and General George S. Patton, have asserted that the current condition of the Sahara is due to the poor farming methods of the current Arab residents and/or the original inhabitants, "the children of the sun." Williams did allow that climactic change played a role, and confessed that he found the geological record "puzzling." The honored teacher should have asked himself the identity of the agent of climactic change; he should have read Velikovsky. Alternatively, he should have left it at "puzzling." Climates do *not* change by themselves. There must be an agent. As yet, nobody has unearthed any evidence of humans burning wood, oil or gas in sufficient quantities to have changed climates. Long term climactic changes are necessarily worldwide phenomena. Volcanoes have been known to affect climates for short periods of time, especially locally. However, volcanoes, especially a number of volcanoes erupting simultaneously, also need an agent. Nothing physical happens without a force.

In any case, poor farming methods could not have been the agent of change. How do we know? We have a historical precedent, at least one. Farming in the American Midwest began about 1800. By the 1930s, the area was a "dustbowl," and reforms were instituted that have at least provided temporary relief from the onslaught of quick profits. The creation of the Sahara could not have been due to poor farming methods over thousands of years. Creating "the dustbowl" took only a little over a century in the United States. Were Americans so "efficient?"

People might be ignorant, but the penalties for violating *The Law of Truth or Consequences* are much swifter than the millennia implied by the assessment of Patton and Williams.

The Patton/Williams assertion represents, to these eyes, a classic example of drawing an erroneous conclusion about social history based on a false premise about natural history. "What is the false premise?" The Newton-Darwin static environment.

Philosophy:

There were also cultural reasons why "the children of the sun" would not have abused their land. These reasons focused on their philosphy, or what is called "religion" by Europeans. Any meaningful discussion of the culture of black people must necessarily examine our "religion." It has permeated *Bilud as Sudan* since anybody can remember or chronicle. The essentials of that "religion" are still the basis for African thought, including the thoughts in African communities around the world.

The African "religion" is not widely understood, and for good reason—the reality conflicts with the Judeo-Christian and Islamic portrayal of black people as idol-worshipping savages. To Jews, blacks were "cursed by God." "Christians" eagerly accepted the convenient tag. To the Islamic world, non-Muslim blacks were "infidels"—fair game for slavery that rivaled the European slavery in its barbarity.

To understand traditional African "religion," one must first understand that, in Africa, "One's religion is what one practices." "Religion" is not simply a creed and a set of rituals to be given a passing nod in a "pragmatic" world. Instead, it is a set of deeply held beliefs by which one governs one's actions. To Europeans, the "commandment" to "keep the sabbath holy" has a certain truth. To people raised in African cultures, the commandment begs a question: *"What is one supposed to do the other six days of the week?"* Jesus, also, had a problem with that particular commandment. See if you can find a scriptural reference to support that assertion. "Can't find one?" Try *Luke* 13:10.

Chancellor Williams, Yosef Ben-Jochannan and Jonathan Kwitny (in his excellent book *Endless Enemies: The Making of an Unfriendly World*) have all noted this essential difference between the European perception of "religion" and the perceptions of people from other cultures. Having said that, I will drop the quotation marks from the word religion, and leave it to the reader to determine by the context whether I am writing about a philosophical construct or the commitment to that construct as evidenced by one's actions.

Before moving further on the topic of religion, it is necessary to present some data:

> ...there is more kinship between the various [black] peoples of Africa than might appear at first sight...This great comparative homogeneity of African society is apparent in the religious sphere...
>
> ...Above all [in traditional African religion] is the Supreme Being...
>
> ...Then there is the popular theory that African religion derives from Egypt...
>
> E.G. Parrinder, *African Traditional Religion,* Hutchinson's University Library, London, 1st edition 1954, 2nd revised edition 1962, p. 11, 24, 32.

Whether traditional African religion derives from Egypt is a question that relates back to the previously addressed issue about the epicenter of African civilization. If African civilization was born in Central Africa, as is assumed here, then traditional African religion did not derive from Egypt. Rather, Egypt inherited a religion that was several thousand years old and passed it on. If African civilization was born in the eastern section of Africa, then traditional

African religion derives from Egypt. In this latter case, however, the religion would still predate the civilization known as "Egypt" by several thousand years. We do know that the current traditional African religion is unchanged in essentials from the religion practiced during the height of Egyptian civilization.

"The children of the sun" perceived a universe that existed on two planes of reality: the physical world and the spiritual world. The theology can be graphically portrayed as a triangle:

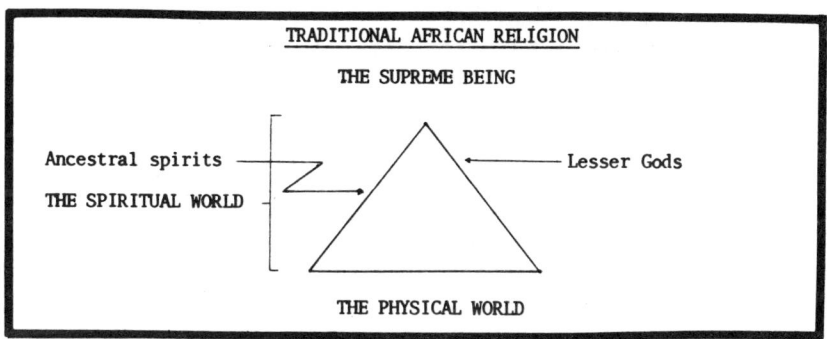

Governing both worlds was the Supreme Being, or the Creator. (Please note that I am using the past tense here because I am describing the religion of "the children of the sun" prior to 4000 B.C. I do not mean to imply that anything of substance has changed.)

The Most High God ruled the universe by eternal laws. The more one learned of these laws, the more virtuous, God-like or "holy" one became. Laws, of course, governed all areas of existence, ranging from ethical laws of behavior to the physical laws of mass and motion. *Learning was engendered by the religion of "the children of the sun."* Obviously, there were no secular/theological conflicts, like the Scopes trials, that have plagued European societies at least since the time of Socrates. Socrates, by the way, was judged guilty of two crimes: offending the Athenian gods and teaching the children to think, "corrupting the youth." It would be a much better world today if Plato, the vampire, had studied Socrates a little more diligently.

...The religion [traditional African] does not anthropomorphize God as a person but finds divinity immanent in the laws and dynamics of the universe...

The Washington Post, 10/17/86, p. B10.

Given that God ruled through eternal laws, politicizing God was difficult. Rarely did "the children of the sun" pray to the Most High Gõd, and for good reason: It was futile. *The solution to problems was to learn God's laws and observe them.*

The Most High God was most often symbolized by a representation of the sun. Europeans and others construed this convention to mean that black people worshiped the sun. That assertion was, and is, a lie. Black people never worshiped the sun, only the life force behind the sun.

Although the Most High God was not anthropomorphic and was therefore not a frequent receiver of plaintive prayers, catharsis was enabled through the institution of lesser gods. These gods were intermediaries on the spiritual plane of reality with jurisdiction over anything from a guild, to a planet, to a village, to a rock. These lesser gods include in their number the more well-known gods of Egypt: Isis, Osiris *et al.* Frequently, allegorical tales were constructed about the goings-on of these lesser gods. These allegories were very similar to the "Uncle Remus"-type stories that African slaves brought to the United States, the nation's first children's stories. Later, much after 4000 B.C., the lesser gods would become politicized. We'll examine the issue later in this book.

"The children of the sun" believed that all of God's creation had a spiritual aspect which usually transcended physical death. This is the concept of the "soul" that was later adopted, and adapted, by Judeo-Christians. Animism, usually spelled with a small "a" by Europeans to demonstrate their ecumenical spirits, is not the belief that inanimate objects have "souls" *per se.* Instead, it is the belief that all is God's creation—a concept not radically different from "the oneness of God" in Islamic literature. Black people didn't worship the idols representing the lesser gods any more than Europeans worship dashboard saints. The idols were only talismanic focal points for meditation or prayer.

Since humans were part of God's creation, humans had a spiritual aspect also. The spirits of deceased ancestors existed in the spiritual world, providing advice and counsel to their descendants in the physical world—"communion." Periodically, these spirits would be reborn in the person of a descendant for a new opportunity to grow—"reincarnation." Physical death was therefore not the worst thing that could happen to a person. Spiritual death was much more severe. It had *eternal* consequences!

The lesser gods of *Bilud as Sudan* are evidence of polytheism to European eyes. Viewed objectively, however, they are no more evidence of polytheism than Christian saints or Jewish angels and demons. That is not to say that there is anything wrong with polytheism, just that there is something very seriously wrong with double standards.

In those European societies that still profess a belief in God at all, much has been made about the separation of church and state. However, if one's religion is what one practices, the church cannot be separated from any human endeavor; and in *Bilud as Sudan,* it wasn't. Neither was there widespread politicizing of the church as there has been in European societies where God Almighty has been used to sanction everything from sexual preference to bigotry to theft.

> ...Before ascribing to their gods this unnatural urge, the Greeks had to come to regard it as respectable. It is true that Homer did not attribute to the warriors of the Achaean host relations that were later called "Greek love," but he tells how the gods abducted the youth, Ganymede, with whom, according to many sources, Zeus fell in love...
>
> Immanuel Velikovsky, *Oedipus and Ahknaton,*
> Pocket Books, New York, 1960, p. 54.

> ...After a black preacher from a nearby city made headlines by trying unsuccessfully to integrate the Plains Baptist Church on the eve of the 1976 Presidential election, Miz Lillian, who was thought to have overcome her Dixie upbringing, snarled: "Somebody should have shot that nigger before he came on the lawn."...
>
> Victor Lasky, *Jimmy Carter: The Man
> & The Myth,* Richard Marek Publishers,
> Inc., New York, 1979, p. 26.

> ...The Lord said to Moses, "Yet one plague more I will bring upon Pharoah and upon Egypt; afterwards he will let you go hence; when he lets you go, he will drive you away completely. Speak now in the hearing of the the people, that they ask, every man of his neighbor and every woman of her neighbor, jewelry of silver and gold."
>
> And the Lord gave the people favor in the sight of the Egyptians...
>
> *Exodus* 11:2-3

During the 1960s, Malcolm X observed that, "Eleven o'clock Sunday morning is the most segregated hour in America." It was a true statement then; it's true today. Thank God!

The physical universe included all of the forces and matter in the cosmos. The physical universe therefore included the land. Originally, land was conceived as a gift from God—a collective gift to the family, clan, tribe, and, later, the province and nation. Individual ownership of land developed much later, and even then, an individual was not free to poison the land. The land was the residence of ancestral spirits. Abuse of the land, as suggested by Patton and Williams, would have been done solely from ignorance. Callousness was precluded by a dominating religion.

On the possibility of ignorance, we draw a blank also. Egypt had grain when others didn't. Abraham's and Joseph's families both went into Egypt seeking grain (among other things). "The children of the sun" had highly developed agricultural science that was six thousand or more years old at the time of Adam. My assertion that General Patton and Chancellor Williams were wrong on the issue of land abuse must be repeated.

Socio-Economic Institutions:

The fundamental building block of the society in *Bilud as Sudan* was the family. The people were referred to as "father of," "mother of," "daughter of," and, yes, "son of." Individualism was held in check, since the actions of an individual reflected directly on his or her family. In view of the achievements that will be discussed subsequently, the restrained individualism does not appear to have restrained progress.

The institution of marriage was quite a bit different from the European institution. Husbands and wives were economic partners. The male was dominant, but the institution was arranged such that a wife wasn't solely dependent on her husband's industry and generosity. Polygamy was allowed. The institution of polygamy might have developed relatively late in black society, but until evidence to the contrary surfaces, I will assume that polygamy was present in *Bilud as Sudan* prior to 4000 B.C. It was not an institution in which brides were bought and sold. There was a certain logic (read: morality) about it.

The family was the fundamental social unit, economic unit and political unit. The male was the arbiter and lawgiver in his household. On reaching the appropriate age and acquiring access to some ancestral land, a man would farm the land and save enough capital to become an eligible bachelor. He would approach the family of a potential bride and ask for her hand in marriage. Sometimes this would be handled through generally respected intermediaries who could attest to the character of the prospective groom. The bride's family and the bride would then approve the marriage, and a "bride price" would be negotiated. The so-called "bride-price" served three primary purposes: (1) It demonstrated the groom's economic achievement; (2) It served to compensate the bride's family for the loss of the bride's labor; and (3) It served to indicate that all parties were in agreement.

Marriage places one partner (usually females) under the protection of the other (usually males). The institution in *Bilud as Sudan* was no different in that regard. Since genetic brothers and sisters were not good breeding pairs, mating with people outside of the immediate family was in order.

The females in the polygamous marriage usually lived in a structure connected to, but separate from, the husband's and the structures that were the homes of the co-wives. Any children of a particular wife lived in that wife's structure. Each wife was assigned a particular plot of land to cultivate, after it had been cleared by the husband. The wife generally did the farming. At harvest time, the labor was probably from both sexes. Ownership of the chattels, such as pots and pans, agricultural implements, *etc.*, was joint between the husband and a particular wife.

Wives also marketed excess production in the marketplaces. The proceeds, again, were jointly owned by the husband and the particular wife. As a result of this institution, a wife's economic welfare was, to a large degree, dependent on her own industry. Women were not confined to "success" based on arbitrary, transient and often political standards of beauty.

Women were also responsible for the primary child rearing duties. Major problems with children were brought to the attention of the husband, but given the dynamics of polygamy (a wife was viewed in the light of her success), mothers would probably have been more prone to administer their own swift justice or to portray a child's problem in a favorable light to the father.

Favoritism by the husband was discouraged by rules governing his relations with multiple wives. A first wife was given a preferential position usually only to the extent that she was physically older than other wives. Age was revered and respected. The logic behind the reverence for age was quite straightforward: The older one became, in most cases, the wiser one became. One must remember the definition of "holy" previously specified.

Divorce was allowed based on traditional grievances by either party. The divorce procedings were administered by the Council of Elders, but it was, and is, very rare in traditional African polygamous societies. Whatever one's personal views on polygamy, it must be conceded by the objective that it worked. What is the chance of an American marriage lasting a lifetime?

Polygamy was not mandated. Many in polygamous societies, and probably most, given the mathematics, were monogamous. Polyandry was a form of marriage that was practiced, and still is today, in some parts of *Bilud as Sudan*.

Men were judged by their ability to keep a harmonious household. Therefore, there was no mad rush to acquire wives, despite the sexual diversity offered. A man could keep only so many women together in a harmonious household. As surplus goods could only be sold to the extent there was a demand, producing excess food was limited by the fact that most people were farmers and the limitations of the manual and animal-driven labor of the time. Wild concentrations of wealth were thus avoided. Nature limited.

Small children were assigned tasks in line with their future duties to teach them responsibility. They were taught manners and the proper forms of address very early. These forms of address were sometimes syrupy, but they were evidently intended to engender a spirit of community and sharing. The spirit of sharing, of course, transcended physical death. Sacrifice to ancestral spirits was a common practice.

Children were introduced to their relatives at clan convocations and at the many festivals required to honor the lesser gods. The nature of their relationship to relatives was explained. This practice was the beginning of teaching the children their history, a sacred trust.

Until puberty, there was a not a marked difference between the training of males and females. On reaching puberty, however, the training was specific to the sexes. Age groupings played an important role in the society, with the idea to extend the spirit of brotherhood beyond the family. Both males and females went through rites of passage, however. These rites sometimes involved scarification, ritualistic circumcision and the receipt of tribal talismans.

Sex education was part of the training for both sexes. Instruction for females included instructions by the older women on how to be a clean, attractive mate for an entire lifetime. Men were taught cleanliness and technique also. As Chancellor Williams and Yosef Ben-Jochannan point out, "the children of the sun" had a very matter-of-fact attitude about sex. Sex, after all, was part of God's creation. Why mystify it?

Female adolescents were taught to be wives. They needed to know how to grow food. They needed to know how to calculate for the marketplace. They needed to know how to raise children.

Males were taught their tribal history and the mechanics of warfare (more on warfare in *Bilud as Sudan* later). Upon completion of the rites of passage, males became warriors responsible for defending the tribe's borders.

After a period as a warrior, the males would be trained by their fathers in a particular craft or they became farmers. Guilds developed from families and clans with hereditary occupations.

The aged were cared for by their extended families. Aging, therefore, was a much more pleasant thing than in today's world. Your children were your "social security," as you were to your parents. The natural cycle of life was recognized and accommodated by the society.

The males selected by the guilds went through apprenticeships that were quite long by today's standards. Some historians have chronicled apprenticeships of a decade or longer for arts such as medicine. The idea was not to limit competition (there was no monetary advantage to doing so), but to produce the best possible physicians (*e.g.*) for the tribe. There were pros and cons to these long apprenticeships. On the pro side, they did produce the best artists, craftsmen and scientists. On the con side, they were few in number.

Literacy was not widespread. Instead, most people were taught retentive skills that would boggle the minds of the best and brightest in today's world. This limited literacy was of little consequence in *Bilud as Sudan* before Adam, where the focus was on harmonious coexistence. Later it would be a disaster.

The guilds each (of course) had a patron god. The practitioners survived on donations to their god. Success engendered success. The temples, or universities depending on one's perspective, honored the patron god while advertising the success of the guild. A guild would not prosper without functioning. Excesses were kept in check by the Council of Elders and the philosophy of unity and sharing engendered from birth.

Political Institutions:

The next building block of the society after the family was the clan. After the clan, there was the village, there was sometimes a district and then a tribal organization. Each of these entities had a Council of Elders selected from the best and the brightest of the organization below in the hierarchy. The debates in these august bodies were "interminable." They still are.

A man who provided the impetus (through war or negotiation) to form a tribe from various clans became the hereditary chief of his tribe. He was the executive who, with the advice and consent of the Council, was responsible for the well-being of his people. He was responsible for maintaining harmony and equity. Each member of the tribe was entitled to be heard in the Council. The chief was the nominal lawgiver and judge. The real power was in the Council. A chief could not be arbitrary, especially with respect to objectives. As the embodiment of everything good in the tribe, his role was primarily that of representing the people to the gods.

Donations—taxes came much later—to the chief were made by the members of the tribe *for use as a social welfare fund*. The fund was not the property of the chief, although his maintenance was sometimes derived from it.

The chief was not a despot. He had unlimited power to carry out the will of the people as defined by the Council, but not to line his pockets. What could he buy? Williams points out quite accurately that "royalty" originally meant "royal worth" not "royal birth." Control of the army of warriors was in the hands of the Council except for the duration of emergencies. After an emergency, control of the army went back to the Council from the chief.

Dissatisfaction with a decision made by a Council could be appealed to the next higher political entity. A litigant also had the alternative of simply leaving the vicinity with his family and/or clan and forming his own political entity in an unoccupied area. This institution served to produce internal harmony, but it also served to create a culturally cohesive, but politically fragmented *Bilud as Sudan*. *Bilud as Sudan* has never been under unified *political* rule in its entire history.

It is interesting to note that one method of appealing a decision was to petition the chief's mother. Such was the reverence for the institution of motherhood. It remains a very serious insult to say something irreverent about another person's mother. Then, as today, one didn't say lightly, "Yo' Mama!" The phrase has an allusive, contextual definition. Roughly, it means: "That which you hold most sacred is corrupt!" Alternatively, it can mean: "The basis of your argument is invalid!" It almost always means that the speaker is quite angry, and the discussion phase of the dispute is terminated. Almost never does it refer to the actual virtues of one's mother.

Chiefs were checked from building "dynasties" (as Europeans define the word) by the institution of matrilineal progression. The heir to the office of chief was not the chief's son, but the son of the chief's sister. Matrilineal progression served to check the accumulation of power for its own sake, opened up the office of chief to the descendants of other males (selected by the chief's sister) and retained the original gifted bloodlines in an administrative position that would benefit the tribe.

Matrilineal progression also gave women a significant role in the political life of the tribe. Is it not power to train a future chief? What mother doesn't influence her son? Matrilineal progression, however, did not survive the trip across cultural boundaries and was later politicized.

Warfare in *Bilud as Sudan* was rather unique. The idea of war was to achieve the political objective at issue, not to see how many enemies one could slay. The tactics involved coordinated maneuver, usually a series of feigned charges (replete with shouts, masks and other paraphenalia designed to terrorize), followed by a series of measured withdrawals aimed at maneuvering the enemy into a position obviously untenable for continuing the hostilities.

If the appropriate compensations could be negotiated, the bulk of the enemy army was allowed to withdraw under feigned blindness. Yes, some warriors got killed. Wholesale bloodshed, no. "The children of the sun" loved their enemies. Chancellor Williams has chronicled armies calling "timeouts" to refresh themselves at a stream and exchange insults and jokes. War was a glorified chess match! Nietzsche, Plato and Goethe would have had apoplexy. War became a much more serious affair later. Even after repeated invasions, however, war was not a central focus of black societies:

...The Pharoahs generally were more interested in pyramids and temples than in war...

The Wall Street Journal, 11/4/86, p. 38.

A reader or two might now be jumping up and down, outraged by the apparent contradiction to the Judeo-Christian scriptures represented by the preceding excerpt. *Sit ---- --- down!* The issue will be examined, but the word "Pharoah" brings immediate attention to the development of monarchy and nations.

As previously mentioned, cultural solidarity with political fragmentation was the rule in *Bilud as Sudan.* The exception to the rule was, predictably, in what is today the eastern end of the land of the blacks—"Sumer" and "Egypt."

To these eyes, the reason for political consolidation in what is to-day the east is obvious: *There was a need.* In West and Central Africa, the political fragmentation was not a problem in such a vast, culturally cohesive area. Few large nations; so what? The people's needs were served by the cultural institutions. Social, artistic and scientific development was occurring at a pace that was unhurried, but the pace was at least as fast as anywhere else in the world. What would large nations have brought to the party? Another level of administration?

In the east, however, there was not cultural cohesion. There were cultural (and coincidently, racial) borders. Philosophy did not tran-scend the borders, and political fragmentation was inconsistent with cultural and physical survival. It was necessary to be politically unified as a result of the close proximity of people who tended to a philosophy closer to those of Nietzsche, Goethe and Plato. Those people didn't completely understand that hammers and anvils both get pounded. They didn't understand that anvils last longer. They didn't understand that both hammers and anvils are the tools of men, and it is more productive to be a man. Who were these people? The roll will be called later. Yes, names will be named.

> ...do not let me be conveyed to the east [the direction of the sunrise] to per-form the festival of the fiends hostile to me...
>
> *The Egyptian Book of the Dead,* Plate XVII.

Unified strength meant survival and mutually benefical trade for both cultures. It is interesting to note that the word "Babylon," a city in the Fertile Crescent, originally meant "gate." It was that. The developments in *Bilud as Sudan* near "the gate" will be examined in subsequent chapters.

Ethos:

Contrary to many portrayals of "Egyptians" as "preoccupied with death," and portrayals of "the children of the sun," in general, as

"blood-thirsty savages," the cultural ethos in *Bilud as Sudan* was—
and is—one of a passionate joy of life.

Think about it. The children were well fed. They had the world's
best physicians. Old age was not a problem. Sex was not a problem.
They had a religion that worked and enabled progress. What *need*
was unmet? I can't think of any. What would rational people do in
that kind of a setting? You guessed it: Party!

There was a festival for this and a festival for that. When those
festivals were over, "the children of the sun" had a festival for this
and that. Music, of course, was necessary to honor the gods and
enhance the festivals. The invention of all but a very few musical in-
struments can be traced to *Bilud as Sudan*. Black music was born.

When I use the words "black music" to white people I am frequently countered with, "Music is music!" We just have to disagree.
There are differences. If one ranks the elements of music, in black
music: rhythm is first, followed by harmony with melody bringing up
the rear. In European music: harmony tends to be first, followed by
melody with rhythm bringing up the rear. In some Oriental music
forms: melody is first, followed by rhythm with harmony bringing up
the rear.

Many black people can appreciate the works of "Wolfie"
(*"Amadeus"* was a great movie) and many other European com-
posers. Flights of fanciful melody, in harmony, take place in black
music. But the focus is on the rhythm, a rhythm of life in which the
most important beat is frequently a rest. In the music of our culture,
the drum is not king—but emperor.

Humor has also always been a major part of black culture. Our
humor, like our speech patterns and art, tends to be allusive rather
than literal. Slapstick is not a popular form of humor. Black humor
tends to the irreverent, however. Pathos and irony are two of the
leading forms. As an example, I offer the following Gikuyu story
which to us humorously describes colonialism in Africa:

...Once upon a time an elephant made a friendship with a man. One day a
heavy thunderstorm broke out, the elephant went to his friend, who had a little hut at the edge of the forest, and said to him: "My dear good man, will
you please let me put my trunk inside your hut to keep it out of this torrential
rain?" The man, seeing what situation his friend was in, replied: "My dear
good elephant, my hut is very small, but there is room for your trunk and
myself. Please put your trunk in gently." The elephant thanked his friend,
saying: "You have done a good deed and one day I shall return your kind-
ness." But what followed? As soon as the elephant put his trunk inside the

hut, slowly he pushed his head inside, and finally flung the man out in the rain, and then lay down comfortably inside the hut, saying: "My dear good friend, your skin is harder than mine, and as there is not enough room for both of us, you can afford to remain in the rain while I am protecting my delicate skin from the hailstorm."

The man, seeing what his friend had done to him, started to grumble, the animals in the nearby forest heard the noise and came to see what was the matter. All stood around listening to the heated argument between the man and his friend the elephant. In this turmoil the lion came along roaring, and said in a loud voice: "Don't you know that I am the King of the Jungle! How dare anyone disturb the peace of my kingdom?" On hearing this the elephant, who was one of the high ministers of the jungle kingdom, replied in a soothing voice, and said: "My Lord, there is no disturbance of the peace in your kingdom. I have only been having a little discussion with my friend here as to the possession of this little hut which your lordship sees me occupying."

The lion, who wanted to have "peace and tranquility" in his kingdom, replied in a noble voice, saying: "I command my ministers to appoint a Commission of Enquiry to go thoroughly into this matter and report accordingly." He then turned to the man and said: "You have done well by establishing friendship with my people, especially the elephant who is one of my honourable ministers of state. Do not grumble any more, your hut is not lost to you. Wait until the sitting of my Imperial Commission, and there you will be given plenty of opportunity to state your case. I am sure that you will be pleased with the findings of the Commission." The man was very pleased by these sweet words from the King of the Jungle, and innocently waited for his opportunity, in the belief that, naturally, the hut would be returned to him.

The elephant, obeying the command of his master, got busy with other ministers to appoint the Commission of Enquiry. The following elders of the jungle were appointed to sit in the Commission: (1) Mr. Rhinoceros; (2) Mr. Buffalo; (3) Mr. Alligator; (4) The Rt. Hon. Mr. Fox to act as chairman; and (5) Mr. Leopard to act as Secretary to the Commission. On seeing the personnel, the man protested and asked if it was not necessary to include in this Commission a member from his side. But he was told that it was impossible, since no one from his side was well enough educated to understand the intricacies of jungle law. Further, that there was nothing to fear, for the members of the commission were all men of repute for their impartiality in justice, and as they were gentlemen chosen by God to look after the interests of races less adequately endowed with teeth and claws, he might rest assured that they would investigate the matter with the greatest care and report impartially.

The Commission sat to take the evidence. The Rt. Hon. Mr. Elephant was first called. He came along with a superior air, brushing his tusks with a sapling which Mrs. Elephant had provided, and in an authoritative voice said: "Gentlemen of the Jungle, there is no need for me to waste your valuable time in relating a story which I am sure you all know. I have always regarded it as my duty to protect the interests of my friends, and this appears to have caused the misunderstanding between myself and my friend here. He invited me to save his hut from being blown away by a hurricane. As the hurricane had gained access owing to the unoccupied space in the hut, I considered it necessary, in my friend's own interests, to turn the undeveloped space to a more economic use by sitting in it myself; a duty which any of you would undoubtedly have performed with equal readiness in similar circumstances.

After hearing the Rt. Hon. Mr. Elephant's conclusive evidence, the Commission called Mr. Hyena and other elders of the jungle, who all supported what Mr. Elephant had said. They then called the man, who began to give his own account of the dispute. But the Commission cut him short, saying: "My good man, please confine yourself to relevant issues. We have already heard the circumstances from various unbiased sources; all we wish you to tell us whether the undeveloped space in your hut was occupied by anyone else before Mr. Elephant assumed his position?" "No, but—" But at this point the Commission declared that they had heard sufficient evidence from both sides and retired to consider their decision. After enjoying a delicious meal at the expense of the Rt. Hon. Mr. Elephant, they reached their verdict, called the man, and declared as follows: "In our opinion this dispute has arisen through a regrettable misunderstanding due to the backwardness of your ideas. We consider that Mr. Elephant has fulfilled his sacred duty of protecting your interests. As it is clearly for your own good that the space should be put to its most economic use, and as you yourself have not reached the stage of expansion which would enable you to fill it, we consider it necessary to arrange a compromise to suit both parties. Mr. Elephant shall continue his occupation of the hut, but we give you permission to look for a site where you can build another hut more suited to your needs, and we will see that you are well protected." The man, having no alternative, and fearing that his refusal might expose him to the teeth and claws of members of the Commission, did as they suggested. But no sooner had he built another hut than Mr. Rhinoceros charged in with his horn lowered and ordered the man to quit. A Royal Commission was again appointed to look into the matter, and the same finding was given. This procedure was repeated until Mr. Buffalo, Mr. Leopard, Mr. Hyena and the rest were all accomodated with new huts. Then the man decided that he must adopt an effective method of protection, since Commissions of Enquiry didn't seem to be of any use to him. He sat down and said: *"Ng' enda thi ndeagaga motegi,"* which literally means "there is nothing which treads on the earth that cannot be trapped," or in other words, you can fool people for a time, but not for ever.

Early one morning, when the huts already occupied by the jungle lords were all beginning to decay and fall to pieces, he went out and built a bigger and better hut a little distance away. No sooner had Mr. Rhinoceros seen it than he came rushing in, only to find that Mr. Elephant was already inside, sound asleep. Mr. Leopard next came in at the window, Mr. Lion, Mr. Fox, and Mr. Buffalo entered the doors, while Mr. Hyena howled for a place in the shade and Mr. Alligator basked on the roof. Presently they all began disputing about their rights of penetration, and from disputing they came to fighting, and while they were all embroiled together the man set the hut on fire and burnt it to the ground, jungle lords and all. Then he went home saying: "Peace is costly, but it's worth the expense," and lived happily ever after.

A Gikuyu story, quoted in *Facing Mt.*
Kenya, by Jomo Kenyatta, Vintage Books,
New York, 1962, p. 47.

"Gentlemen chosen by God?" Jomo Kenyatta's book is an excellent place to acquire an understanding of the culture of an African tribe, the Gikuyu, today. In reading *Facing Mt. Kenya,* I was struck by three overwhelming impressions. First, the author was brilliant. Second, when one compares the Gikuyu culture described by Kenyatta with the historical culture of Africa as chronicled by Chancellor Williams, Yosef Ben-Jochannan *et al,* very little of substance has changed in terms of cultural essentials. The last impression is one that presents itself in much of the literature on traditional culture in Africa. That impression is the high degree to which "the children of the sun" modeled their society on the role model of real lions; essentially social animals, not "monsters filled with joy."

It's time now to leave this abbreviated look at "the children of the sun" before Adam. We must say good-bye to the Right Honorable Mr. Elephant *et al* and go find Adam. Where is that little rascal?

Chapter 3

THE ALTAIC RING—A WORKING HYPOTHESIS

In order to find Adam, one must first determine who Adam was. The common European portrayal of Adam is that he was, either literally or figuratively, the first human. That common portrayal is not entirely supported by the scriptures.

According to *Genesis*, Adam and Eve had two sons, Cain and Abel. Cain killed Abel. That left only three humans on the planet, if the scriptures are interpreted literally. Cain, however, was exiled into the Land of Nod, where he married. *Whom did Cain marry?* Literalists, when confronted with that issue, wax very creative. Some say God created some people after Adam and Eve, and Cain's wife was one of those people. Some go so far as to say that Cain married his sister. However, those explanations are *not* supported by the scriptures.

Figuratists, of course, point out that *Genesis* is metaphorical, and one cannot expect the metaphors to withstand literal challenges. Okay, nooooo problem. But, if we agree that *Genesis* is metaphorical, then it is fair game for interpretation—anybody's interpretation. I am an anybody. I will try to observe the admonishment of the great teacher, Jesus. I shall judge for myself what is right.

One doesn't necessarily have to interpret Adam as a metaphor for the first human. Alternative interpretations are not necessarily less justified, and they just might be more justified. The fundamental assumption here will be that *Adam is a metaphor for early Hebrews and not a metaphor for the first human.* If one assumes that Adam is a metaphor for early Hebrews, one needs only to look to the original homeland of the Hebrews to find Adam. Problem: Where is it? We know that it wasn't in the Fertile Crescent or to the west of the Fertile Crescent, where the current nation of Israel exists. As previously shown, even the Hebrew literature (*Genesis* 2:10-14) identifies those areas as within the Land of Cush—some *Bibles* say Ethiopia. Sumer was not a Hebrew culture. Where should we look?

As previously mentioned, Adam was created in an undefined place to the north of the Garden of Eden and moved south by "the Lord" across four rivers. The first two rivers are not definitely known and probably now nonexistent or relocated. The last two are (3) the Tigris and (4) the Euphrates. Because of the geographic orientation of these rivers the conclusion here is that, unless they have been drastically reoriented, "the Lord" moved Adam from what is today the north. *Genesis* identifies a land, Hav'ilah, between Adam's birthplace and the garden of Eden. Recall the Right Honorable Rev. Brown's conclusion about the "primieval Cush in Central Asia." I agree with Rev. Brown's conclusion. Rev. Brown also concluded that it was impossible to match the biblical description of the four rivers described in *Genesis* 2:10-14 *"as they now exist."* The emphasis is Rev. Brown's. Rev. Brown also pointed out that many biblical scholars have identified the Pishon, the first river, as the Phasis. The Phasis is a tributary of the Black Sea—repeat: *Black* Sea. The Gihon, the second river, has been identified as the Araxes or Aras river. The Aras is a tributary of the Caspian Sea. If these identifications are correct, Adam came *through* the Caucasus mountains into the Land of Cush. Okay, that's all we know about geography at this point.

Is there a physical description of Adam? Perhaps. An early connotation of the word "Adam" includes the color red. The plain vanilla interpretation of that redness is that it refers to the red soil from which Adam was allegedly made. An alternative interpretation is available. The redness could refer to Adam's red/blond complexion. Adam could have been a white man with classic Caucasoid features. If the soil was red, wouldn't Adam have been red also?

> ...ADAM. The name given in the Scripture to the first man. It apparently has reference to the ground from which he was formed, which is called in Hebrew *Adamah*. The idea of *redness of colour* [emphasis original] seems to be inherent in either word...
>
> Improved Dictionary of the Bible, *Brown's Self-Interpreting Bible,* John E. Potter and Company, Phila., 1873, p. 2.

I now have a serious problem. Red/blond is not the stereotype for Semites, and the Hebrews are today called Semites. The stereotype for Semites is swarthy, not red/blond. But changes in the complexions of various ethnic groups are well documented. Today, after slavery, American blacks range in complexion from Caucasoid to the original black of "the children of the sun." The Greeks are described in *The Iliad* as "fair-haired Achaeans." Today, after Greek invasions of Turkey and Turkish invasions of Greece, Greeks are, on average, darker in complexion than the average European.

So now we know that in the 6,000 years available to us since roughly 4000 B.C., there is more than ample time for Hebrews to have become darker than Adam. We have documented the possibility and the process, but is there any evidence of the event—of Hebrews intermingling with people of darker races? Yes, there is evidence. "Where?" The *Bible*.

Isaac is described in *Genesis* as marrying both Hittite and Aramaean wives. The clear implication is that Isaac was neither a Hittite or an Aramaean. Isaac fathered two children by his Aramaean wife; twin boys, Jacob and Esau:

...And the Lord said to her, "Two nations are in your womb,"...

Genesis 25:23

Esau was the oldest child (nation) of Isaac and Rebecca. He is described as a red-haired, hairy hunter. Jacob, the younger brother, is of unspecified complexion, but he isn't hairy. He is described as "smooth." Jacob's name means "supplanter," or he who replaces. His mother (recall that she was not a Hebrew by blood) favored Jacob over Esau. Esau was favored by his father. Jacob's mother assisted him in conniving Esau of his birthright as the oldest child. Later, Jacob went to live with his mother's family in the east.

Even before Isaac, Abraham is described as marrying a "Chaldean," an Afro-Asian. We won't count the child that Abraham fathered by his Egyptian slave girl, Hagar. Hagar's child was sent away. Conclusion? Hebrews intermingled with a number of people of darker races. The intermingling probably resulted in obfuscation of the original complexion of the Hebrews at the time of Jacob and Esau; metaphorical people to be sure.

Is there any other evidence that Adam was a Caucasian besides metaphorical interpretation of the scriptures? Language certainly provides some evidence. Note the language tree on the next page. Several points are noteworthy: (1) The languages all sprang from a common root or trunk, (2) there is no "Semitic" language on the tree and (3) there are no native African, Native American or Oriental languages on the tree at all. This last point indicates that the excluded languages sprang from different roots.

The early common and unwritten language is Proto-Indo-European or Indo-European:

...The term Indo-European is expressive of the geographic extent of the family, from India to western Europe (including Britain and Iceland), an area

44

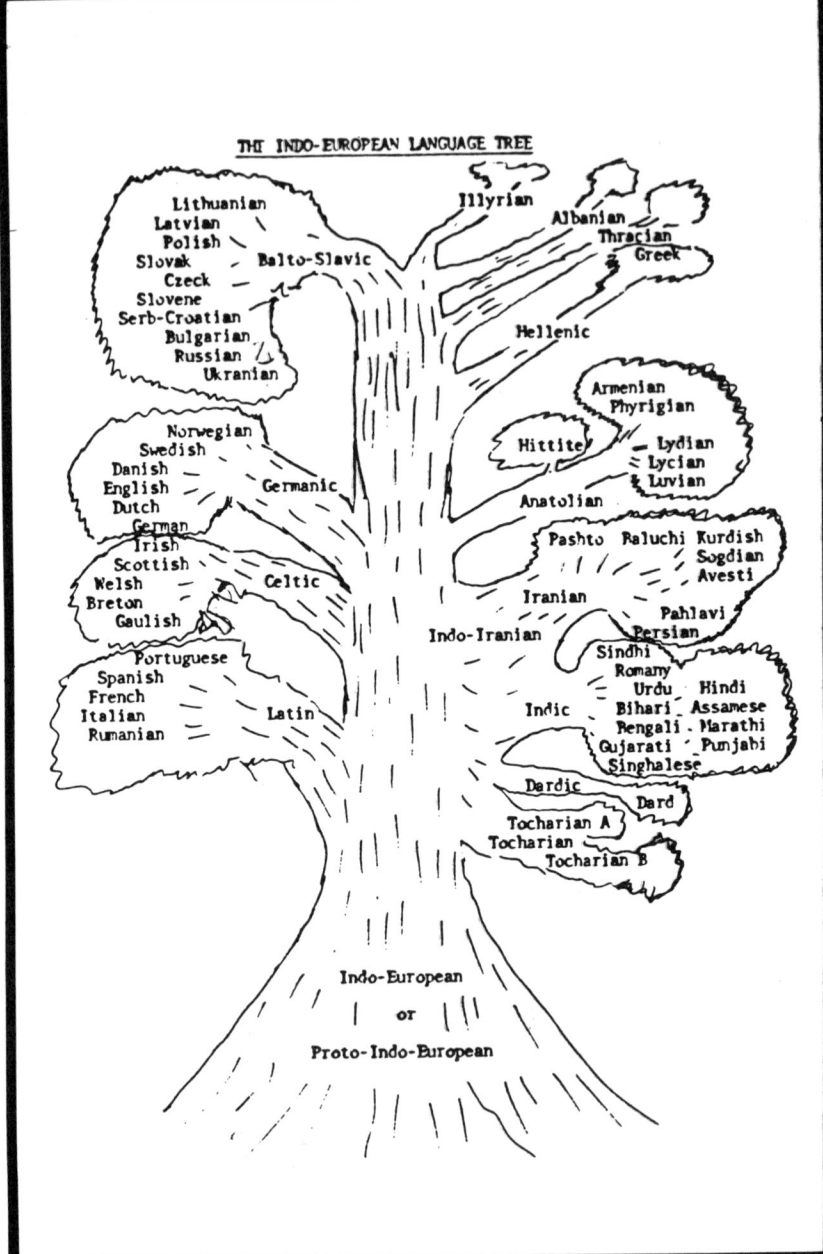

later expanded with the European settlement of the New World. The original home of the Europeans is believed to have been somewhere in east central Europe. Because there is a common IE word for copper (seen in Latin as aes), but none for bronze or iron, it is thought that the Indo-Europeans lived through the New Stone Age as a single tribe speaking a common language. Some time before the beginning of the Bronze Age, the tribal unity came to an end, and portions of the tribe migrated at first probably southeast from central Europe and into western Asia as far as India...

> *The Random House College Dictionary,*
> Revised Edition, Jess Stein: Editor-in-
> Chief, Random House, Inc., New York, 1982,
> p. xi.

The intermingling of the Hebrews with people who were neither Hebrews or Cushites ("the children of the sun") was described previously. Who were these people? They were Hittites and Aramaeans.

The *original* Hittites were the ancestors of many of today's Turks, and inhabited much the same territory that Turkey occupies today. These *original* Hittites are an unnamed people. They were invaded by Indo-Europeans around the time of Jacob, and the invaders became known as Hittites. However, at the time of Adam, *circa* 4000 B.C., the "Hittites" were an Altaic-speaking people:

> ...The Hittites, whose origin is unknown, spoke an Indo-European language. They invaded the region which became known as Hatti, about 1900 B.C. and imposed their language, culture and rule on the earlier inhabitants, a people speaking a non-Indo-European agglutinative language...

> *Funk & Wagnall's New Encyclopedia,* Funk &
> Wagnall's, Inc., New York, 1979, Vol. 12,
> p. 397.

Why is it that Random House can figure out where Indo-Europeans came from, but Funk & Wagnall's cannot? In any case, the original "Hittites" spoke an agglutinative language. Altaic languages are agglutinative. The Hittites at the time of Jacob were probably Indo-Europeans. Isaac married both Hittite and Aramaean wives. It is written that he preferred his Aramaean wives. I deduce from that assertion that the Aramaeans were more advanced than the Indo-European Hittites at the time of Isaac. Naturally Isaac would have preferred the more advanced civilization.

The Aramaeans were from Southwest Asia, northeast of the Fertile Crescent. Most reference books describe Aramaeans as "ancient

Syrians." However, we know from *Genesis* 2:10-14 that what is to-
day Syria was part of the Land of Cush at the time of Adam. The
Aramaeans must have come to what is today Syria at a later time.
Their homeland could not have been farther west than what is today
Iran at the time of Adam, *circa* 4000 B.C. Ethnically, the Aramaeans
were probably the extreme western wing of people native to
Afghanistan, Pakistan, Kashmir and northern India. They were of
mixed black and Oriental ancestry.

Aramaean is a Semitic language. Semitic is most often described as
"Afro-Asian." Could the early Hebrews have adopted Aramaean
patterns on an oral base that was Indo-European? The possibility
does not sound far-fetched. Many Kenyans speak English, but Kenyans are not Indo-Europeans. Jacob did "supplant" Esau, didn't he?

> ...We now know, for instance, that the pious belief of later Judaism and
> Christianity that Yahweh/Jehovah was from the beginning a "pure" desert
> god, utterly opposed to popular fertility cults of contemporary Canaan, was
> quite false. He can now be philogically related to the Indo-European Zeus,
> and their common name interpreted from its Sumerian origin to mean "Sper-
> matazoa," the sacred juice of created life...

> John M. Allegro, *The Chosen People,*
> Doubleday & Co., Inc., Garden City,
> New York, 1972, p.xii.

Alphabets		
English Letter	Hebrew Name	Greek Name
A	Aleph	Alpha
B	Beth	Beta
C	Ghimel	Gamma
D	Daleth	Delta

We can correlate the preceding information to the Jacob and Esau
metaphor. Esau, the hunting, red-haired and hairy oldest child, was
an Indo-European. Jacob, the smooth, younger supplanter, reflected
his mixed Indo-European and Afro-Asian ancestry. Aramaean is a
later development of Sumerian. It is most probable that Afro-
Asians—called Sumerians, Phoenicians or Aramaeans—taught both
Greeks and Hebrews to write. However, the oral base of both
languages is Indo-European, just like the concepts of the divinity in

both cultures were Indo-European: white, male warriors. The language development followed the extra-ethnic contacts. We'll come back to the development of the Hebrew language in the next chapter. Racially, the groups who resided between the place where Adam was created and *Bilud as Sudan* were brown people. In *Genesis* 10:9, Hav'ilah is described as a son of Cush. It isn't unreasonable to assume that Hav'ilah was between Adam and the Cushites in complexion. Maybe it means that Hav'ilah's culture was derived, at least in part, from the Cushites. Maybe both.

Let's go back to appearance for the moment, back to our natural history. God gave "the children of the sun" the gift of black skin to cope with the then (before Adam) more direct and closer heat of the sun. The earth was hotter than today, on average. We are going to assume that nature doesn't waste anything, including skin pigmentation, and that all are equipped to deal with their environments. If Adam was red/blond, what was his native environment? Given a red/blond complexion, logically one has to assume that Adam's native environment was Artic, or at least Nordic. Was Adam given gifts to cope with his native environment?

Certainly a thin Caucasoid nose is designed for warming air to a larger degree than a wide Cushite nose. Certainly pale complexions were not designed for the climate in the Middle East. A Middle East that was even hotter at the time of Adam presented an even greater problem for pale complexions. Certainly thin lips are designed for retaining, not dissipating, heat. Certainly a hairy body is not designed for steamy realms. Adam was given gifts.

I have another problem: European Russia is temperate in climate—on the cold side during certain periods of the year, but temperate. TODAY, it is temperate. What if the region, say Minsk-Moscow-Gorkiy, centered on a polar region before Adam, before *circa* 4000 B.C.? North or South Pole makes no difference—a polar region at least in climate, if not geographically and/or magnetically. Given that nature doesn't waste anything, including skin pigmentation, would one expect the average complexion of any people seen to get darker as one moved from a polar region to the tropics? I would expect it.

Oh, oh. Reader number 12 just said she doesn't give a good, healthy hoot about what *I* would expect, she wants some evidence. I like your style number 12. Let's see if we can bound the aforementioned area of east central Europe with a ring of non-Indo-European speaking people:

ALTAIC: The family of languages made up of Turkic, Mongolian, Tungusic and Korean subfamilies.

Say what number 12? "That only bounds east central Europe on the east and the south?" Right you are:

SAMOYED: A member of a Ural-Altaic people dwelling in Northwest Siberia and along the Northeast coast of European Russia.

What now, number 12? Ahhh, "The west is still open." There's no fooling you, is there:

FINNO-UGRIC: A subfamily of Ural-Altaic languages including Finnish, Estonian, Lapp and Hungarian.

The Altaic Ring is now closed. There is a map on the next page to show others what number 12 was hollering about. But what would have caused Adam to migrate, especially toward regions where the heat must have been difficult for him?

...The most ancient catastrophe of which Schaeffer discerned vestiges took place between 2400 and 2300 before the present era..."Ethnic migrations were, no doubt, the consequence of the manifestation of nature."*...

...These catastrophes occurred when Egypt was in the Bronze Age and Europe was entering the Neolithic Age...

...In a recent article, S.K. Runcorn of the University of Cambridge reports that "the evidence accumulates that earth did reverse its [magnetic] field several times." The unavoidable conclusion, according to Runcorn, is that "the earth's axis of rotation has changed also. In other words, the planet has rolled about, changing the location of its geographic poles."**...

*Claude F.A. Schaeffer, *Stratigraphie comparee et chronologie de l'Asie Occidental (IIIe et IIe millinaires),* Oxford University Press, 1948, p. 534-67.

**S.K. Runcorn, "The Earth's Magnetism," *Scientific American,* 9/55.

Immanuel Velikovsky, *Earth in Upheaval,* Pocket Book reprint of the original, New York, 1977, p. 177, 51 & 132. Originally published in 1955.

Adam migrated as a result of a cataclysm? An "ethnic migration?" The earth's poles rolling about? The devil, you say!

Schaeffer's earliest catastrophe was around the 24th century B.C. I have accepted the Mosaic dating of Adam as *circa* 4000 B.C. Do I have a problem? I don't think so. Certainly cataclysms much more severe than the very severe cataclysms that we're talking about here

THE ALTAIC RING

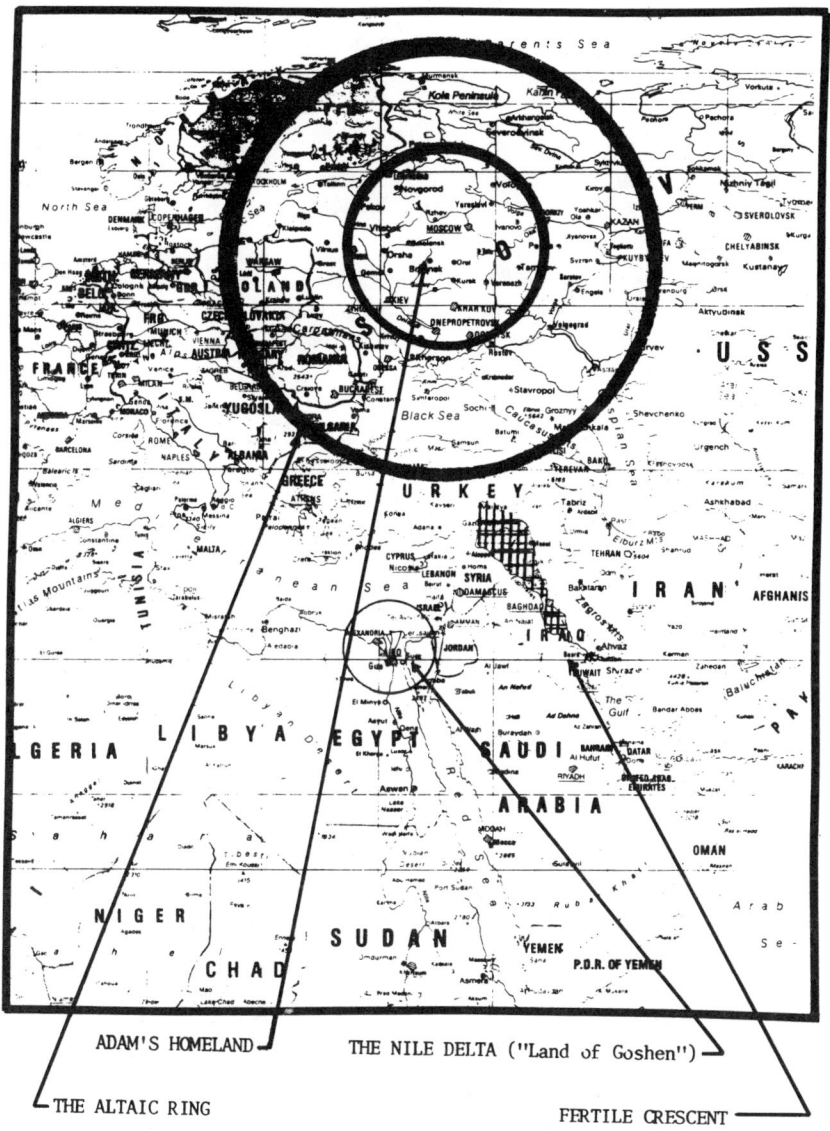

ADAM'S HOMELAND⌐   THE NILE DELTA ("Land of Goshen") ⌐

└THE ALTAIC RING   FERTILE CRESCENT ⌐

happened before 2400 B.C. A cataclysm brought the Age of Reptiles to a close. The preceding excerpt is offered to illustrate the process, not the event. To my knowledge, the identification of a cataclysm *circa* 4000 B.C. is novel here. Certainly something significant happened in that time frame:

> ...In the year of the world 2453 [1495 B.C.], according to certain authorities, a comet was seen in Syria, Babylonia, India in the sign Jo, in the form of a disc,*...
>
> * J. Hevelius, *Cometographia,* 1668, p. 794.
>
>> Quoted in *Worlds in Collision,* by Immanuel
>> Velikovsky, Pocket Book reprint of the
>> original, New York, 1977, p. 97.
>> Originally published in 1950.

Hevelius wrote in Latin and was referencing a Roman calendar in the preceding excerpt. From the information in the excerpt, we know that the beginning of time was evidently calculated in Rome at 3948 B.C. How do we know that? What is 2453 plus 1495? Was Latin one of the languages on the Indo-European language tree? You bet your sweet bippy it was. Look! I *know* that number 12 is checking it out.

But if Adam was affected by a cataclysm, wouldn't the Altaics, Aramaeans and others have been affected? Seems reasonable to me:

> ...About 4000 B.C. a people known in archeology as Ubaidians established settlements in the region known as Sumer...
>
> *Funk & Wagnalls New Encyclopedia,* Funk
> & Wagnalls, Inc., New York, 1979, Vol. 22,
> p. 307.

Chancellor Williams wrote about white people coming into contact with black people sporadically beginning about 4500 B.C. The contacts accelerated after 4000 B.C., according to Williams. That testimony seems to fit the working hypothesis here. But what was Adam's homeland like?

Adam was a hunter native to a very cold, overcast region. He probably survived hunting limited game, much as today's (Altaic) Eskimos do. The area of Adam's homeland closest to the tropics after the cataclysm would have warmed first. The branch of Adam's racial (white) and linguistic (Indo-European) families in that area (that is today southern Russia) would have seen their traditional game disappear first. Adam's traditional game that survived the cataclysm would have moved toward the new polar region seeking their natural environment—the shrinking, relocating ice.

Adam had few, if any, skills in agriculture. No growing season; no agricultural science. Culture follows nature. The survivors in Adam's family following the cataclysm would have been, to say the least, desperate. No agricultural science, little game, a hunting culture...military adventures into the Altaic Ring and *Bilud as Sudan* almost *had to* happen. But why didn't such adventures happen before 4000 B.C.?

Before the cataclysm *circa* 4000 B.C., Adam was not strong or desperate enough. The Altaic Ring and *Bilud as Sudan* were not weak enough. Certainly a cataclysm that moved a polar region would have had worldwide impacts. The social structure in *Bilud as Sudan,* the Altaic Ring and everywhere else in the world had to have been disrupted. The populations had to have been reduced.

With Adam desperate (hunger makes one that way) and moving through a fluid Altaic Ring on his way to *Bilud as Sudan,* the world would never be the same again. ADAM WAS ON THE LOOSE! Again, why did he migrate? Answer: A cataclysm such as the subsequent cataclysm described in the following excerpt.

...the goddess Rhea [Nut], the wife of Helios [Ra], was beloved by Kronos [Seb]. When Helios discovered the intrique, he cursed his wife and declared that she should not be delivered of any children in any month or any year. Then the god Hermes, who also loved Rhea, played at tables with Selene and won from her the seventieth part of each day of the year, which added together made five whole days. These he joined to the three hundred and sixty days of which the year then consisted...

The Egyptian Book of the Dead—(The
Papyrus of Ani), Translation and
Transliteration by E. A. Wallis Budge,
Dover Publications, Inc., New York, 1967,
p. xlix. Originally published in 1895.

Note well that the Greek names for the gods named above (as well as the Egyptian names in this context) refer to celestial bodies. Rhea is the earth. Helios is the sun. Kronos is Saturn. Hermes represents Mercury. Selene represents the moon. Also note that the excerpt alludes to a lengthening of the terrestial year and some impact on the moon. If the planets actually were put into disorder causing a cataclysm, and Adam—as a result of similar events *circa* 4000 B.C.—migrated to the hut of "the children of the sun," then we should be able to find evidence in *Genesis* and other books of the *Bible.* Let's test the hypothesis.

52

ONE POSSIBLE TERRESTIAL REORIENTATION

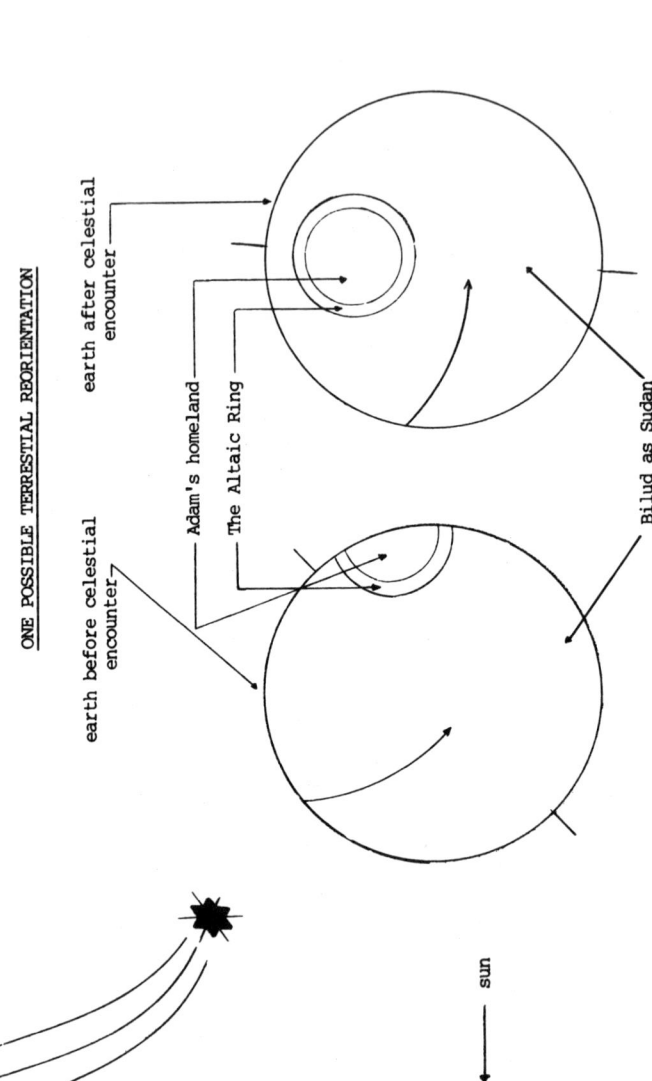

earth before celestial encounter

earth after celestial encounter

Adam's homeland

The Altaic Ring

Bilud as Sudan

sun

In the possible terrestial reorientation illustrated above, the earth encounters a celestial body and is moved away from the sun. The year is therefore lengthened. In this particular possibility, the geographic pole is in a constant position on the terrestial sphere, but the orientation of the pole relative to the sun is changed. Areas that got no direct sunlight prior to the cataclysm, get direct sunlight after the cataclysm. There are many possible reorientations including movements of the earth's crust around the substrata, and/or relocation of the geographic poles, and/or changes in the ecliptic, and/or reorientation of the poles as shown above.

Chapter 4

ADAM'S PATH

Let's summarize Adam's probable circumstances based on the assumptions that he is a native of a cold, overcast region in a world that has just experienced a natural cataclysm:

1.) Adam is a hunter, not a farmer.
2.) He probably has little experience even with wild plants. His native environment didn't provide those things.
3.) His social graces are not the best. His experience with collective action would have been only the temporary alliances of collective hunts.
4.) His commercial experience is very limited. He might have seen the Altaics and/or "the children of the sun" exchange goods through barter or for gold.
5.) His language skills are probably very limited. A written language is out of the question. Prior to the cataclysm, Adam spent his time (full-time) surviving. Cerebral pursuits were irrelevant. No need.
6.) Adam's personal toilet is suspicious, at best, and he is not a steward of the environment. One doesn't steward ice, and germs don't multiply very fast in a sub-freezing environment. "Racism?" No, legitimate historical inquiry. Have you never wondered why the phrase, "the diseases of the white man," appears so frequently—even in Adam's history books?
7.) Philosophy...not a whole lot to say. Nietzsche was Adam, essentially unchanged after about 6,000 years. Adam has "the pure conscience of a beast of prey."
8.) His cultural ethos is that of an individualistic hunter. His disposition is anything but sunny, and the trials in the post-cataclysmic environment didn't help his demeanor one whit.
9.) Adam is prone to quick "solutions." In his native environment, an animal—a scarce animal—had to be *quickly judged* as prey or predator.
10.) Adam is well-armed. He's desperate!

Now let's see if we can trace Adam's path through *Genesis*.

Genesis 1:

If one avoids the literal trap, which we must do until someone figures out where Cain's wife came from, *Genesis* 1 is consistent with the assumptions about Adam. Here are some examples:

...the earth was without form and void, and darkness was upon the deep...

Genesis 1:2

A polar region, especially one without today's polar tilt and today's ecliptic, could be in virtual year round darkness. Alternatively, the polar region could have long periods of dim light followed by long periods of almost no light. In both cases, there is no inconsistency with the assumed physical description of Adam and his homeland.

...God separated the light from the darkness...

Genesis 1:4

The polar region is moved by the cataclysmic event, and now gets more direct sunlight. The polar overcast is dissipated and relocated. The phenomena of days and nights are seen.

...And God said, "Let the waters under the heavens be gathered together into one place."...

Genesis 1:9

The ice cover, especially in the part of Adam's homeland closest to the tropics, melts. The run-off floods move to the low areas.

...The earth brought forth vegetation, plants yielding seed, each according to its kind, upon the earth. And it was so...

Genesis 1:11

Dormant vegetation warmed by the rays of the sun begins to appear. Note that plants but not trees appear.

...Let us make man in our own image, after our likeness...

Genesis 1:26

Three points are noteworthy in *Genesis* 1:26. First, Adam could not have been created "on the sixth day." Why? If he was, who saw the events on days one through five? The passage describes a survivor of the cataclysm.

Point two is that Adam is made in gods' image. The gods, therefore, are anthropomorphic; and the gods certainly are not female, Oriental or black. Note well that Adam was created in the image of the gods at the time of Moses (15th century B.C.), when *Genesis* was written. *Retroactively,* Adam was created in the image of the gods.

Point three, as you may have guessed, is that God is plural. How could this be? It's not true? "In *our* image," is unmistakably plural. "After *our* likeness," is unmistakably plural.

There is a very simple explanation as to why God is plural in *Genesis* 1:26 (and in many places throughout *Genesis*). Remember that *Genesis* was written in the 15th century B.C., evidently building on some oral traditions back to the time of Adam. Make no mistake, there are many political embellishments relating to the time of Moses, but there is also, to these eyes, an oral tradition on which the tangled web was woven.

The Hebrews at the time of Moses, and for centuries after Moses, were largely polytheistic. The plural references to the gods are slips, revealing deeply felt beliefs. In describing the oral tradition of Adam, the author(s) of *Genesis* strayed from the monotheism that Moses was trying to impose. Why was Moses trying to impose monotheism? We'll examine the point later. Now let's look at all of *Genesis* 1:26-28.

...Then God said, "Let us make man in our image, after our likeness; and let them have dominion over the fish of the sea, and over the birds of the air, and over the cattle, and over all the earth, and over every creeping thing that creeps upon the earth.

So God created man in his own image, in the image of God he created him; male and female he created them.

And God blessed them, and God said to them, "Be fruitful and multiply, and replenish the earth and subdue it; and have dominion over the fish of the sea and over the birds of the air, and over every living thing that moves upon the earth."...

Genesis 1:26-28

There are some severe problems for literalists in the preceding passage, but none for the hypothesis that assumes that "the Creation" was not the Creation. Problem number one is that God created a male *and a female*. But "EVE" ISN'T CREATED UNTIL LATE IN *GENESIS* 2 AFTER "THE LORD" TAKES ADAM TO THE GARDEN OF EDEN. A redundancy? A narrator getting ahead of the story? I think not. The females created in *Genesis* 1 mean that females, as well as males, survived the cataclysm. The meaning of "Eve," the female "created" in *Genesis* 2, will be examined later.

God instructed the males and females in *Genesis* 1 to "replenish" the earth. HOW CAN ONE "*RE*PLENISH" THAT WHICH HAS ALLEGEDLY NEVER BEEN PLENISHED? Some later *versions* of the *Bible* have neatly solved this particular problem by replacing the verb "replenish" with the words "fill the earth." It is perhaps appropriate at this point to remind the reader of the operative definition of the word "version:"

> **VERSION:** A personal or particular account of something, possibly inaccurate or biased; different from the original.

The verb "subdue" is also quite interesting. Subdue what or whom? God has already placed humanity over the birds, fishes and animals. Subdue??? We'll come back to that point.

Recall that in our assumed circumstances for Adam, he is not a farmer and has limited knowledge of plants. Adam's game is depleted and relocating. How did he survive the "ethnic migration?" Adam learns, out of necessity, to eat nuts and berries that are produced on the recently dormant vegetation in his homeland. Later, Adam would employ another method of survival.

> ...And God said, "Behold, I have given you every plant yielding seed which is upon the face of all the earth, and every tree with seed in its fruit you shall have them for meat."...
>
> *Genesis* 1:29

Again, the reader must be cautioned that some later *versions* of the *Bible* have the word "food" substituted for the word "meat." However, the older *versions* are consistent with the assumptions about Adam. He's a carnivore by tradition and circumstance. He has no agricultural science. He's foraging. He's foraging toward the tropics, where he would encounter trees.

We could go on and on with *Genesis* 1, and a case can be made relative to our assumptions. However, some of the obvious issues are more appropriately dealt with in the light of *Genesis* 2. Another terrible pun, whew!

Genesis 2-5:

These chapters have to be examined collectively because they are so interrelated.

Adam moved to what is today the south. He has limited knowledge of fabulous wealth in that direction from the early sporadic contacts. He doesn't know how to grow food. His game supply is depleted. Anybody in Adam's way is in serious trouble. Adam has not yet learned the more subtle techniques of the Right Honorable Mr. Elephant. Philosophically, however, Adam, Mr. Elephant and Herr Nietzsche are neck and neck...and neck.

Adam moves across the first river through the land of Hav'ilah. The Altaics are, of course, weakened by the cataclysmic upheaval. So is *Bilud as Sudan*. Since *Genesis* states that Adam crossed the Tigris and the Euphrates, which were wholly within the land of Cush, it must be concluded that Adam came to the hut of "the children of the sun." Adam sees wonders such as he has never seen before: writing, agriculture, architecture, medicine, metal work, *etc*. These wonders are operating at half speed, mind you, but they're there. There, in *Bilud as Sudan,* according to *Genesis* 2, plants begin to grow. The author(s) of *Genesis* also have a problem with the narrative that they try to fix retroactively:

...In the day that the Lord God made the earth and the heavens, when no plant of the field was yet in the earth and no herb of the field had yet sprung up—for the Lord God had not caused it to rain upon the earth, and there was no man to till the ground...

Genesis 2:4-5

...The Lord God took the man and put him in the Garden of Eden to till it and keep it...

Genesis 2:15

But plants were created in *Genesis* 1:11. "And it was so." Now, in *Genesis* 2, a man is necessary to till the ground. Why? POLITICS!

Did Adam till the ground in the Garden of Eden? According to the assumptions here, he couldn't have. "Why?" He didn't know how. *Genesis* later indicates that whatever is meant by *Genesis* 2:15, Adam did not till the ground in the Garden of Eden. Where is that indicated? *Genesis* 3:19:

..."In the sweat of your face you shall eat bread."...

Genesis 3:19

According to *Genesis* 3, one of Adam's punishments for his disobedience was to work for a living. How could Adam have worked *before* the punishment? How did he survive in the Garden of Eden?

Adam burst through the Altaic Ring into *Bilud as Sudan,* surviving at first on forage and then on what he could take and hold. He was a conqueror. In less trying times, conquering *Bilud as Sudan,* even a small portion of *Bilud as Sudan,* was out of the question. With the cataclysmic disorder, it wasn't that hard. The population of *Bilud as Sudan* had to have been reduced. The socio-political structures had to have been disrupted. The cultural ethos in *Bilud as Sudan* was one that Adam didn't understand. Adam looked at "the children of the sun" as stupidly compliant, instead of gracious hosts. He took every advantage and lived the life of Riley—wine, women and song.

Adam and his allies established a military and political base in the Nile Delta region. That area, with its many river tributaries, is a natural military fortress. It is referred to frequently in the *Old Testament* as "the Land of Goshen."

Let's look at another dual creation in *Genesis*: animals. In *Genesis* 1, animals are "created" on the fifth day:

> ...And God said, "Let the earth bring forth living creatures according to their kinds: cattle and creeping things and beasts of the earth according to their kinds." And it was so...
>
> *Genesis* 1:24

Note that animals are created very late in the prodigious "week" of "the Creation." Why? In Adam's native environment, there were not a lot of different kinds of animals. A seal, a walrus, maybe a polar bear or two. All of these are swimming animals. As Adam moves toward the tropics, he sees surviving land animals of an area that, before the cataclysm, was temperate. Then animals are reinvented in *Genesis* 2 after Adam reaches the Garden of Eden.

> ...So out of the ground the Lord God formed every beast of the field and bird of the air, and brought them to the man to see what he would call them; and whatever the man called every living creature, that was its name...
>
> *Genesis* 2:18

You have probably already surmised that these recreated animals in *Genesis* 2 are animals native to a torrid or tropical climate. Adam only encountered them after coming to the Garden of Eden; after crossing the rivers into the Land of Cush.

It's time to do some housecleaning. Remember way back in the last chapter when Adam and his homeland were identified? Adam was identified as an Indo-European. I ran into a problem because Hebrew is not usually classified as an Indo-European language. It is usually classified as a Semitic, or Afro-Asian language. Well, what have we here in *Genesis* 2:18? Is Adam sharpening up his language game, or what? If he was in Africa, the "Afro" of Afro-Asian is taken care of, but what about the Asian?

At the time of the cataclysm, it is doubtful that Adam alone would have had the wherewithal, however desperate, to occupy *Bilud as Sudan*. Not even the eentsy little corner of *Bilud as Sudan* called the Fertile Crescent and the Land of Goshen. He had to have had allies. Who were they?

Certainly, he had to have passed through the Altaic Ring. Certainly he had to have come in contact with "ethnic migrations" coming from what is today the east. We identified a tribe with whom Adam (Isaac) later intermarried, the Aramaeans. Their homeland was identified as southwest Asia, to the east-northeast of the Fertile Crescent. Neither the Altaics nor the Aramaeans had agricultural science as advanced as "the children of the sun" at that time. Adam certainly had nothing that those two groups would have wanted, besides his fighting talents. "The children of the sun" were obviously in harm's way. Adam, polishing up his language game in *Genesis* 2:18, is, no doubt, putting the "Asian" in Afro-Asian on an Indo-European base.

Adam's language could not have been highly developed in 4000 B.C. In the howling cold and darkness of his homeland, conversations over tea were not indicated. Poetry? For what? Poetry didn't put meat on the table.

What survived of Adam's family, the women and children, would have moved south also following the warrior spearheads:

... "This at last is bone of my bones and flesh of my flesh; she shall be called Woman."...

Genesis 2:23

Eve arrives on the scene. Forget the bit about the rib. That's just Adam's sexual politics of which all men are guilty to a degree. Sit down, ladies, you play politics too. Adam was perhaps a little more guilty than the rest of us, however. There is no telling what his boy/girl game was like before he came to *Bilud as Sudan*. Only after coming to the hut of "the children of the sun," does Adam get into a marriage thing; polygamy to be sure, but marriage:

...Therefore a man leaves his father and his mother and cleaves to his wife...

Genesis 2:24

"Wife" is singular in the above excerpt. Why did I say that Adam was polygamous? Well the singular wife could have been a convenient *version* of the original text supplied by later Hebrew or Christian translators. But remember, this author is a black man. To me, one's religion is what one practices. Was Isaac monogamous? Abraham? David? How about that rascal, Solomon? Please, let's be real. "Eve" is generic.

But Adam has a problem with Eve. She was allegedly beguiled by a serpent. The serpent, as can be discovered in almost any halfway decent history book on the period, was the "Egyptian" symbol for wisdom, or knowledge. Knowledge was something expressly forbidden by Adam's god. We're not talking about just any old kind of knowledge here. *Genesis* 2:17 is quite specific on the point. The forbidden knowledge is "the knowledge of good and evil." Although commonly portrayed as an apple, the *Bible* does not specify the metaphorical fruit of which Adam and Eve partook to gain the forbidden knowledge of good and evil. The *Koran* identifies it as a banana, a *tropical* fruit.

What kind of a god would forbid knowledge of good and evil? Isn't that the whole point of gods? Adam's god forbade it! Adam's god was Nietzsche's and Plato's god. Adam's god was David's and Moses' god:

> ...The Lord said, I will bring my people again from Bashan, I will bring my people again from the depths of the sea; That thy foot may be dipped in the blood of thine enemies, and the tongue of thy dogs in the same...

> *Psalm* 68:22-23 (A Psalm of David)

> ...The Lord is my strength and my song, and he is become my salvation, this is my God, and I will praise him, my father's God, and I will exalt him. The Lord is a man of war; the Lord is his name...

> *Exodus* 15:2-3 (The Song of Moses)

One could go on and on with examples, but the point is clear: Adam's god was (is) a warrior god. Warriors are not supposed to know about good and evil. "Don't think; kill on order!" Obedience is in order for warriors, not thinking.

Okay, Adam was a warrior. He worshiped a warrior god. But he made a mistake. He disobeyed. He partook of the tree of forbidden fruit. What does that mean? It means that Adam became "soft." He's now into marriage, language, and he probably has acquired some basic skills in agriculture and animal husbandry. Bad! Warriors don't do those things. Adam is no longer the lean, mean killing machine. The very rough edges of his warrior ethos have been honed by wine, women and song on demand, and I do mean "demand." What are "the children of the sun" doing?

The children were, without doubt, devastated by the cataclysm and the subsequent "ethnic migrations." Their tradition of leaders leading from the front must have cost them dearly in the early encounters with Adam and his allies. Adam & Co. did not understand chess match wars. I mean we're talking, in the words of *"Dr. Detroit,"* "scorched earth, no survival, wholesale destruction" in this war. The war evidently went on intermittently for hundreds of years. The children had their boundaries pushed down to just north of Thebes. Adam, the Aramaeans and the Altaics operated out of their fortress in the Land of Goshen.

Finally, in 3100 B.C., Menes moved down the Nile to what is today the north and kicked "the Triple A Alliance" out of *Bilud as Sudan.* Menes is generally acknowledged as the first Pharoah of the First Dynasty of Egypt. What is not generally acknowledged is that he was a black man, as were the other Pharoahs of the first six dynasties of Egypt. It is frequently said that Menes united "the two kingdoms." What two kingdoms? The Eurasian kingdom in the north or Lower Egypt with the African kingdom in the south or Upper Egypt. Menes founded the so-called "Old Kingdom."

I believe that the words "Old Kingdom" are misleading. They are misleading because if Menes united two kingdoms, then Egypt had to have been a kingdom prior to 3100 B.C. Having said that, I will drop the quotation marks from the words Old Kingdom.

How was Menes able to conquer Adam? The only thing that Menes really had to do was convince his people of the nature of the beast. "The children of the sun" were already more skilled than Adam, the Altaics and the Aramaeans. Whereas warfare in *Bilud as Sudan* was the glorified chess match type of warfare previously described, the principles of coordinated maneuver applied to warfare in general. It didn't matter whether one looked the other way at the conclusion of the match. One could maneuver, not look the other way and issue many obituaries also.

Adam was soft. Menes was more skilled. The children had regrouped in the south. Menes kicked Adam's butt:

> ...He drove out the man, and at the east of the garden of Eden he placed cherubim, and a flaming sword which turned every way to guard the way to the tree of life...
>
> *Genesis* 3:24

62

Adam could not directly acknowledge the defeat. Despite Viet Nam and Lebanon and Korea, have the U.S. Marines *ever* been defeated? Did Germany make peace in 1943 when any rational nation would have? Warriors just don't say, "We got whipped." Adam was a warrior. He did the only rational thing. He blamed the defeat on Eve's provocation of God. Adam couldn't have gotten soft. Eve was the culprit. *She* provoked God. It sounded better, because Adam equated feminine with soft, and he, after all, was a warrior.

·If Adam had had the chance to watch lions over thousands of years, he would have known better than to equate feminine with soft. Lionesses teach everybody to hunt, male and female alike. Lionesses do most of the hunting. But Adam didn't know that, of course. Nzinga, a female warrior, was one of the greatest military leaders in the history of Africa. What is the old line? "Hell hath no fury..." Adam didn't know.

Well, what happened to him? Adam returned to the north, and evidently had a civil war on his hands on the way. The war was between those sections of his family that wanted to stay in *Bilud as Sudan* and those who were compelled to go.

It should be pointed out that Menes kicked the political leadership out of *Bilud as Sudan,* not the masses. The masses were allowed to stay. Some of them became integrated into the society, and some acted as enemies within during Adam's periodic returns. Here is the evidence of the civil war in Adam's household:

...Abel was a keeper of sheep, and Cain a tiller of ground...

Genesis 4:2

The story goes on. Cain killed Abel and did not return to the unspecified place to which Adam and Eve went. Additional evidence that this metaphorical murder represents a civil war will be offered later. I am stating, despite the absence of a scriptural reference at this point, that Adam and Eve returned to the north. That evidence will be offered later in this book also.

Chancellor Williams was quite down on Menes for allowing the masses of invaders to stay in the hut of our ancestors. (The honored teacher and yours truly *live* our history.) In view of the subsequent actions by some of Adam's descendants, there is *a lot* to be said for that perspective.

It must also be realized, however, that Menes might not have had a choice. The complexion of the Fertile Crescent and the Nile Delta had lightened to a large degree as a result of murder, rape and marriage during the long occupation by Adam, the Aramaeans and the Altaics. The population of *Bilud as Sudan* had, no doubt, been reduced by the cataclysm and the long war. Racial lines had to have been obscured. Cultural identification could only be tested by crisis. Why didn't Menes pursue Adam and annihilate him along with his partners? Do lions pursue an invader once the invader is out of the pride's territory? Were there not cultural (read: religious) reasons for not pursuing the invader into his territory? Did "the children of the sun" *ever* invade anybody else's territory?

> ...Among the so-called "Bush Negroes" of Surinam—descendants of West Africans taken to this Dutch colony after 1600 who had escaped to the forest and conserved their independence- ...the spirits of the Earth were regarded as the possession of the original inhabitants, of the "Indians" whose ancestors had first inhabited this land.*
>
> This attitude is in marked contrast to that of European cultures. While the black Africans customarily fused with other peoples, and adopted the gods and ancestors of the original inhabitants of any new place, Europeans have dispossessed the original inhabitants of their lands and gods and imposed European gods upon them. At the same time they segregated themselves from the native population in a superior social position...
>
> *M.J. Herskovits, *The Human Factor in Changing Africa,* Routledge, London, 1962.
>
> Michael Bradley, *The Black Discovery of America,* Personal Library, Toronto, 1981, p. 37.
>
> ..."I saw a Kuke [a member of the Gikuyu tribe] jump off the train as it was pulling into the station this morning," a white hunter told us blandly. "I pulled out my gun and called 'Halt!' and damn it all, the fellow halted. I could have bagged him easily."...
>
> John Gunther, *Inside Africa,* Harper & Brothers, New York, 1955, p. 359.

The cultural propensity of "the children of the sun" might easily have been overcome by the ugly actions of Adam and his allies during the long occupation. Culture notwithstanding, people are people. But the cultural propensity was not overcome. The religion might have been strong enough by itself to prevent a campaign of vengeance. We will never know. We won't know because there was political rein-forcement for the policy dictated by the religion. Separation of the two justifications, the philisophical and the political, is therefore highly speculative. What was the political angle?

In addition to the aforementioned demographic conditions in *Bilud as Sudan* after the invaders' political leadership was routed, there is the simple fact that *Adam had nothing of value.* He had no chattels. He had little knowledge. Thinking people know that wars are fought for wealth. For that reason, African leaders were traditionally expected to lead from the front. Control, real control, of the army was in the hands of the Council of Elders. Those institutions helped to reduce the likelihood of leaders leading their constituencies into wars for wealth.

In European societies, the children are taught that wars are fought for the most noble causes: "democracy" (in many, many flavors), phoney aggression ("Remember the Maine!"), "God" (always a favorite), and the honor and glory of women (like Helen of Troy). The real deal is, of course, money (pronounced mun' naay in Black English).

... "but he desired to take away my Trojan plunder, all I had fought and bled for."...

The Odyssey, Book 13

So much for Helen's beauty. So much, that is, if one reads. If one reads, one doesn't have to die for somebody else's "Trojan plunder." The phenomenon of wars for bogus reasons and its antidote were described succinctly by Don Corleone, *The Godfather* in Mario Puzo's novel of the same name: "DON'T DIE FOR STRANGERS!" The necessary material to read is not available in American high school history books, and probably never will be; but it's available:

...The fighting that broke out at dawn on June 25 [1950], saved Syngman Rhee [the South Korean dictator] from ruin and gave President Truman the pretext he required for seizing Formosa. No one who studies the evidence can doubt that the Korean War began with an attack upon North Korea launched by Syngman Rhee with the support of the American Military Advisory Group...

Sir John Pratt, Former Head of the Far
Eastern Section of the British Ministry
of Information.

Quoted in *The People's Almanac* by David
Wallenchinsky and Irving Wallace, Doubleday
& Company, Inc., New York, 1975, p. 240.

A society designed to engender television watching instead of reading extracts a high price from those who go for the fake and don't read. However, some of us learn the hard way...and pass it on. Truth will out:

...."And this country befell upon us one big atrocity. It lied. They had us naive, young, dumb-ass niggers believin' that this war [Viet Nam] was for democracy and independence. It was fought for money. All those big corporations made billions on the war, and then America left."...

> Specialist 4 Arthur E. "Gene" Woodley, Jr.
> Quoted in *Bloods, An Oral History Of The Vietnam War By Black Veterans,* Wallace Terry, Random House, Inc., New York, 1984, p. 264.

...."When I was in Vietnam, it was not important to me where I died. Now it is very important to me. I made a promise in Nam that I would never risk my life or limb to protect anybody else's property. I will protect my own. So this country is not going to tell me to go out again to stop the spread of communism. In Germany [at the time of the Viet Nam War] we were buying beef for the GIs that came from Communist countries. They telling us to fight the spread of Communism, but they be helping the Communist economy. I don't walk around blind anymore. If another war breaks out and they want me to go, I'd rather die. I'll fight anyone here in America. But if they come and get me to send to some other country, I'm going to have my gun ready for them."...

> Specialist 4 Charles Strong.
> Quoted in *Bloods, An Oral History Of The Vietnam War By Black Veterans,* Wallace Terry, Random House, Inc., New York, 1984, p. 64.

What did the masses of black people think about the Eurasian invaders? Well the children certainly didn't like the Eurasians, but they loved them:

...for every shepherd is an abomination to the Egyptians...

> *Genesis* 46:34

...As a fact this [the above idea] is shown by the monuments of Egypt. In the sculptures shepherds always appear 'dirty and unshaven;' and at Beni-Hassan and the tombs near the pyramids of Ghiza [Giza], they are found caricatured as a deformed and unseemly race (Wilkensen). But the cause of it is not so clear. The most probable explanation is that a foreign race of shepherds had got possession of Egypt, and had for a long time tyrannized over the inhabitants. The Egyptians had thus been taught to hate all shepherds. Joined in this may have been the fact that Egypt was an agricultural and commercial country, and that the shepherds and tribes were rude and barbarous nomads and were therefore held in contempt...

> Explanatory notes to *Genesis* 46:34 by
> Rev. John Brown, Late Minister of the
> Gospel at Haddington and Professor of
> Divinity to the Associate Synod, *Brown's
> Self-Interpreting Bible,* John E. Potter
> and Company, Phila., 1873, p. 60.

"Dirty and unshaven?" Hmmmmm! Before commenting on the preceding excerpts it is necessary to review some wisdom from Chancellor Williams:

> ...Indeed, it is doubtful whether anyone, even a devil, could write a book completely devoid of the truth...
>
> Chancellor Williams, *The Destruction of,
> Black Civilization,* Third World Press,
> Chicago, 1976, p. 33.

Thank you, honored teacher.

Now for the comments on *Genesis* 46:34 and Rev. Brown's assertions relative to that passage. There is no question that the Right Honorable Rev. Brown is correct that people, who were shepherds (recall Cain's and Abel's occupations) and who were "rude and barbarous," invaded and controlled a part of *Bilud as Sudan* prior to the Old Kingdom, which began in 3100 B.C. We can date the invasion because Memphis, now known as Cairo, of which Giza is a suburb, was only built in the First Dynasty. But the monuments of Egypt do not reflect *all* shepherds in caricature.

Egyptians kept herds of cattle and sheep. The Altaics and Aramaeans kept herds. Adam might have had or acquired some rudimentary skills as a herdsman; the Lapps keep reindeer. The tombs of Egypt show Egyptians herding animals, and the Egyptians aren't characterized as "dirty and unshaven" or "rude and barbarous." Only those shepherds who *acted* "rude and barbarous" are so characterized. Who were they? Does the *Old Testament* describe soldiers maneuvering among herds of animals? Was Adam the culprit? The Altaics? The Aramaeans? All of the above? In any case, "the children of the sun" didn't "hate" anybody then, and we don't "hate" anybody now—after many "jungle lords" and "rude and barbarous" shepherds:

...''I'm not a hate monger. Nor do I ever advocate anybody else that is. I love myself so therefore I do love all people. I don't necessarily like all people, but I do love them.''...

> Mrs. Leftwich,
> A black mother of a PCP victim, quoted in
> *The Washington Post*, 8/25/85, p. B3.

...''I don't believe in hating people,'' Blocker said. This [boxing] is a business. My job is to beat him and his job is to beat me. There's no need for hate.''...

> Maurice Blocker,
> Welterweight contender and a champion
> if he never wins another fight. Quoted
> in *The Washington Post*, 4/18/87, p. D3.

Some will say that the words of two people don't mean anything. But the words of a zillion would mean nothing to some, and perhaps those who doubt should listen to the voice of an English historian, speaking in one of his more enlightened moments:

> ...This over-all humane and essentially religious attitude of the blacks led Arnold Toynbee to say that mankind may have to emulate them if civilization is to be saved...

> Chancellor Williams, *The Destruction
> of Black Civilization,* Third World
> Press, Chicago, 1976, p. 197.

Back to Adam's path. The fact is that, of the section of Adam's family that chose to remain in *Bilud as Sudan,* many became fully integrated in black society. They got to watch and participate in the development of the highest known achievements to date of ''the children of the sun.'' Menes had started the Old Kingdom. The serpent, wisdom, again ruled in the place of a warrior god. Menes was more than a warrior, a ''hammer.'' Menes was a man. He reigned for over sixty years, built Memphis (the city is named after him) and constructed a canal between the Nile and the Red Sea. The Red Sea was a source for reeds that produced papyrus, the paper of ''the children of the sun.'' This last fact, by the way, tends to indicate that the Red Sea was not, at that time, salt water. Some may have doubted what has been offered about cataclysms here. *Think* about it. Other evidence is offered in Velikovsky's works. *Read* them.

I should also point out that, at least 6,000 years ago, Egyptians had the technology to produce paper from reeds—not trees. That achievement illustrates how a technology can be oriented to *accommodate* nature. Today, after 6,000 years of "progress," Adam destroys trees for his paper and passes off the destruction as benign. The Egyptian paper seems to have lasted reasonably well, wouldn't you say? Why is Adam destroying the trees? Will the world's children have rain forests? Will there be children? Destruction of the environment is not necessary for progress. To the contrary...

During the Old Kingdom, "the children of the sun" were so advanced that they were performing surgery on the human skull, trepanning operations. African medicine was more oriented to dietary and medicinal cures than surgery, however. Chemistry, therefore, became highly developed. Psychological healing was practiced. There is evidence of hynoptic cures for ailments such as skin disorders also. According to the information available in *Jesus: The Evidence* by Ian Wilson, "Egyptians" induced the hypnosis with "a light source."

It is an irony of ironies that today we have the Bakke decision. "The children of the sun" are not qualified on "merit" to be physicians. We be genetically deficient. Mr. Elephant's tests say so. What was Mr. Elephant's medicine like during this time period? Where is the European Imhotep?

Some readers are now saying, "Imwho?" The question is understandable. Imhotep was a genius in many fields. He was especially brilliant in architecture and medicine. His advancements served as the basis for medical science in Egypt for centuries. He was honored by physicians as late as the time of Jesus. *Imhotep was "the father of medicine"* before "the war of the scholars" passed that title to Hippocrates. *Hippocrates lived about 2,000 years after Imhotep.* Hippocrates might have been an excellent physician in his time, but he couldn't have carried Imhotep's tongue depressor!

Some readers might now be saying, "Black propaganda!" Say whatever you want to say, no problem. But go find out where the early Greek physicians got their training. It certainly wasn't in Heidelberg or Johns Hopkins or Cambridge or Athens. Today, I can find Hippocrates' name in *The American Heritage Dictionary of the English Language.* Imhotep? Yo, Brother Imhotep. A futile call! Another battle lost in "the war of the scholars." False premises... false policy...self-destruction.

Civil engineering was also advanced during the Old Kingdom. Canals were built. Agricultural science and productivity were thus advanced. When was the first Roman canal built? Answer: About 2,500 years later.

The Pharoahs of the Old Kingdom weren't stupid. They had experienced a cataclysm followed by "ethnic migrations." Of necessity, they further centralized political authority. Power shifted from the Council to the chief. The Pharoahs maintained strength to keep the "rude and barbarous shepherds" out of *Bilud as Sudan*.

Chancellor Williams estimated that during this time frame 20,000 war chariots could be dispatched out of Thebes, acting under a single commander. (The Egyptian Thebes of a hundred gates, also known as Luxor and Karnak, preceded the Greek Thebes of seven gates by at least 4,000 years.) A long period of peace was guaranteed by the strength of 20,000 war chariots.

Adam, the Altaics and the Aramaeans understood power. Chess match wars, no; but power was a language that they spoke fluently. The amalgamation of that power had its price. Instead of the customary representatives of the people to the spiritual universe, the Pharoahs became the divine representatives of God to the people. In that seemingly subtle change, "the Triple A Alliance" had won a long-term victory. Its impact will be discussed later.

It is doubtful that the people, or the Pharoahs, believed that the Pharoahs were literally gods (in the Western sense of the word). The title was one bestowed to designate royalty and the awesome power now entrusted to the leaders. From the perspective of the children, the change was justified by the long and unpleasant experience with the "rude and barbarous" invaders. I can hear the voices of the children now, "ANYTHING to keep those *'muchachos'* out!" It was a mistake. "Anything" is seldom the right answer.

On the whole, the leaders kept the new social contract. They kept the expletives out of *Bilud as Sudan*. The leaders retained the essence of the traditional religion. Learning flourished. The children were well-fed. Their cities had drainage and sewer systems. Medicine was highly advanced. The music still played. Let's stop a minute and ask ourselves, "When did Europe get such things?" Have Europeans, to this day, ever been able to feed themselves without the use of other people's land? Is 15% of the USA hungry at some time during every month? More? Let's move on.

The new leaders demanded extreme luxury, stone houses and such, and all the trappings of office. I wonder where the idea of extreme luxury for the leaders came from? The Pharoahs sometimes acted whimsically, but *they fed the people*. But the Pharoahs were bad guys. No less an authority than Hollywood says so. If you ever want to watch a movie with hodge-podge history, "doublethink," watch

"The Ten Commandments." We have Seti, Ramses and Moses—
people who lived hundreds of years apart—there, in living color,
poisoning people's minds. Beware the illusion makers, brothers and
sisters.

The children honored their new leaders with new and improved
monuments to their reigns. The pyramids and the Sphinx at Giza
were built during the Old Kingdom. The Sphinx, a portrait of
Khafre, a Pharoah of the 4th Dynasty, was created about the 27th
century B.C. Adam, the Aramaeans and the Altaics understood the
message of the sphinx. Euphemistically, the message was as follows:
"HERE LIVES A SOCIAL LION WHO WILL RISE AND
ASSIGN AS MANY GRAVES AS NECESSARY, IF YOU COME
OVER HERE ACTING UGLY AGAIN!" The Greek myth about
"the riddle of the Sphinx" is at least 1500 years younger than the real
Sphinx at Giza. There was no "riddle." The message was very
straightforward.

Now some readers are saying, "Where is the tendency for bloodless warfare referenced previously?" It was mitigated, no doubt, by
"the Triple A Alliance," but it didn't die.

Note carefully that the Sphinx is a manlion. The Sphinx is lying
down, protecting his children and checking to make sure that no an-
tisocial lions come into the area to bother the children. He reflects
strength and vigilance. The Sphinx maintains his vigil with pride,
serenity and dignity, as real male lions are prone to do. He is not
snarling or fighting. The Sphinx is a *civilized* warning.

Now look at a Lowenbrau bottle and/or the emblem of Richard-
the-Lionhearted. What do you see? Those lions are certainly not
serene. Could it be that those lions are "monsters filled with joy?"
"No?" Okay, my mistake.

Oh, oh. Some readers are now grumbling about "the Conquering
Lion of Judah" that was used as the emblem of some later Emperors
of Abyssinia—later known presumptuously as Ethiopia. Dear
grumbling readers, where is, or was, Judah? Part of ancient Israel?
Did not the early Jews convert some early Abyssinians to Judaism?
Didn't the Jews have military colonies at Elephantine and other
places in East Africa? Where did the *Falashas* come from? "The
Conquering Lion of Judah" is not a *native* African symbol. Sorry,
your grumbling is not justified on this point.

The racial identity of the Sphinx was so clear that Europeans found
it necessary to shoot off his Cushite nose. The nose of the Great

Sphinx at Giza did not weather off. By the way, the Sphinx faces east-northeast.

Enough about the Sphinx. What about the pyramids?

For many, many centuries prior to the founding of the Old Kingdom, Africans buried their chiefs in pyramids. They can be found in abundance in Upper Egypt, in the south. When Menes built Memphis, pyramidal tombs were built in that region. Perhaps the idea was to reaffirm the title to that land after the Eurasian occupation. However, to the best of my knowledge, not a single Pharoah has been found in a pyramid at Giza.

Graverobbers? That idea doesn't make sense to me. Why would anybody steal a corpse with a fortune in gold and silver all around? After all, thieves are capitalists. They're in business not because they like to steal, but to make money. Well what did happen to the bodies of the Pharoahs? Either the pyramids at Giza were ceremonial tombs to begin with, or the bodies of the Pharoahs were later removed to prevent their capture and interred elsewhere. The bodies of the Pharoahs that have been found were found further south in the Valley of the Kings near Thebes. That makes sense, if we remember the religion of "the children of the sun." In the south, the spirits of the Pharoahs could commune with their ancestors and with the living.

The pyramids are wonders of architecture, built without power machinery. The Great Pyramid at Giza was the tallest manmade structure on earth for over 3,000 years. But doesn't that fact present a problem to the cataclysmic natural history assumed here? How did the pyramids survive the subsequent cataclysms?

No big problem. The pyramids, first of all, were designed strong. The pyramidal structure is inherently strong. There is very little free internal space. The sides are slanted upward to the exterior. Any earth shaking, therefore, would cause the sides to fall inward on the small amount of free space. The so-called "burial chambers" are covered with large slabs of stone placed in such a way that they would crack under stress, but the structure would be preserved. The slabs *are* cracked.

The workmanship is another reason for the longevity of the pyramids. The stones were fitted with a degree of precision that would be hard to duplicate with today's "high tech." The shift inward from earth shaking served only to make the fit tighter. Mathematics *had to have been* highly developed. The architects almost had to have known about earth shaking. Is such workmanship possible from oppressed slaves such as the Hollywood epics portray the workers on the pyramids and other temples?

I don't think so. Many of the stones on the monuments of Egypt are engraved with the names of the work gangs. Oppressed slaves or people honoring their leaders? What was the African institution of slavery all about? The following excerpt gives us a listing of some of the rights of slaves in traditional African societies:

> ...entitled to own property, to marry free persons and beget free offspring, to achieve their own freedom by various methods, in some societies to rise to positions of wealth and great authority...
>
> John D. Hargreaves, *West Africa: The Former French States,* Prentice-Hall, Inc., Englewood Cliffs, N.J., 1967, p. 46.

Basil Davidson, in his book *The Lost Cities of Africa,* confirms the relatively benign nature of slavery in Africa. Davidson points out that it was hard to tell who was a slave and who wasn't. Slavery was, in essence, an institution for working off debts, concentrating labor and protecting the destitute. It had next to no relationship to Eurasian slavery. *Nobody was defined as less than a human.*

All right, let's sum up the era. "The children of the sun" had a run of about 750 years of unmatched progress. The people were fed. Scientific progress took place. Social inequities were minimal. Any disturbances by the Altaics and the Aramaeans in the Fertile Crescent were easily dispatched. Adam wasn't raising any hell. Right into the Sixth Dynasty the children were moving right along. What happened then?

CATACLYSM! What follows a cataclysm? Right, "ethnic migrations."

Genesis 6-50:

Before moving on with the megahistory, let's understand a little about this particular cataclysm. This cataclysm is the first cataclysm that was mentioned by Schaeffer, "the Deluge" or "the flood of Noah." It began in the 24th century B.C., in the middle of the Sixth Dynasty of the Old Kingdom in Egypt. It might have continued intermittently until the time of Abraham and Lot in the 21st century B.C., and a case can be made that it should be considered two cataclysms. I don't argue the point. What caused the cataclysm? It was caused by the same thing that caused all of the other cataclysms: disturbances in the solar system caused by the electromagnetic and/or mechanical interactions of celestial bodies. Where's Adam? Where did we leave the rascal? Didn't we leave him returning to the north, licking his wounds? What did he do when he got there? Not very much. *Genesis* 5 and 6 describe a relative period of tranquility in Adam's history. Adam didn't do much more than make babies during that period.

Adam is a little different at this point than he was when he first came into *Bilud as Sudan*. He now knows the difference between right and wrong, after a manner. He picked up a few agricultural and husbandry skills in *Bilud as Sudan*. He probably still can't write too well, if at all, but he knows about it. His philosophy, however, is unchanged. *Genesis* 6 has him proclaiming the earth as "corrupt." Nobody is "good" but *his* descendants who survived the cataclysm. Of course!

Why "of course?" Because Adam now knows the difference between right and wrong. It is now necessary to rationalize his actions. He no longer has "the pure conscience of a beast of prey." His conscience is still that of "a beast of prey," but it isn't pure. He must now use divine authorization to justify his actions. He *half-learned* about good and evil. Evil is what other people do. Accordingly, those evil other people are fair game for whatever. God makes a pact with Adam, now called Noah, to destroy those other evil people, but Adam (Noah) will have salvation. No question!

The retroactive prophecy was obviously self-fulfilling. Those members of Adam's family who survived the cataclysm were, of course, the "good" people. Where do we find Adam after the cataclysm?

...the ark came to rest upon the mountains of Ararat...

Genesis 8:4

Adam survived the high-water catastrophe in the highlands of what is today southern Russia. Ark? No ark. Some animals would have rushed to the high ground also. Adam might have shepherded some animals up the mountains. An ark? No ark.

But haven't people reported seeing the ark that the thoroughly evil Russians won't let good Christians view? People have reported seeing

74

a lot of things. Would the Russians risk the wrath of God? Are they that stupid? If they are that stupid, why do we spend so many billions of dollars to prepare for their aggressions? "They don't believe in God?" With an ark in hand, they wouldn't have to *believe*, they would have evidence. Show me the ark, and I will say, "I was wrong."

At this point in history, Adam did not have the technology to build a boat of sufficient size to house pairs of all of the animals in the world. The construction itself, the required waste disposal system, not to mention the capture and transport problems with the animals, are simply beyond credibility—nonsense! If Adam (Noah) didn't have the technology to build a large boat in the 24th century B.C., where did the idea come from? Never, ever forget that the *Pentateuch* was written in the 15th century B.C., at the time of Moses. Moses probably didn't have the technology to build a large boat either, but he saw the large boats of the Egyptians. About 500 years after Moses, Solomon had to enlist foreign artisans to build his temple in Jerusalem. Yet we are asked to believe that Noah built a boat of sufficient size to house pairs of all the animals in the world 900 years before Moses and approximately 1400 years before Solomon.

"Divine intervention?" Well, we are at a religious impasse. I am a black man. My God operates through the eternal laws of the universe. My God does not bend the rules for anybody. Let's agree to disagree until such time as somebody shows me the ark.

"The deluge" was not a high-water catastrophe everywhere. It was a catastrophe everywhere, but not necessarily a high-water catastrophe. The amount of water in the ecosphere is finite. High-water in one area implies low-water in another area. People, plants and animals from all over the world survived the cataclysm...without an ark. In Adam's (Noah's) area, however, the cataclysm was initially manifested by high-water.

Noah, his wife, three sons and their wives survived the cataclysm: *Genesis* 8. A very curious thing happens in *Genesis* 9 and 10. Noah gets drunk and falls asleep naked in his tent; not a building mind you, but a tent. If Noah had the technology to build an ark, why is he sleeping in a tent? Anyway, one of his sons, Ham, walks in on him. Ham goes outside and tells his brothers, "Hey, the ol' man is drunk and naked in his tent." Noah wakes up. Ham's brothers tell Noah what Ham said, which was, after all, "true." For the heinous crime of saying what was true (in the context of the story), Noah cursed Ham's son (Canaan) and all of his descendants:

..."Cursed be Canaan; a slave of slaves shall he be to his brothers." He [Noah] also said, Blessed by the Lord my God shall be Shem; and Let Canaan be his slave. God enlarge Japheth, and let him dwell in the tents of Shem; and let Canaan be his slave."...

Genesis 9:25-27

...A most decisive derogatory racial tradition stems from the biblical interpretation of Noah's curse of Ham. The Bible did not apply any racial label, but the idea of race later became attached to the descendants of Ham. A collection of Jewish oral traditions in the Babylonian Talmud from the second to sixth century A.D. holds that the descendants of Ham were cursed by being black* and this belief received even greater elaboration during the Middle Ages when, according to one source, Noah's curse was explained.

"...it must be Canaan your firstborn, whom they enslave...Canaan's children shall be born *ugly* and *black*!...Your grandchildren's hair shall be twisted into kinks,...their lips shall swell;..." Men of this race are called Negroes; their forefather Canaan commanded them to love theft and fornication, to be banded together in hatred of their masters and never to tell the truth.**

Indeed, that passage includes not only a pretty clear description of the color and physical type of the "cursed" people, it also presents the principal stereotypes associated with the blacks—thieves, fornicators and liars...

*Thomas F. Gosset, Race: The History of an Idea in America, (Dallas, 1963), p. 5.
**Robert Graves and Raphael Patai, Hebrew Myths, (New York, 1964), p. 121.

Joseph E. Harris, Africans and Their
History, New American Library, New York,
1972, p. 14.

Now wait a minute. According to the Old Testament, Lot's daughters slept with their father; at least one man masturbates in public; Jacob connives his own brother of his just inheritance; David takes another man's wife... In short, "the chosen people" lived a pretty licentious existence. Among these people are the leading patriarchs of the Hebrews. What did Ham do that was so bad? Noah was drunk; Ham wasn't. Why would a man who was favored by God curse a whole race of people for accidently seeing him drunk and naked? Some have suggested that the passage describes a homosexual encounter, and that was the cause of "Noah's" snit. However, if that *was* the real deal, it was between two *white* men: Noah and Ham. Why even mention black folks?

In reading the tangled web that is Genesis, the reader must never, ever forget that Genesis was written in the 15th century B.C., at the time of Moses. Noah survived a flood that happened in the 24th century B.C. At the time of Moses, the author(s) of the *Book of Genesis* knew about three invasions of *Bilud as Sudan* in which the Hebrews had participated. One of those invasions, Adam's, has already been examined. The other two will be examined subsequently, but they came after Noah and before Moses. Moses and company are leaving Egypt with gold and silver that the "the Lord" told them to "borrow" from the Egyptians. How is it that black people are "thieves, fornicators and liars?" ...And who the hell were the Jews calling "ugly?" What is the real deal here?

The real deal is that Moses was nation-building. In his perverted philosophy, truth did not serve his purposes. He resorted to lies. Despite the assertion of the *Old Testament,* humanity did *not* all spring from the descendants of Noah. We are not *that* incestuous. According to the Eurasian theory of "the sons of Noah," Ham's grandchildren were to be born black with thick lips and kinky hair. Therefore, the alleged "curse" could not have taken place until after the 24th century B.C., when the flood took place. If that is true, then obviously the Sphinx (built in the 27th century B.C.) doesn't have thick lips. There obviously were no "Negroes" before the 24th century B.C. Sure! Look at the Old Kingdom statues. To whom does the description "the children of the sun" pertain? White people?

Black people have suffered and continue to suffer from this perverted nonsense almost beyond description. Without equivocation or hesitation I say to the spirit of Moses, *YO' MAMA*! May you burn in hell forever and beyond, and then may you burn some more. Many friends and relatives who read the manuscript to this book admonished me to temper the above statements. Their rationale was generally as follows:

1.) Moses is honored and respected by a lot of people.
2.) The statements will be construed as "anti-Semitic."
3.) The statements are "un-Christian."
4.) Moses married a black woman, and he, therefore, could not have been a bigot.
5.) Don't judge people of the past by today's standards.

To point 1: Moses might be honored and respected by a lot of people. Those people are entitled to their opinions as people. Similarly, I am entitled to my opinion. But Moses wrote, or caused to be written, the assertion that my people are less than human or, at the very best, humans cursed by God. Should I approve of that? Should I pander to bigotry? Should I honor and respect Moses? Why?

To point 2: I acknowledge that the statements could be *construed* as "anti-Semitic," but so could anything. I have to heed the lesson of the historical record:

> ...Did such rebellions [as Nat Turner's] set back the cause of emancipation, as some moderate abolitionists claimed at the time? An answer was given in 1845 by James Hammond, a supporter of slavery:
>
> > But if your course was wholly different—If you distilled nectar from your lips and discoursed sweet music...do you think you could prevail upon us to give up a thousand millions of dollars on the value of our slaves and a thousand millions of dollars more in the depreciation of our lands...
>
> Howard Zinn, *A People's History of the United States,* Perennial Library, New York, 1980, p. 170.

The lesson of the historical record is: *THERE IS NO SUCH THING AS A "MODERATE ABOLITIONIST."* It's like the title of the old song: *"Iz You Iz Or Iz You Ain't, My Baby?"* To quote Malcolm X, "You're either part of the problem or part of the solution."

To point 3: As to the absence of Christianity, we'll examine that point later. In the meantime, read *John* 8:44 and then explain to me why my statement is "un-Christian."

To point 4: According to the *Bible,* Moses "married" a woman or women alternately described as Midianite and Cushite. In my view, such a development proves nothing except that the woman or women held some personal attraction for Moses. Thomas Jefferson fathered more black children than most black men, but that fact did not stop him from defining his own children as chattel. Moses might have "married" a Midianite woman or women. So?

> ...Then they brought the captives [Midianites] and the booty and the spoil to Moses and to Eleazar the priest, and to the congregation of the people of Israel, at the camp in the plains of Moab by the Jordan at Jericho. Moses, and Eleazar the priest, and all the leaders of the congregation, went forth to meet them outside the camp. And Moses was angry with the officers of the army, the commanders of thousands and the commanders of hundreds who had come from service in the war. Moses said to them, "Have you let all the women live? Behold, these caused the people of Israel, by the counsel of Balaam, to act treacherously against the Lord in the matter of Peor, and so plague came among the congregation of the Lord. Now therefore, kill every

male among the little ones, and kill every woman who has known man by lying with him. But all the young girls who have not known man by lying with him, keep alive for yourselves."...

Numbers 31:12-18

How can *anybody* admire Moses? *This* is the great lawgiver of Western "civilization?" Does *Numbers* 31 describe attempted genocide perpetrated by Moses against his "in-laws," or am I missing something? Speak up, children of Shem and Japheth.

·*To point 5:* It is frequently suggested that one shouldn't judge historical personages by today's standards. I disagree with that suggestion for several reasons. Foremost among my reasons is the question: *WHOM DO WE 'WANT OUR CHILDREN TO ADMIRE, AND WHY?* Moreover, judging Moses by his own professions, Moses comes up as a hypocritical, lying, raping, murdering thief. The events of *Numbers* 31 and many similar events happened *AFTER* Moses offered the *Ten Commandments* as rules of behavior. Did Moses love his neighbor? Did he murder? Did he steal? Did he covet? Did he bear false witness? Why should I have my children admire Moses? I don't want them to be psychological slaves or any other kind of slave.

In summary, friends and relatives, we cannot love anybody unless we love ourselves. We cannot bite our tongues and turn other cheeks, unless we like getting bloody tongues and slapped cheeks. Are the Hebrews who don't admire Adolph Hitler anti-German? As to Moses, brothers and sisters, you have a tough sale here. I respect and appreciate candor, and I hope other people do also. If other people don't appreciate candor, so? Who benefits, if one is intimidated? Our children? I view my statements about Moses as pro-human, not anti-anything or anybody. Back to the megahistory.

With the knowledge of the three prior invasions and one that was going on at the time of Moses, Moses was able to make something that was already accomplished look like a prophecy. He took credit for the vast destruction going on during the cataclysm in his time, "the plagues of *Exodus.*" The cataclysm during Moses' time was made to be the work of *his* tribe's god. The stealing that Moses was doing was therefore "authorized." Certainly!

We have to give credit where credit is due. It was a neat maneuver. Call the people from whom you stole, whom you raped and whom you lied about, "thieves, fornicators and liars." Nobody who participated in the crimes, the Altaics and the Aramaeans, would have any interest in revealing the travesty. People who *worshiped* truth would become known as "liars." What was Moses really afraid of? Why would he do such a thing? Moses was nation-building. He wanted a "glorious" history like that of "the children of the sun." Since he didn't have a very remarkable history, he invented one. The fraud has been perpetrated ever since. The Hebrews, like everybody else, had been devastated by the cataclysm at the time of the exodus from Egypt. Recall the testimony of the rabbinical tradition in which it was stated that 98% of the Hebrews died in "the plague of darkness." Moses' group was therefore weak, like everybody else. Despite being "chosen people," they encountered some Semitic tribes moving into Egypt when the Hebrews were leaving and did not have unbridled success in the inevitable military encounters. The Amalekites, for example, evidently gave as good as they got in their battle with the Hebrews—despite fighting "chosen people." Moses chose mysticism as a weapon to buy time for nation-building. The myths would protect him from the advances of people in a disoriented world—for a time. "Don't mess with us, our god destroyed Egypt. You want us to turn our god loose on you?" Read *Exodus* 18.

Who could offer contrary testimony? Correct, "the children of the sun." They saw the Hebrews die right along with everybody else. The children knew Moses' history and Adam's history. Knowledge was "Ham's" *real* crime:

...And Ham, the father of Canaan, saw the nakedness of his father...

Genesis 9:22

Ham saw "the nakedness" of his father. This is not physical nakedness. It is historical nakedness. Moses couldn't have it.

Moses could not have the truth told. He wanted to build a nation. Solution? Call the truth-worshipers "liars." Nobody would believe them. The cataclysm destroyed records. One of *our* very early mistakes was not to make literacy widespread. We went for long periods of time after the cataclysms with very few literate people. Subsequent invaders, each having his own *version* of history to write, further obscurred the truth. Moses' curse worked for a while, but it came back to bite his descendants. "How?"

The so-called Christian world, Adam's erstwhile brothers, eagerly adopted the Hebrew legacy of "chosen people." We'll go into detail on the mechanics of this later, but here is a small sample of the historical record from the Right Honorable Rev. Brown:

...Multitudes too of the posterity of Japheth in Asia and America, but chiefly in Europe, have been persuaded of God to embrace the true religion, and become his church, ever since the Jews were rejected. The far greater part of that race known to us do, and for many ages have, at least in word, made professions of the Christian faith, while very few of the descendants of Shem or Ham have so much as pretended it. ...The Hamites as a race have been 'servants of servants,'...under perpetual servitude under the Shemitic Israelites, and the Japhetic Greeks, Romans and Saxons. Japheth has been enlarged. His descendants occupy at this day the territories of Shem and constitute the leading nations of the civilized world...

Explanatory notes to *Genesis* 9:26-27, by
Rev. John Brown, Late Minister of the
Gospel at Haddington and Professor of
Divinity to the Associate Synod. *Brown's
Self-Interpreting Bible,* John E. Potter and
Company, Phila., 1873, p. 15.

Whoa! What does all this garbage mean? It is simply a summary of the historical interpretation of the meaning of Christianity by what Pope John Paul II called, "our Christian civilization." What does it say? First one has to know the players.

In "Christian civilization," Ham is generally interpreted as the father of black people. Shem is generally interpreted as the father of brown (including "red" and "yellow" people). "Christian civilization" classified Hebrews, not according to their original Indo-European origins, but as descendants of Shem. So did the Hebrews, when it was convenient. The point will be examined later. White people, of course, were classified by "Christian civilization" as the descendants of Japheth: "Greeks, Romans, Saxons" and what have you. Now that we know the players in this tragedy, it is possible to do the analysis.

Point one is Rev. Brown's assertion that "the Jews were rejected." *WHO* rejected them? Why "God," of course. This blasphemy is the same garbage that Moses started in the 15th century B.C. with his "chosen people." The so-called Christian *version* of the Hamitic events was some of the same garbage used to justify Hitler's holocaust. That is why Moses' (Noah's) curse of Ham came back to bite his own descendants. We have an expression in black America, "What goes around comes around." Hebrews have a similar expression, "The sins of the fathers..." Properly interpreted, both expressions mean that if you start out wrong, you're going to end up wronged. I am *not* endorsing Hitler's holocaust. I am pointing out the fact, as many historians have, that it was a historical inevitability.

"Master races" and "chosen people" cannot coexist. *It just won't work!*

One can have pride in one's race for its gifts and legitimate achievements, and no rational person should have a problem with such pride. However, once one starts to say that one's race is *superior* to other races by divine selection, forces are set in motion that result in the devastation of the select. Look at "the flower of Hypoborean youth" slain on the plains of Russian, killed by "subhuman" Slavs. There are many, many other examples. The Most High God does not bend the rules *for anybody*, no matter how many "hammers" are included in one's army.

Point two about Rev. Brown's commentary is that the descendants of Japheth, white folks, do not have to *believe* in Rev. Brown's interpretation of Christianity. All that is required for salvation is "a profession—at least in word." This assertion is known as "amazing" or "mysterious grace." *Ain't a damn thing mysterious about it.* The "salvation" is the white skin. It is racism, period!

European "scholarship" rushed to support the story of Noah's perverted curse of Ham. A language grouping was created called "Japhetic." And I do mean "created," when I say "created." The grouping could not stand even the most cursory challenges, and one can find some words like the following without too much effort:

JAPHETIC: Designating a discredited linguistic grouping that attempted to associate Basque, Etruscan, Sumerian and Elamite with the Indo-European languages.

Lies upon lies upon lies. One can't help but be reminded of the "science" of Darwin.

Okay, what happened next? In *Genesis* 11 and 12, Noah dies, and his descendants allegedly migrate all over the world. The Japhetic descendants moved west. The sons of Canaan moved south-southwest. They actually survived the cataclysm in their native lands without an ark. The descendants that Noah (Moses) favored moved again south-southeast. A harmonious rebuilding effort is described as going on in the Fertile Crescent at Babylon. The Hebrew word for Babylon, *Babhel,* identifies the area.

According to *Genesis* 11, this harmonious effort was *not* favored by God:

...And the Lord came down to see the city and the tower, which the sons of men had built. And the Lord said, "Behold, they are one people, and they have all one language; and this is only the beginning of what they will do; and nothing that they propose to do will now be impossible for them. Come, let us go down, and there confuse their language, that they may not understand one another's speech." So the Lord scattered them abroad...

Genesis 11:5-7

It is unclear to me whether "the Lord" is a reference to the continuing cataclysm or an effort by the Hebrews to bring disharmony through subterfuge. Either could be the case. Note carefully that God is plural again: "let *us* go down."

The Hebrews evidently continued on down the Fertile Crescent and settled in Ur, near the Persian Gulf. After much begetting, Abram, later known as Abraham, was born. In *Genesis* 15, one of the baldest lies in the *Old Testament* takes place:

...Then the Lord said to Abram, "Know of a surety that your descendants will be sojourners in a land that is not theirs, and will be slaves there, and they will be oppressed for four hundred years; but I will bring judgment on the nation which they serve, and afterward they shall come out with great possessions."...

Genesis 15:13-14

The reader knows, I assume, that the land referred to is Egypt. The story of "four hundred years" of oppression is quite widely believed. *It is a lie!* However, for now let us use the four hundred year period to date the alleged oppression. If Moses was the leader who took the allegedly oppressed Hebrews out of Egypt, then all one has to do is count backwards four hundred years from Moses to date the start of the oppression. When did Moses leave Egypt?

Chancellor Williams, a son of Ham; Immanuel Velikovsky, a son of Shem, and the Right Honorable Rev. Brown, a son of Japheth, all put Moses on Mt. Sinai between 1491 and 1495 B.C. That group should eliminate the politics of the date. Let's be arbitrary and use 1495 B.C. as the date, just for convenience. Four years, in megahistory, is the epitome of nit-picking. I don't really give a damn which one is used. Count backward 400 years. We are now at 1895 B.C. This must be the approximate time of the beginning of the alleged oppression of the Hebrews by "the children of the sun." *IT COULD NOT HAVE HAPPENED,* as will be shown. What is happening with the children after the cataclysm?

The Sixth Dynasty in Egypt ended early in the 23rd century B.C., amid a great deal of turmoil. Chancellor Williams was down on the brothers and sisters of the Sixth Dynasty for neglecting defense of the Motherland and their accomodative policies with the invaders. If, however, there was a natural cataclysm that weakened *Bilud as Sudan,* accomodation might have been the only choice available. When did Schaeffer say his earliest cataclysm took place? Answer: Between the 24th and 23rd century B.C. The cataclysm was followed by the usual "ethnic migrations." Again, "the children of the sun" did not go into anybody else's land. Japheth and Shem came into our land. The same religious and political reasons existed at this time to support the stay-at-home policy that existed at the time of Adam, the first Adam. Japheth and Shem still had nothing that we wanted: no chattels and no knowledge. The initial wave would have been the Aramaeans, who were probably the more advanced of "the Triple A Alliance." Adam and the Altaics would have followed.

> ...It should be noted that the greatest Hebrew invasion of Egypt occured about 600 years before Moses...
>
> Chancellor Williams, *The Destruction of Black Civilization,* Third World Press, Chicago, 1976, p. 89.

If the honored teacher is correct that the greatest Hebrew invasion of Egypt occurred about 600 years before Moses, and all of Noah's sons place Moses at *circa* 1495, then the greatest Hebrew invasion of Egypt had to have taken place about 2100 B.C.

Is there any supporting evidence for Williams' assertion in the *Bible?* Sure there is. Abraham leaves Ur in *Genesis* 11. In *Genesis* 12 through 23, he moves into Palestine. After a famine, he goes into Egypt, comes out wealthy of course, and then goes on a rampage in the Middle East where he is also *given* wealth. In sanitizing the events, the author(s) of the *Books of Moses* state that the wealth was *given* to Abraham as a result of a Pharoah and a king in the Middle East trying to avoid God's wrath. These people had incurred God's wrath by taking liberties with Abraham's wife, whom Abraham portrayed as his sister. All I can say is that she *must have been* a fine somebody.

The 7th through 10th Dynasties in Egypt represent an Egyptian dark(?) age. Learning came to screeching halt. No pyramids were built. Destruction was the order of the day. During this period, the Pharoahs, who had become separated from the people by the practice of making themselves lesser gods, tried to reach accomodation with the Eurasians through widespread intermarriage. Since the progression to the throne was matrilineal, a Eurasian marrying the sister of a Pharoah would produce the heir to the throne. The children revolted, and the sordid deeds ended up producing what Williams called "the new breed." "The new breed" were brown Egyptians. They were racially brown and culturally brown, especially in the leadership ranks. They came to look upon their erstwhile brothers and sisters as inferior. The blacks, who didn't want to forceably integrate with the Eurasians (who had so oppressed the children), retreated south toward the place of origin of their civilization.

Finally, "the new breed" succeded in throwing the invaders out around the middle of the 21st century B.C. Chancellor Williams says 2040. This date would put the expulsion about half a century after Abraham's "sojourn" that made him wealthy. The date marks the beginning of what is generally called "the Middle Kingdom." The dates seem to fit, but Egypt would never be the same again. The list of dynasties after the Old Kingdom is one long tangled web of "who knows?" The tangled web reflects the intermittent wars for control between Eurasians in the north, "the new breed" in the center and the original Egyptians, "the children of the sun," in the south. The 11th Dynasty, for example, began about 75 to 95 years before the end of the 10th Dynasty. Fighting with little, if any, learning was the rule during the Seventh through Tenth Dynasties, sometimes called the First Intermediate Period.

Abraham buried his wife in the land of the Hittites, and then he died. These facts would tend to indicate that Adam went north again, but maybe not completely out of the Middle East. We next run into the story of Isaac, Jacob and Esau. Isaac marries an Aramaean. The Hebrews evidently engaged in widespread intermarriage with the Aramaeans at this point in time.

Jacob and Esau split up after Jacob connived Esau of his birthright. Jacob, the "smooth," goes to live with his mother's family in the east. He does some foul deeds there, and returns west (rich) to Canaan, where he is temporarily reconciled with Esau, the "red-haired and hairy." Esau and Jacob again have their differences, and Esau moves southeast out of Canaan (Palestine) and founds the tribe called Edomites. The Edomites were later repeatedly assaulted by people called the Israelites, descendants of Jacob.

During this time, "the new breed" in Egypt was alternately progressing and fighting civil wars. Who was fighting the wars? "The new breed" and "the children of the sun." Eurasian tribes saw an opening with the internal discord in Egypt. They moved in for the kill:

> ...Among these invaders were the Hyksos, the "Children of Israel" according to the historian Josephus. This invasion of Egypt in 1720 B.C. was ruthless and aimed at nothing less than the extermination of the Egyptian people...
>
> Chancellor Williams, *The Destruction of Black Civilization,* Third World Press, Chicago, 1976, p. 88.

Many readers will not accept the testimony of Chancellor Williams alone about this attempted genocide and its perpetrators. No problem. We sons of Ham(bone) have come to expect such attitudes. We are what Frantz Fanon described in his compulsory book of the same name, *The Wretched of the Earth.* Somehow we lost the tag of "faultless" that Homer put on us. Do *not* take Williams' word about this attempted genocide. Go to the the library and read *Against Apion* by Josephus Flavius, sometimes written Flavius Josephus. Josephus was a Jewish citizen of Rome.

Why is it that assertions by black historians are difficult to get into print, shunted to dusty shelves and generally ignored? There are several reasons. First, some do not want alternatives to accepted dogma available. "The Velikovsky affair" gets repeated daily for black people in "the land of the free and the home of the brave." Second, we in the black community have not developed our own market sufficiently such that we can enable the ideas of our young men and women to flow for the benefit of all. If others don't want to listen, that's their loss. But our children *must have* access to all ideas and the education and training to evaluate those ideas. A third cause of this lack of opportunity is, like the second, self-inflicted. Too many of us take the position that only the accepted dogma is valid. We become imitators instead of initiators. This third cause is part and parcel of the previously examined "Moses-was-a-good-guy syndrome." If we do not *think* for ourselves, somebody else will do it for us—for *their* purposes. Back to the megahistory.

Is there biblical evidence to validate the testimony of Chancellor Williams and Josephus? Yes, there is. It is sanitized to the maximum possible degree, but it's there. It is, coincidently, the story of Joseph. Forget the bit about some evil Pharoah oppressing Joseph. The Hyksos, frequently referred to as the Amu Hyksos, came to power during this time period, at least in the Nile Delta region. This is the period of the Hyksos Dynasties of Egypt. The Right Honorable Rev. Brown also puts Joseph in Egypt at the end of the 18th century B.C. The occupation, *the third* major occupation since 4000 B.C., had devastating results for the people of Egypt.

There was no damn dream about seven fat cows and seven lean cows. The story simply means that Joseph did what capitalists always do; he created a shortage. Pharoah didn't favor him for saving the people. "Joseph" *was* the Pharoah (or a vassal to a non-Egyptian Pharoah) at least over part of Egypt. He fought a war and enslaved the Egyptian people. Here is an excerpt which describes the conclusion of Joseph's war on Egypt. The excerpt is from the *Bible.*

...And when that year was ended, they [the Egyptians] came to him the following year, and said to him, "We will not hide from my lord that our money is all spent; and the herds of cattle are my lord's; there is nothing left in the sight of my lord but our bodies and our lands. Why should we die before your eyes, both we and our land? Buy us and our land for food, and we with our land will be slaves to Pharoah; and give us seed, that we may live, and not die, and that the land may not be desolate."

So Joseph bought all the land of Egypt for Pharoah; for all the Egyptians sold their fields because the famine was severe upon them. The land became Pharoah's; and as for the people, he made slaves of them from one end of Egypt to the other. Only the land of the priests he did not buy; for the priests had a fixed allowance from Pharoah, and lived on the allowance which Pharoah gave them; therefore he did not sell their land. Then Joseph said to the people, "Behold, I have this day bought you and your land for Pharoah. Now here is seed for you, and you shall sow the land for Pharoah. And at the harvests you shall give a fifth to Pharoah, and four-fifths shall be your own, as seed for the field and as food for your little ones." And they said, "You have saved our lives; may it please my lord, we will be slaves to Pharoah." So Joseph made it a statute concerning the land of Egypt, and it stands to this day, that Pharoah should have the fifth; the land of the priests alone did not become Pharoah's. Thus Israel dwelt in the land of Egypt, in the land of Goshen, and they gained possessions in it, and were fruitful and multiplied exceedingly...

Genesis 47:18-27

Readers should be cautioned that some *versions* of the *Bible* substitute the word "servant" for the word "slave." Some *versions* substitute the words "removed them to the cities" for the words "made slaves of them."

"Joseph bought the land of Egypt for Pharoah???" Let's use a little mother wit. If all that Joseph did was "remove them [the Egyptians] to the cities," how were the Egyptians going to give 20% of their crops off the top to the Pharoah? Were they going to grow crops in the cities? Be real.

The passage describes the surrender of starving people in Egypt. The Amu Hyksos came to the throne of Egypt, operating again out of the Nile Delta, the Land of Goshen. They ruled from about 1720 B.C. until approximately 1600 B.C., perhaps as late as the 1540s. Learning again came to a screeching halt during this period. No advances in science, the arts, literature—nothing. The Amu Hyksos were still not cerebral people. They still didn't like the snake. They still worshiped a warrior god. By the way, "Amu" has been translated as "Asian" and "Hebrew." Hyksos was originally translated as "shepherd kings." Later translations yielded "foreign kings." Either works.

The institutional changes described here were disastorous. Of foremost importance is the death of economic democracy in Egypt. The land was now owned by a central government, not a family or tribe. The second change was taxation, its collection and use. Taxation was high (20% off of the top) paid directly to the central government. Prior to this time, taxes, if they existed at all, were paid or given by the people to the treasuries of their respective tribes. A portion of those funds were then given to the next higher administrative unit. *The new, centralized taxation was not used to benefit the people who did the work.* The new taxes benefited only the Israelites in the Land of Goshen, who became "fruitful and multiplied exceedingly." Nobody could accept those arrangements. The Egyptians didn't. They overthrew the Hyksos about 1600 B.C., maybe as late as the 1540's.

A third disastorous institutional change was the bribery of the learned leadership and the further separation of the people from the leaders.

Now it's time to do some housecleaning. Recall that Abraham came into Egypt in the 21st century B.C. Joseph came in about 1720 B.C., and Hebrews stayed on the throne until at least 1600 B.C. Moses left in 1495 B.C. WHEN DID THE ALLEGED 400-YEAR PERIOD OF OPPRESSION OCCUR? There could not have been a 400-year period of oppression, because there aren't 400 years in which the oppression could have taken place between Abraham's invasion (during which he got rich), Joseph's invasion (during which he got rich) and Moses leaving with "borrowed" gold and silver. *It is a lie!* Moses, I curse your spirit again for an infinite number of eternities. May you roast slowly in high heat.

There is nothing in the Bible between Joseph and Moses. NOTHING!

"Scholarship" again tried to come to the rescue of the Judeo-Christian lie. If there was no 400-year period of enslavement, the sons of Shem and the sons of Japheth would create one to keep the sons and daughters of Ham(bone) in our place. The result was, of course, the very common dating of Moses in the 13th century B.C.. One could squeeze out 400 years between Joseph and Moses with such a dating. *Another lie!*

Velikovsky, a son of Shem, pointed out, in his book *Ages in Chaos,* that the Israelites had been in Canaan for over two hundred years by the 13th century B.C. Any dating of Moses subsequent to the 15th century B.C. leaves no time for the events of the *Book of Joshua* and the *Book of Judges.* The time frame covered by those books is generally conceded to be *at least* two hundred years. One cannot date Moses in the 13th century B.C. and reconcile other known dates such as the Babylonian Captivity, while allowing sufficient time for the reigns of the other Hebrew patriarchs described in the *Old Testament. Take that statement as an academic challenge,* children of Shem and Japheth. The 13th century B.C. dating of Moses is a lie, and without the lie there could not have been a 400-year period of Hebrew enslavement in Egypt. We are left with only the sequence of *events* described in the *Old Testament:* (1) The Hyksos (Joseph) enslaved the Egyptians (beginning about 1720 B.C. and ruled until *at least* 1600 B.C.); (2) A new king (Pharoah) overthrew the Hyksos; (3) After a brief period, Moses left Egypt in the midst of a natural catastrophe (cataclysm) with "borrowed" gold and silver. Again, there is nothing in the Judeo-Christian *Bible* between Joseph and Moses. The new king, "who did not know Joseph," is *the same king* who allegedly oppressed Moses. It's right there in *Exodus* 1. Read it! Now do you understand why some protested so vehemently against the publication of Velikovsky's book, *Worlds in Collision*? The myth of a 400-year period of Hebrew enslavement in Egypt was simply an attempt to stigmatize the Egyptians, people who had been repeatedly invaded by the Hebrews. Velikovsky's book endangered "the 400-year myth" as well as the myth of divine intervention. It also endangered by myth of the infallibleness of Western "science."

Oh, I almost forgot. Any children of Shem and Japheth—or Ham (bone)—who decide to accept my academic challenge should be mindful of the scriptures:

> ...And it came to pass in the four hundred and eightieth year after the children of Israel had come out of the land of Egypt...he [Solomon] began to build the house of the Lord...

> *1 Kings* 6:1

Solomon had been dated as early as the 11th century B.C. Most historians date him in the 10th century B.C. The latest dating that I have been able to find anywhere is early in the 9th century B.C. The temple in Jerusalem, which was built by non-Israeli artisans, was begun in the fourth year of Solomon's reign. This was 480 years after the exodus from Egypt, according to the scriptures that is. Is it possible for Moses to have left Egypt in the 13th century B.C.? Is it possible for there to have been a 400-year period of oppressed Hebrews in Egypt? You figure it out!

But Velikovsky's hands weren't clean either. He went to great lengths in the aforementioned book trying to prove that the Hyksos, who were notoriously cruel and barbarous, were a Semitic tribe other than the Hebrews, the Amalekites, naturally. He said that the Hyksos were only entering Egypt when the Hebrews were leaving. What then of the Hyksos Dynasties that preceded Moses? Why did I write the Amalekites "naturally?" Because Velikovsky followed the Mosaic tradition. He could accept a "radical" natural history, but on the social history that obviously went along with that natural history, he protected "vested interests."

> ...And the Lord said to Moses, "Write this as a memorial in a book and recite it in the ears of Joshua, that I will utterly blot out the remembrance of Amalek from under heaven." And Moses built an altar and called the name of it, The Lord is my banner, saying, "A hand upon the banner of the Lord! The Lord will have war with Amalek from generation to generation."...

> *Exodus* 17:14

Velikovsky described Egyptians as "the oppressors" of the Hebrews. Velikovsy moved the Hyksos Dynasties from before Moses to after Moses. In whose land were the Hebrews? How did they get there? From where? Velikovsky's account can only be described as "tortured." I wish you were still living, Dr. Velikovsky. I would ask you three questions: (1) Who was Joseph of *Genesis*, an Amalekite? (2) Was Josephus Flavius really wrong? (3) Where is the 400-year period of oppression? May you anguish over those questions next to Moses for contributing to the libel of my people. We will take whatever heat is due us for our sins. Lies never!

Exodus:

The Egyptians overthrew the Amu Hyksos around 1600 B.C., possibly 20 to 60 years later. The defeat is again not referenced directly in the scriptures, but it's there:

> ...Now there arose a new King over Egypt, who did not know Joseph...
>
> *Exodus* 1:8

The story, and I do mean story, goes on to state that the new Pharoah attempted to kill all of the newborn Hebrew males. *It is another lie!*

According to the account in *Exodus*, Moses was saved from this attempted genocide by Pharoah's daughter. She drew him out of the Nile where Moses' mother had allegedly placed him to avoid the wrath of the new Pharoah. Pharoah's daughter rescued Moses. Uh-huh! Moses, while you turn there on the spit, could you tell me if Aaron was so rescued also? Where did the battle-aged Hebrew men who fought the Amalekites come from? Were the Hebrew warriors all women? If you have no answers, enjoy the heat. If you have answers for those questions, I have about sixty other questions to ask you about the episode.

These lies have served to oppress black people for almost 3,500 years. *Their time has come.* If the sons and daughters of Shem and Japheth will not ask obvious questions about the alleged oppression of the Hebrews by the Egyptians, then we sons and daughters of Ham(bone) must ask. Whom shall we ask? Each other, of course. The "best" universities of Shem and Japheth do not see fit to eliminate 500-year gaps in their fantasies called "history." Obviously, as a group, they are not interested in the truth. Let us sons and daughters of Ham(bone) ask each other the questions that need asking. Back to the megahistory.

The Egyptians, "the new breed," started a rebuilding period after the terrible occupation by Joseph. What happened then? CATACLYSM! What follows a cataclysm? Right, "ethnic migrations." We are now at the "plagues of *Exodus*."

These are not the first "plagues" described in the *Bible*, but they are the only ones described in detail. Earlier plagues happened in the time of Abraham and Lot. They are briefly mentioned in *Genesis* 12:17. These later plagues are, however, described in detail by the author(s) of the *Books of Moses*. Moses knew about these plagues; *he saw them.* As previously mentioned, they affected everybody, and

Velikovsky did a pretty fair job specifying the cause of each plague as a result of a defined celestial event. Read *Worlds in Collision*, and you will see—for your consideration—a cause of each of the plagues described in *Exodus*. I have alternative interpretations for some of the plagues, but, in general, I agree with Velikovsky's interpretations. See what you think.

Exodus itself stamps "lie" in many, many places to the story of 400 years of oppressed Hebrews in Egypt. Here's an example:

> ...And the whole congregation of Israel murmured against Moses and Aaron in the wilderness, and said to them, "Would that we had died by the hand of the Lord in the land of Egypt, when we sat by the fleshpots and ate bread to the full; for you have brought us out into this wilderness to kill this whole assembly with hunger."...

> *Exodus* 16:3

Does it sound like "the whole congregation of Israel" recollects being made to make "bricks without straw?" Sitting next to the meat in those days were powerful people, not oppressed slaves. What American slave could say such a thing? Can the sons and daughters of Ham(bone) say that they aren't hungry today? The preceding testimony does not describe oppression. The following testimony (from a son of Japheth) describes oppression:

> ...It is oftentimes loosely said, that America has been settled by the European races, and different portions are distinguished, as settled by the English, French, Spanish and Portuguese. The truth really is, that America, including its islands, has been settled chiefly from Africa, and by negroes; and it is only in our own immediate times, that its colonization by Europeans has been commenced upon a scale of any magnitude. Prior to the commencement of the current century, the number of negroes brought hither probably exceeded the whole number of Europeans of all nationalities, who had emigrated hither, twenty-fold, or even more; and down to within less than twenty years ago, the African slave trade still brought in more people than did voluntary white immigration...

> In reference to the number of negroes taken in Africa for transportation to America, the *Encyclopedia Americana* (1851) says it has been "calculated to amount during the last three centuries to above forty millions, of whom fifteen or twenty per cent die on the passage."...

> When it is considered that the stock of negroes in the United States is due mainly to natural increase, and not to importation, and contrast these vast importations with the comparatively small number of negroes now existing in other parts of America; it is seen how immense a sacrifice in human life has

been made, to enable the civilized world to be supplied at cheap prices with
sugar, rum and coffee...

> George M. Weston, *The Progress of
> Slavery in the United States,* published by
> the author, Washington, 1857, p. 154.

Let me emphasize to the reader that the preceding estimate is very,
very conservative in the range of estimates of people killed in the slave
trade. I just can't help but wonder what Mr. Weston's definition of
"civilized" was? It should also be pointed out that Mr. Weston
wasn't arguing in his book for an end to slavery because it was wrong
per se. He argued against slavery primarily because it had devastating
impacts, both economic and social, on the *whites* in America—
especially the poor whites. Back to the megahistory.

It must be noted that this particular cataclysm, "the plagues of *Exodus,"* was perhaps the worst of the four assumed in the natural
history here. I mean we're talking *megadeaths.* Remember 98% of
the Hebrews died in just one of the plagues. Populations worldwide
must have been similarly affected. I don't know if 98% is the right
number, but it was a high number in any case. The world population
was *drastically* reduced.

The continent of Africa was mutilated. The Albion Sea, Lake
Triton, in the Sahara drained into the Atlantic and Mediterranean.
The Great Rift in East Africa was created. That split in the African
continent was described by early astronauts as the most prominent
feature on earth. The sea that once occupied the American Midwest
was probably drained in this cataclysm also. Velikovsky collected
worldwide accounts of this disaster. They are not pretty scenes.
Water standing above the mountains; fire raining from the sky; "a
thick darkness" (choking gasses)...It's all there in *Worlds in Collision.* Read it. Then read *Earth in Upheaval.* Then decide if you think
those things really happened.

I think they did. The mystery about them came from Moses utilizing the events to his political advantage, as previously described. The
Red Sea did part, but Moses didn't part it. Hebrews, right along with
the sons of Ham(bone), drowned when it came back together. Read
the books.

So much for *Exodus.*

Leviticus, Numbers **and** *Deuteronomy:*

These *Books of Moses* essentially describe rules (which were
fragmentary borrowings from Egyptian rules—see: *The Egyptian*

Book of the Dead) that Moses was trying to impose on the Hebrews. Rules! In the basic rules, *The Ten Commandments*, revealed in *Exodus* and *Deuteronomy* (they're different), Moses attempts with his first rule to impose monotheism on the Hebrews. Why?

Remember that Moses was trying to use the cataclysm as a weapon. He wanted to portray it to the world as an act of the god of the Hebrews. It could not be portrayed as an act of everybody's God. If the cataclysm was portrayed as an act of everybody's God, Moses would, of course, have lost the weapon. Moses substituted a sometimes polymorphic (recall "the burning bush"), but mostly anthropomorphic tribal god for the traditional Hebrew planetary gods. The new god, of course, was seen ONLY BY THE SELECT. Hebrew "monotheism" was political and geopolitical, not spiritual, in origin. Similarly, the Hebrews were told not to make any images of the new god. If they did and the images reflected the cataclysmic events, the illusory weapon would have been lost. Why? Because everybody saw the same events, all the survivors that is. Native Americans saw them. People in India saw them. The Egyptians saw them. Everybody saw them. It has been suggested that "the Star of David" was a slip, portraying a head-on view of the comet that caused the cataclysm, "the plagues of *Exodus*." "The Star of David" originally was not exclusively a Hebrew symbol. Indeed, many people around the world used the symbol. What does that fact tell you? Moses also gives the party line about the lineage of the Hebrew people in *Deuteronomy*:

> ..."And you shall make response before the Lord your God, 'An Aramaean ready to starve was my father; and he went down into Egypt and sojourned there, few in number; and there he became a nation great, mighty, and populous. And the Egyptians treated us harshly, and afflicted us, and laid upon us hard bondage'..."
>
> *Deuteronomy* 26:5

Here we go again. O spirit of Moses, may you never know what air conditioning is like! I weary of cursing that wretched soul. Readers should be cautioned that some *versions* of the *Bible* substitute the word "wandering" for "ready to starve." In the revised *version* of the events, we are asked to believe a tribe of people was born on the run—no home, just "wandering!" Do oppressed people become "mighty and populous?" Africans in the Americas today probably do not exceed the number taken out of Africa during the overt slave trade. How did the Hebrews become "mighty and populous" if they were "afflicted?" Does Moses say that the Hebrews were dragged into Egypt? Why does he have to remind the Hebrews of their alleged recent oppression?

Why would Moses claim *only* Aramaean heritage? Isaac *married* an Aramaean. Isaac was *not* an Aramaean. Adam was red. Esau was red. Why would Moses claim *only* Aramaean ancestry? He had to have known the story of Jacob and Esau. The story appears in the *Books of Moses*! There was a reason. The reason was political.

At this point in time, *circa* 1500 B.C., the sons of Japheth were nowhere. There was no Greek Empire, no Roman Empire and Nietzsche was just a gleam in some Frank's blue eyes. Moses has visions of a homeland for the Hebrews in Canaan (Palestine). Remember that God gave that land to the Hebrews in the books written no earlier than *the time of Moses*. God forgot to tell the Canaanites that their land had been given away, and the war is, of course, still going on. The Canaanites will win eventually, when they solve their leadership problems.

Since the Canaanites were largely Indo-Europeans and Altaics at that point in time; the Hebrews had intermarried most heavily with the Aramaeans, and the Aramaeans were potential allies against the Indo-Europeans and Altaics, Moses chose to trace his ancestry to the Aramaeans. Not Esau, the red and hairy; but Jacob, the smooth. It was a *temporary* victory.

Why was Moses trying to impose rules on his followers? Moses had a big problem on his hands. His people had survived, since Adam, by taking from other people. That was all fine and dandy as long as the Hebrews were in somebody else's country, like Egypt. During the exodus from Egypt, there was no host country from whom to "borrow" things. Moses' group could not survive with internal theft, murder and what have you. Therefore, he tried to establish rules. He failed.

Why did he fail? Moses didn't understand that rules, laws, can *only* yield justice in an environment where there is an underlying philosophy on which one can apply the rules. In the absence of such a philosophy, the rules become weapons for the Inner Party to use against the proles (members of the proletariat) and members of the Outer Party. Among black Americans, there is an expression: *"The bitch peeks!"* The bitch is, of course, the blindfolded statue of *"Justice"* who presumes to stand in front of many American courthouses. A philosopher who lived about 1,500 hundred years after

Móses understood the philosophical requirements for justice. That philosopher was, of course, Jesus:

... "Woe to you lawyers also! for you load men with burdens hard to bear, and you yourselves do not touch the burdens with one of your fingers...

Woe to you lawyers! for you have taken away the key of knowledge; you did not enter yourselves, and you·hindered those who were entering."...

Luke 12:46 & 52

What evidence is there that Moses' rules without a viable underlying philosophy failed? Read the *Old Testament* from *Exodus* to the end! It is one long, sordid tale of theft, rape, murder, wars and rumors of war. As a friend of mine observed, "It's hot!" Despite the sanitizing of the events, the message comes across very clear: Moses failed with his rules. Justice and prosperity did not come to the Hebrews—domestically or internationally.

It was just fine to destroy the city of Jericho. No problem when this king and that king were slain and their people marched into a horrible form of slavery. It was okay to "borrow" gold and silver from the Egyptians; "the Lord" said so. The land of Canaan was okay to steal; "the Lord" said so. Morality, in Moses' mind, did not transcend borders. Philosophically, therefore, he had no basis to build his nation. There is no record of scientific achievements in the nation of Israel, as there was in the Old Kingdom of Egypt. If there was, show me. Show me an Israelite pyramid! Arts? Science? Nothing but wars and rumors of war.

What was happening in Egypt after Moses died and Joshua founded Israel? Obviously the cataclysm wrought havoc. Semitic tribes did invade. They were eventually thrown out, and "the new breed" of Egyptians eventually regained power.

Great nations don't just, one day, collapse. Usually, the process is rather extended. Rot sets in and eats away at the socio-politico-economic structure. On what *day* did the Roman Empire collapse? The Greek Empire? Hard to pick a day, isn't it? Such was the case with Egypt. A new era, the Age of Ramses, began about 1200 B.C. During the Age of Ramses, Egyptians defeated the Greeks and Persians in naval battles. Egypt was therefore again formidable around 1200 B.C.

One of these "new breed" rulers understood the mistakes of his predecessors. His name was Akhnaton, or Ikhnaton. He is known as "the great reformer." What did he attempt to reform? He attempted to reform the religion of the Egyptians, "the new breed" of Egyptians.

Three cataclysms have been mentioned already. After each of those, there were "ethnic migrations" into Egypt. There was also the Hyksos invasion, Joseph. These Eurasian invasions had corrupted the institutions of *Bilud as Sudan*, especially religion. The Most High God had fallen into disfavor. The individual guilds and their priests no longer operated to learn the truth of a part of the Most High God's creation. They no longer operated to serve tribe, clan or national interests. They operated under the principle: "I got mine, get yours!" In short, they had become individualistic and powerful. It was a formula for disaster, and Ihknaton knew it.

Even though he was the physical product of what was, by then, inbred and significantly Eurasian royalty, he identified with the culture of his maternal ancestors. He disdained the culture of his Eurasian fathers. He tried to reform the religion of the Egyptians such that the nation would have a philosophical base for further progress. He, therefore, imposed the emblem of the sun, the traditional representation of the Most High God, on the statues and temples of Egypt. This change is, of course, frequently construed by the scholarship of the sons and daughters of Shem and Japheth as worshiping the sun. It was not that at all.

Ihknaton was trying to reimpose the traditional religion of "the children of the sun" such that *Bilud as Sudan* could progress after retrogressing so badly following the cataclysms, invasions and civil wars. He never worshiped the entity of the sun. He was trying to resurrect worship of the truth.

By the time of Ihknaton, however, the "vested interests" in Egypt had become quite powerful. Ihknaton failed, but his effort must be mentioned. May your spirit enjoy eternal bliss, Brother Ihknaton.

Ihknaton *was* a prophet. Predatory economics, priests vying for power, Eurasians in the Delta still clamoring for power...it was not a formula for success, peace and prosperity. Along came another cataclysm. When? It began in the 8th century B.C. and continued into the 7th century B.C. Eurasians poured into Egypt again. They were thrown out again. Who threw them out, "the new breed?"

No, it wasn't "the new breed." It was "the children of the sun."

erating out of the Sudan, Piankhi defeated the Eurasian kings, Tefnakhte and Bocchoria, late in the 8th century B.C. His successor, Shabaka, completed the liberation of *Bilud as Sudan* all the way to the Mediterranean. This event marked the beginning of the Twenty-fifth Dynasty. As Chancellor Williams points out, it is the *only* dynasty that the "scholarship" of the sons and daughters of Japheth and Shem acknowledges as being black. Don't even worry about it, brothers and sisters. It's on them, not us.

"The children of the sun" couldn't hold, however. Assyrians became the first of a parade of conquerors in *Bilud as Sudan*: Assyrians, Persians, Greeks, Romans, Turks, Arabs, Frenchmen, Englishmen, Belgians, Dutchmen, Spaniards, Italians and Germans. Why couldn't the children stand up to these people?

There were three main reasons, as I see it. First, there was the iron weaponry of the invaders. Chancellor Williams lamented about the late development of iron in *Bilud as Sudan*. He attributed that late development to Iron Guild politics in Egypt. That might have had something to do with it, but I don't think it's the complete answer.

In the earliest times in *Bilud as Sudan*, gold was the metal of choice because of its abundance. Bronze, an alloy of copper and tin, was developed. The reason for the late exploitation of iron could not have been technical. Any society that had the technology to make bronze had the technology to work in iron. Bronze is an alloy. Iron is an elemental metal. Why did "the children of the sun" develop iron *after* bronze? As Williams pointed out, there are iron deposits all over the ground in some sections of Africa. Africans worked with iron, in small quantities, for a very long time before the Iron Age. Was it only Iron Guild politics? I don't think so.

Iron is an element found in the earth's core. The cataclysms described here freed molten iron to rise closer to the surface of the earth. Additionally, some of the celestial bodies that rained debris on the surface of the earth evidently had some iron content. The development of iron came after bronze *worldwide,* not just in *Bilud as Sudan*. Why would an elemental metal be developed after an alloy? The only thing that makes sense to me is that the iron wasn't always there in sufficient quantities to exploit. Did Iron Guild politics have the same retarding effect worldwide? I don't think so. Were there not also Bronze Guild politics?

What was the second reason for the parade of conquerors in *Bilud as Sudan*? The second reason was food. *Bilud as Sudan* was mutilated in "the plagues of *Exodus.*" The Sahara became the Sahara. Therefore, "the children of the sun" could no longer support a population as large as that of previous times. European Russia and the Ukraine, on the other hand, were now fertile areas. The ascendancy of Japheth was thus assured. Seems like a conscious "act of

God," doesn't it? It wasn't. Has Japheth found salvation? Or has he known only inquisitions, wars and rumors of war in an increasingly polluted world?

The third reason was the repeated corruption and destruction of the leadership in *Bilud as Sudan.*

Other Adams:

For now, it is important to point out the similarities between the Hebrew actions and the actions of the other members of Adam's Indo-European family. The Hebrews were in no way unique, except that they were among the first to break out of the cold, dark Indo-European homeland. Here is an example:

...Archeological evidence indicates that a primitive Mediterranean people closely akin to the races of northern Africa inhabited the southern Aegean area as far back as the Neolithic Age, before 4000 B.C...

...During the second millennium B.C. began a series of invasions by the tribes from the north who spoke an Indo-European language that was the precursor to Greek...The most prominent of the early invaders were the Achaeans...

...As Hellenic race pride developed, the pre-Hellenic inhabitants of Greece called the Pelasgians (*q.v.*) came to be considered an inferior race...Out of the mythology that became the basis of an intricate religion, the Hellenes developed a geneology which ascribed to themselves aspects of divinity...

Funk & Wagnalls New Encyclopedia, Funk & Wagnalls, Inc., New York, 1979, Vol. 11, p. 439, 440 & 441.

Is the pattern obvious? "No?" Okay, let's go through it. Before 4000 B.C. there were some brown people in Greece, probably Altaics. After a couple of cataclysms, some "rude and barbarous" people came out of the north. They developed a false pride about themselves. In their eyes, they become "chosen." The "chosen," of course, take the possessions of the unchosen. A noble cause, like the beauty of a woman, is offered to the squeamish in campaigns for "Trojan plunder." Is there a real difference between Helen's beauty and "the Lord's" gift of Canaan to the Israelites, or "Manifest Destiny?"

The black and brown (including "yellow" and "red") people who happened to be in the way of the "rude and barbarous" nomads, who were "ready to starve," initially welcomed the nomads. For their hospitality, these "niggers" were given genocide, either immediately or when it was convenient:

> ...This empire [the Frankish Empire] reached tentatively to the Carpathians and extinguished the alien Avar [Altaic] power in central Europe...
>
> > Peter Calvocoressi and Guy Wint, *Total War*,
> > Ballantine Books, New York, 1973, Vol.1,
> > p. 29.

> ...Numbers: An estimate of the number of Native Americans in 1492, when the Europeans arrived in the "New World" is about 1,115,000 indigenous people in what was to become the contiguous U.S. Various native American groups insist that there were 2.5 million. Whatever the figure, the native American population declined steadily after 1500 A.D. as a result of wars with the whites, contact with unfamiliar diseases, deliberate extermination, and the introduction of grain alcohol (Benjamin Franklin suggested that rum would be most efficient in the extirpation—his word—of the savages). By 1890, there were fewer than 90,000 native Americans in the U.S...
>
> > David Wallachinsky and Irving Wallace,
> > *The People's Almanac #2*, Bantam Books,
> > Inc., New York, 1978, p. 130.

Today, in 1987, Franklin receives the *highest* American honor. His face disgraces American money. Today, the United States is building a "Holocaust Memorial," allegedly to mark the inhumanity of Hitler's holocaust. Why? What was the difference between Adolph Hitler and Ben Franklin or any of the other "Founding Fathers" who shared Franklin's view on "extirpation?"

"You can't answer the question because you don't know what 'extirpation' means?" No problem, I'll save you the trip to the dictionary:

EXTIRPATE: To pull up by the roots; to destroy the whole of; exterminate.

Now that you know the meaning of "extirpate," I will also give you the answer to the question about the difference between Adolph Hitler and the American Founding Fathers:

> ...Bismarck himself preferred to live in a state of equilibrium with the Russian and Habsburg empires to the east of it, but the Germanness of the Habsburg empire was a standing invitation to all Germans to go east, to regard the Slavs as their Red Indians or 'fuzzy-wuzzies' to embark on one of the great movements of European expansion and colonization—only this time within Europe itself and at the expense of peoples whose systems were neither so alien nor so technically backward as the Asian and African societies which other Europeans subjugated. Like all Imperialists the Ger-

mans easily convinced themselves that they were benefiting inferior people by interfering with them—until eventually the Nazis dispensed with the idea of benefiting anybody but themselves...

> Peter Calvocoressi and Guy Wint, *Total War*,
> Ballantine Books, New York, 1973, Vol. 1,
> p. 21.

So...Calvocoressi and Wint have given us the answer to the question. *Hitler's genocide was different from Franklin's by reason of the color of the niggers.* Is there another difference? Pray make it known. We, in black America, labor under a misconception, and so evidently did Calvocoressi and Wint. What of Moses' treatment of the Midianites described in *Numbers* 31?

The pattern described above can be seen EVERYWHERE that Adam's family, Indo-Europeans, went. Sometimes one has to dust the politics off the truth, but the truth is still there:

> ...About the middle of the 3d millennium B.C., Dravidian India was subjected to the first of a sustained series of invasions by tribes of Indo-European linguistic stock...
>
> *Funk & Wagnall's New Encyclopedia,* Funk &
> Wagnall's, Inc., New York, 1979, Vol. 13,
> p. 196.

The article from which the preceding excerpt was taken goes on to say that the racial identity of the Indo-European invaders is "unknown." Riiight! Then the article describes "remnants" of the Dravidian people fleeing north into the hills and south into the Indian subcontinent. "Scholarship!"

Okay, some readers say that Greece, Germany, India, and the United States are isolated examples. What about Australia?

> ...Religion among the Austroloids is closely bound up with the social system. Each of the clans is totemic, and the totem animal or plant of the clan is regarded as embodying sacred attributes and is sanctified. By extension, all living things are regarded as having a close kinship with man. The Australoids universally believe in reincarnation and, frequently, in the existence of a supreme deity. It has been estimated that at the time of the first settlement in 1788, the aboriginal population of Australia was between 150,000 and 300,000. The population declined to its present level of about 80,000 because of a lack of resistance to the diseases of the white man, disruption of the aboriginal way of life, and, in the early period, government indifference to the aborigines...
>
> *Funk & Wagnall's New Encyclopedia,* Funk &
> Wagnall's, Inc., New York, 1979, Vol. 2,
> p. 456.

There's that phrase again: "the diseases of the white man."
Let us apply some mother wit to the "scholarship" exhibited in the preceding excerpt. Were not the Australoids neglected by Adam's government *before* 1788? Obviously, the answer is yes. If such was the case, then how could continued neglect, "indifference," contribute to the drastic reduction in the Australoid population?
Again, it is obvious. Neglect by Adam's government had nothing to do with the reduction in population. What was the real deal? The real deal was that Adam was "extirpating" some more niggers, "fuzzy wuzzies."
Okay, some readers say that Greece, India, Germany, the United States, and Australia aren't sufficient evidence. Okay. What about Africa? Wasn't the long story of "the children of the sun" sufficient? "No?" How about a later episode? Let's look at a typical *version* of the events through Adam's eyes:

...the origin of the Atlantic [slave] trade was the discovery of America and the consequent development of rich sugar plantations in the West Indies. When the American aborigines were killed off, as they were promptly, a labor force had to be found somewhere, and slaves were a marvelously cheap and convenient device to this end. The trade brought fantastic profits...

For every three slaves that got to America alive—so frightful were conditions in the boats or on shore before departure—seven died...

A case can be made for slavery and even for the slave trade. It is that tribal wars took place in the African interior without cessation, and that it was better for a man to be taken prisoner and made a domestic slave, or even sold into slavery, than to be killed and perhaps eaten. On a slave raid the object was to get the prisoner alive, and, with luck, he might survive the trip to America or Arabia. On balance, the slave trade (despite its inferno-like horrors) may have saved more lives than it cost...

John Gunther, *Inside Africa,* Harper &
Brothers, New York, 1955, p. 752 & 753.

Mr. Gunther was affronted because the Nigerian press railed against his qualifications to write a history of Africa. To these eyes, there is no question about his lack of qualifications, and the brothers and sisters in Nigeria are to be commended for their perceptiveness. I really shouldn't dignify his "case for slavery" with a response. But I will.
Before addressing the "rude and barbarous" Mr. Gunther's "case for slavery," let me first point out my views on his mind-set. He skips right over the genocide of the Native Americans to get on with his "case for slavery." In fact, the Native Americans are not

people—they are "aborigines," something evidently less than human. Therefore, their genocide can be skipped over with no problem. Is this an *atypical* attitude? For the answer, let us turn to another learned son of Japheth whose recent theories on humanity found a great deal of favor and marked the beginning of the "conservative" resurgence in American social and political thought:

> ...Shock waves are rolling through the U.S. educational community over a frank and startling reappraisal of differences in classroom performance between whites and Negroes.
>
> In a lengthy article, taking up most of the winter issue of the "Harvard Educational Review," one of the nation's leading educational psychologists, Dr. Arthur R. Jensen of the University of California at Berkeley, presents these major findings:
>
> —Negro scores averaging about 15 points below the white average on I.Q. tests must be taken seriously as evidence of genetic differences between two races in learning patterns...
>
> *U.S. News & World Report,* 3/10/69, p. 48.

The preceding excerpt about the "frank" reappraisal of learning differences is quoted in Sam Yette's excellent book, *The Choice: The Issue of Black Survival in America.* Yette went on to describe Dr. Jensen in a question-and-answer session at which Jensen expounded on the essentials of his theory:

> ...In the question-and-answer period, a black reporter asked to raise a "slightly unorthodox question, but one not nearly so difficult as those Stanford-Binet questions you have been putting to the black children." Jensen, somewhat patronizingly, assured the black reporter that any question would be welcomed.
>
> "Who discovered America?" the black reporter asked.
>
> After a long silent pause, Jensen began by saying: "I know that the answer I'm going to give is not the answer you're looking for." But the reporter assured him that such was the nature of test questions. Then Jensen offered his answer: "Christopher Columbus discovered America."
>
> Someone in the audience suggested that it might have been Leif Ericson. The reporter asked if all of them wouldn't agree that it was "some European" who discovered America.
>
> "Definitely," Jensen and the others agreed.
>
> "What did they find here?" the reporter pressed.
>
> There was another long pause, and Jensen finally said: "Aboriginal tribes...Indians, I guess."

"People?" the reporter asked.

Reluctantly, Jensen said, "Yes, people."

"Then, who discovered America?" the question came again.

Jensen indicated that the point of the question was not clear, so the black reporter elaborated: "Suppose, just suppose for a moment that I came to your home tonight and 'discovered' it, killed off your family and beat you, then restricted you to some reserved area of the house. And in another section of the house, I beat and chained some men, women and children I kidnapped in the park on my way to your house. Then, under penalty of death, I denied all of you hostages the knowledge of the house and how to run it; and, then, if I devised a test over the things I had denied you to learn, and if you failed that test—just as I had intended—would I be fair or correct to call you stupid? And if I did call you stupid, for what purpose would I do it?"...

> Samuel F. Yette, *The Choice: The Issue
> of Black Survival in America*, Cottage
> Books, Silver Spring, Md., 1971, p. 250.

Sam Yette's book is a book that *every* black American should read. If you can't find it locally, write to Sam Yette c/o Cottage Books, P.O. Box 2071 Silver Spring, Md. 20902.

Back to Mr. Gunther's mindset. It is by no means atypical. Nor is it new. Recall Mr. Gunther's fascination with the *profits* that were made in the slave trade. Remember this?

> ...and the gold of that land is good...
>
> *Genesis* 2:12

Today, in these waning days of the reigning empire, black Americans are being told that we don't work hard enough. That is the root of our problems. Nothing else, just a lack of "the work ethic." Well maybe some genetic inferiority thrown in, but basically we suffer from a lack of "the work ethic."

In the excerpt from John Weston's book, it was shown just who built this hemisphere into a European bastion. John Gunther, *en passant,* confirms that "Negroes" were needed for a "labor force." *WHY COULDN'T THE SONS OF JAPHETH WORK?* When did they develop this alleged "work ethic?" Mr. Gunther, of course, did not or would not see the bankruptcy in his train of thought(?).

And now to address Mr. Gunther's "case for slavery." Essentially, Gunther's case for slavery is that Africans were removed from incessant wars, cannibalism, *etc.,* by the slave trade. They were given a chance, "with luck," to survive by the slavers. Absolute fantasy! I can find no better example of the devastation caused by the slave trade than the contrast of society in West Africa presented by Michael Bradley in his book, *The Black Discovery of America.* Bradley first presented the testimony of an Arab traveler on conditions in the area of Benin about 1300 A.D., before the slave trade began:

> ...[They] are seldom unjust, and have a greater abhorrence of injustice than any other people. Their sultan shows no mercy to anyone who is found guilty of the least act of it. There is complete security in the country. Neither traveler nor inhabitant in it has anything to fear from robbers or men of violence. They do not confiscate the property of any white man who dies in their country, even if it be uncounted wealth. On the contrary, they give it into the charge of some trustworthy person among the whites, until the rightful heir takes possesion of it...
>
> Ibn Battuta (Mohammed Ibn Allah), *Travels in Asia and Africa,* trans. H.A.R. Gibb, (1929) (Morocco, 1356)

I wonder where Mr. Gunther would propose that I look in Europe of 1300 for a society such as the one described above? *Today,* where would I look? Bradley contrasted the above society with the same area after about 400 years of the slave trade:

> ...Truly has Benin been called a city of blood. Its history is one long record of savagery of the most debased kind...
>
> R.H. Bacon, *Benin, The City of Blood,* (London, 1897)

The slave trade saved *nobody,* black or white, from savagery. To the contrary, it promoted savagery "of the most debased kind."

Gunther went on to say that Africans brought the slaves to the coastal areas, and I guess he thought that somehow that fact mitigated the European horror. It happened. Blacks did sell blacks to the whites, just like some Jews collaborated with the Nazis and some Indians collaborated with the whites. The initial sellers probably did not know the nature of European slavery. The later ones knew and couldn't do much about it. One sinner put tremendous pressure on the next man. If he traded his brothers and sisters for advantage, then his brothers and sisters had two enemies. There is no question that it was wrong on our part. Obviously we didn't know who the enemy was. However, that collaboration in no way mitigates the greater crime, and you do not need to accept *my* assessment on the weight of the respective crimes:

..."Temptations to sin are sure to come, but woe to him by whom they come."...

Luke 17:1

"Who said that?" Open up your *Bible* and find out who said it. If you disagree with the assessment, then obviously you think that no drug peddlers should be prosecuted. "No?" What is their crime? Okay, we've looked at the legacy of Adam in the United States, twice in Africa, Australia, India, Greece and Germany. Sordid tales about Latin America abound.

Chancellor Williams described Portuguese chronicles of Africans on the slave marches as simply willing themselves to death—dying on will. No poison. No rope. No sword. Just dying at revulsion of the European horror. Quite frankly, I found that hard to believe. But Michael Bradley alluded to the same phenomenon in the Americas. Here is a brief example from another work about Adam's footprints in Latin America:

> ...The Taino Indians, the native people [of Puerto Rico], called the island *Boriquen,* "Land of Courage." They were the first to be conquered and they were the first to rebel. The Taino Indians—they numbered 50,000 when the Spanish arrived—lived in tribes along the sea and along the rivers. The European invaders called them "savages," but for several thousand years they had developed civilization and a culture.
>
> The Tainos were mainly a farming people. They grew corn, yuca and tobacco; they domesticated animals and hunted small game; they wove cotton fabrics and used the fibers of the rubber tree. Taino doctors used herbs and roots to cure illness and disease; their musicians played flutes and drums and their poets preserved their history in legend and song...
>
> In the social life of the Taino, political and religious organization was one and inseparable; democratic councils governed the tribes...
>
> [After the Spanish came] The Indians who worked the mines were given just enough food to allow them to live and labor another day...The Taino "savages" were given "souls" by Christian missionaries and brought into the fold of the Catholic Church. Bishops and priests, with few exceptions, used their religion as a weapon against native peoples. The *Bible* was used to justify brutality...
>
> By 1514 only 3,000 Indians were still alive; in 20 years the Spanish exterminated over 45,000 people or 95% of the population. Seven years later only 600 Taino Indians were alive...
>
> The Peoples Press Puerto Rico Project,*
> *PUERTO RICO—The Flame of Resistance,*

Peoples Press, San Francisco, 1977, p. 6,
8 and 10.
*Lincoln Bergman, Gail Dolgin, Robert
Gabriner, Maisie McAdoo, John Baskin &
Jane Norling.

What was this religion that Columbus brought to the "New
world?" Was it something new? No way, José:

> ...Gold is the most precious of all commodities; gold constitutes treasure,
> and he who possesses it has all he needs in this world, has also the means of
> rescuing souls from purgatory and restoring them to the enjoyment of
> paradise...

Christopher Columbus

Remember *Genesis* 2:12? "The gold of that land is good." From
the preceding excerpts, the repetitious pattern is prominent. Adam
came upon people who were doing quite nicely and took gold, his real
god, from them. And then Adam simply "extirpated" the people. It
didn't make any difference that the people gave up the gold. Adam
"extirpated" them *anyway!* The last of the Inca emperors,
Atahualpa, gave the gold to Pizarro. Pizarro had him strangled. I
could document case after case of the same situation, from the Halls
of Montezuma to the shores of the Congo. The "savages" gave up
the gold and were strangled *anyway.* Why? All of these Adams faced
Moses' dilemma. Nobody could be allowed to tell the real deal. It
would lead to disruption in Adam's family. Stealing could not be
authorized. Of course, taking possesions from niggers with no souls
was different. Those beings were simply the "aboriginal tribes" of
Dr. Jensen and the group of reporters. No stealing there. Certainly
not. Where does it say "stealing" in our children's history books?

Oh, oh. Some readers are now saying, "There is nothing offensive
about the word aborigine." Agreed! "Aborigine" simply means
"original inhabitant." There is nothing *per se* offensive about the
word. However, although we might disagree as to its location, Indo-
Europeans were the original inhabitants of *someplace.* Have any of
you grumbling readers ever heard Europeans referred to as
"aborigines" with respect to their original homeland? There are
many similar words: "tribesman," "villager," "primitive,"...Back
to the river of history.

The Spanish took potato plants, among other things, back to the
"Old World." Those plants kept Europe's peasants from starving for
centuries. The events are chronicled in such works of art as *"The*

Potato Growers" and *"The Potato Eaters."* But the Spanish had murdered most of the people who knew about growing potato plants. The results of the genocide of the Indians included the Irish Potato Famine. The Spanish took back only *one* strain of potato. When a blight arrived to which that strain had no resistance, Irishmen died in large numbers. The Incas, the "savages," had known about genetic diversity for centuries. But as a result of the foul deeds of the Spanish, there was nobody able or willing to fix the problem with the potato crop in Europe. "The English?" Be real. Adam never loved his neighbor, not even his family. Good works aren't required. Augustine said so, and the Pope said Augustine was "the common father of our Christian civilization." Don't think. Get away from that serpent. Obey! Gold, baby. That's the route to salvation. Columbus said so, and Columbus is a hero. Open any American grammar school history book. You'll see.

The same thing happened in the USA with the corn crop in the South during the early 1970s. Adam still isn't a farmer. One "high tech" strain of corn was planted. Seventy percent of the crop was wiped out. Americans got ripped off at the supermarket. "No big deal?" "Ordinary pain?" What happens when the next genetically engineered disaster occurs, a disaster that nature is not disposed to deal with lightly?

I could offer many more examples of what happened along Adam's path, but if I offered a million examples, or a trillion, the blind would not see, and the sighted already know. So let us summarize the megahistory.

A Summary of Adam's Path

Adam's path is megahistory. It is a history of races just as Du Bois said it is. There is nothing really mysterious here. There was a cataclysmic event *circa* 4000 B.C. that changed the social history of the world. The world was definitely changed, but was it for the better?

Subsequent cataclysmic events also had significant impacts on the social history of the world. Adam has seen fit to cloud these events in mysticism (sometimes called religion), jury-rigged history and racist "science."

Certainly people of all races have done some foul deeds. I am not suggesting anything to the contrary. As was stated early in this book, a subject as broad as megahistory can only be approached with the convention of "norms." I believe that the cultural norms are as I wrote them. Readers might have different opinions. Make your opinions known. In the meantime, I have to go with the assessment of Michael Bradley:

> . . . We [Adam's family] have voyaged—and murdered, enslaved and tortured—on a greater scale than any other people. . .
>
> Michael Bradley, *The Black Discovery of America*, Personal Library, Toronto, 1981, p. 18.

If you disagree with the historical assessment of Michael Bradley and yours truly, present some credible evidence. Until such time as such evidence becomes available, Bradley's assessment will be operative here—which brings us to the question of WHY?

Certainly there is the temptation to say that Adam is genetically "evil." That assertion is a lie with no salvation for anybody. The many members of Adam's family who have participated in the struggle for freedom, justice and equality argue against that lie. There is physical evidence also. Obviously, humanity is one species. We can mate and produce biologically viable offspring. Our physical differences are relatively minor when compared to our similarities. At some point in the distant past, humanity—initially all black—became separated. It was well before the "tower of Babel," or *Babhel*. It was well before Adam, the first Adam.

To produce a pale race, Adam had to have been in the arctic arena for quite some time. There is a popular theory today that humanity originated in Africa and migrated all over the world. I don't necessarily buy that idea. It's possible, but I don't necessarily buy it. If such was the case, however, Adam had to have migrated before some early cataclysm put European Russia in an arctic zone. On behalf of black people, let me presume to say that we would not have voluntarily walked into the cold. *NO DAMN WAY!*

If Adam migrated before his homeland was frigid, then Adam probably represents the survivors of people who accidently got caught in the cold. The development of a race of pale, hairy, thin-lipped, narrow-nosed people had to have taken place over many thousands of years. Adam was in the frigid zone for quite a while. While the rest of the world was developing progressive social institutions, Adam was SURVIVING. Consequently, when Adam came out of the refrigerator, he was several thousand years behind in terms of social development. His belligerence, impatience and overall "rudeness" are reflections of this early period when Adam spent his time hunting to survive. Predation permeates essentially all of Adam's social institutions. Scarcity engenders predation.

The first Adam was truly without sin. Yes, he committed horrible torts against his neighbors. No, he didn't sin. There is no crime without intent. All subsequent Adams, however, cannot use that defense. They knew and know the difference between good and evil. Either they know, or they have culpable ignorance:

> ...They [the ruling classes of Western Europe] were acquainted with 'inferior' races as well as 'inferior' classes, so the social structure and the imperial experience of Europe combined to establish an order of values and a pragmatic indifference to inequities which could sometimes be reconciled with ideals of justice and decency only by not inquiring too closely into what was going on...
>
> Peter Calvocoressi and Guy Wint, *Total War*,
> Ballantine Books, New York, 1973, Vol. 1,
> p. 29.

> ...The West insists upon seeing the world as it wishes it was, or thinks it should be. All our claims to rationality, objectivity and the scientific approach stop at the borders of our own culture. We will pay heavily for this failure on our part to extend the fairness of objectivity to other peoples and their history. Somewhere in our collective instinct we know it, and we clearly prefer to melt the entire planet (or pollute it past redemption), destroying life totally, rather than become recipients of Third World charity in the form of humanitarian and psychological insights...
>
> Dr. James B. Webster, Professor of African
> History, Dalhousie University, Halifax,
> Canada, (In the Foreword to *The Black
> Discovery of America* by Michael Bradley).

Well, we know why Adam started out the way he did, but why does he continue to be so "rude and barbarous?" Let us turn to Brother James Baldwin for an answer:

> ...At the center of the European horror is their religion: a religion by which it is intended one be coerced, and in which no one believes, the proof being Black/White conditions or options, the horror into which the cowardly delusion of White supremacy seems to have transformed Africa, and the utterly intolerable nightmare of the American dream...And, futhermore, we were not so much permitted to enter the church as corralled into it, as a means of forcing us to corroborate the inscrutable will of God, Who had decreed that we should be slaves forever...

What a cowardly, not to say despicable, vision of human life; what a dreadful concept of the divinity...

James Baldwin, *The Evidence of Things Not Seen,* Holt, Rinehart and Winston, New York, 1985, p. 82.

What *is* Adam's religion? Well...remember the section at the beginning of this book about one's religion being what one practices? We're going to put that aside for a minute and talk about "professions." Recall that the Right Honorable Rev. Brown felt that profession was all that was required for a son of Japheth to gain salvation. Today, Adam generally professes Christianity, if he professes anything at all. "God rejected the Jews," you will recall. So Baldwin must have been writing about that profession known as Christianity. Is the indictment new? Well, you were shown an excerpt from a book, *PUERTO RICO—The Flame of Resistance,* in which it was alleged the "bishops and priests...used their religion as a weapon." That book was published in 1977, eight years before Baldwin's book. But the indictment goes back way before 1977:

...It was estimated that a hundred Negroes died that day [in 1917] in East St. Louis—a tragedy that aroused bitterness in the hearts of many black Americans. The Negro poetess Leila Amos Pendleton wrote these lines in honor of those who died by lynching during these years.

Hang there, O my murdered brothers, sons of Ethiopia,
our common Mother! Hang there, with faces upturned,
mutely calling down vengeance from the Most High God!
Call down vengeance upon this barbarous nation;
a nation of hypocrites, time-servers
and gold worshippers...
Hang there until their eyes are unsealed and they
behold themselves as they are and as they appear to
an amazed world! Hang there until their foresworn
souls perceive the true meaning of Liberty and Justice,
until they catch a glimmer of the meaning of Christianity!

Steven Jantzen, *Hooray For Peace,
Hurrah For War: A History of World War I,*
A Borzoi Book, New York, 1971. p. 236.

So Baldwin's assertion was shared at least seventy years ago. It is actually a lot older than that. Many examples could be shown, but none so poetic as the example of Sister Pendleton—and her poem has the necessary ingredients for analysis. What is "the meaning of Christianity?" Is it the "amazing" or "mysterious grace" of Augustine and Pope John Paul II? If it is, I have to believe that Jesus would be shocked to find out that such is the case. What did Jesus say his philosophy was all about?

> ...But when the Pharisees heard that he [Jesus] had silenced the Sadducees, they came together. And one of them, a lawyer, asked him a question to test him. "Teacher, which is the great commandment in the law?" and he said to him, "You shall love the Lord your God with all your heart, and with all your soul, and with all your mind. This is the great and first commandment. And a second is like it, you shall love your neighbor as yourself. On these two commandments depend all the law and the prophets."...
>
> *Matthew* 23:34-40

"Of course, of course," the television ministers will say, "we love God." Sure they do, but we have to make sure that everyone is singing out of the same hymnbook here. Who was the God whom Jesus was talking about in his response to the lawyer? Did he mean gold? Very doubtful. Recall the camel, the eye of the needle and the rich man.

Did Jesus mean himself? According to testimony in all four gospels, Jesus didn't mean himself by any stretch of a rational imagination:

> ...And Jesus said to him, "Why do you call me good? No one is good but God alone."...
>
> *Mark* 10:18 (*e.g.*)

If Jesus didn't consider gold to be God, and he didn't consider himself to be divine, in Adam's sense of the word, who was "the Father" of whom Jesus spoke so frequently? The answer can be derived by examining Jesus' concept of "the devil."

> ..."You are of your father the devil, and your will is to do your father's desires. He was a murderer from the beginning, and has nothing to do with the truth, because there is no truth in him. When he lies, he speaks according to his nature, for he is a liar and father of liars."...
>
> *John* 8:44

If the devil's essence is a lie, then what is God's essence? One doesn't have to be a genius to figure that out. The essence of God is truth. Is God necessarily anthropomorphic, just because Jesus allegedly used the human metaphor? Of course not!

If God is not necessarily a being, like man, how can one "love" God? Easily, as long as one understands that "love" is not necessarily an extension on the same plane of "like." "Love," in this context.

means to totally embrace the essence of something. Acknowledge the reality. Be real! Start with a true premise.

Given that God is the truth, it follows—to some people—that one should love one's neighbor. Nobody has to *like* their neighbor, but love is indicated:

> ..."It is pretty difficult to like some people. Like is sentimental, and it is pretty difficult to like someone bombing your home; it is pretty difficult to like somebody threatening your children; it is difficult to like congressmen who spend all their time trying to defeat civil rights. But Jesus said love them, and love is greater than like."...
>
> Rev. Martin Luther King, Jr.
> Murdered American Nobel Peace Laureate

How can one "love" a person that one doesn't like? Easily, as long as one understands that the essence of the disliked person is his or her humanity. A person's appearance, behavior and manner have nothing to do with the person's essence. Those things are very superficial and subject to change. However, nobody can change his or her humanity. All of us are "God's children." Given that Jesus' first commandment was to love the truth, the second commandment— "is like it"—flows logically from the first. It is true that we are all God's children. Therefore, one should love one's neighbor. Why?

If I say that you and I are both human, then a mind-set for progress is established. Why? Because I can then start with a true premise and act rationally. I have acknowledged the *reality* of our equal humanity. "Love your neighbor *as yourself.*" If, however, I start out thinking that you are an "aborigine," then I have started my policy based on a false premise. That policy must necessarily fail in the long term—and the long term becomes the short term at some point in time.

It is logically possible, with the aforementioned concept of "love," to love one's neighbor while hating the neighbor's actions.

God, in Jesus' philosophy, was not Moses' anthropomorphic tribal god who gave away other people's land and authorized theft. Neither was God the god of the Right Honorable Rev. Brown, who blessed the sons of Japheth while cursing the sons of Shem and Ham(bone). Jesus' philosophy was about logic—pure, cold, irrefutable logic.

> ..."Consider the lilies, how they grow; they neither toil nor spin; yet I tell you, even Solomon in all his glory was not arrayed like one of these. But if God so clothes the grass which is alive today and tomorrow is thrown into the oven, how much more will he clothe you, O men of little faith? And do not

seek what you are to eat and what you are to drink, nor be of anxious mind. For all the nations of the world seek these things; and your Father knows that you need them. Instead seek his kingdom, and these things will be yours as well.". . .

Luke 12:27-31

The beautiful logic reflected above was corrupted. People were trained that God is anthropomorphic, *literally* a man-like being who would somehow take care of everything. If not, there was "the pie in the sky" to keep the masses docile. Meanwhile, the "bishops and priests" ran off with the gold. Jesus was talking about EDUCATION in the preceding passage. Seek God; seek the truth. "Know the truth, and the truth will set you free." Jesus was not talking about some state of passivity, with your eyes rolled back in your head—while the "bishops and priests" run off with the gold.

One doesn't need a whole lot of faith, "the evidence of things not seen," to see the truth in what Jesus was saying. There are certainly historical precedents. The society of "the children of the sun" was a society in which the truth was worshiped. *EVERYBODY* was fed. The Taino Indians seemed to have fed themselves quite nicely before Adam showed up. Can Adam feed himself today, with all of his "high tech?"

Jesus didn't go for the fake; he loved the snake. Now do you remember the operative definition of "love?" The Mosaic disdain for the truth was *completely* rejected by Jesus:

. . . "Beware the leaven of the Pharisees, which is hypocrisy. Nothing is known that will not be made known to you.". . .

Luke 12:1-2 (*e.g.*)

. . . "The secret things belong to the Lord our God; but the things that are revealed belong to us and to our children forever, that we may do all the words of this law.". . .

Deuteronomy 29:29

Why can't Adam see the error in his ways? He sees them. He chooses not to do anything about them. When some event arouses anger in black America, the following explanation is sometimes offered for Adam: *"He came from nothing, so he acts like nothing!"* In that street wisdom is the truth.

Adam burst through the Altaic Ring having spent many thousands of years SURVIVING. He had no social institutions to speak of. He saw that other people used gold to acquire things that he had never had. Adam's thought processes were not developed to the point where he could understand the complex social arrangements necessary for an exchange of gold to be productive. He simply thought, with his hunter's mind, "Get the gold!" The result was, of course, the transformation of "the Golden Rule" to its current state of philosophical bankruptcy: "He who has the gold makes the rules."

Adam missed a "golden" opportunity when he murdered the philosopher Jesus. Jesus' message was corrupted shortly after his death, unfortunately for all.

In the 1st century A.D., Saul of Tarsus, subsequently known as Saint Paul, imposed his philosophy on the actual philosophy and history of Jesus. Paul might have had good intentions, but essentially the philosphy that he imposed on the original teachings of Jesus was a pessimistic philosophy. Jesus' philosophy was, to the contrary, optimistic.

Paul did not believe that humanity *alone* could ever achieve a civilization of freedom, justice and equality. Paul's solution was described acutely by a brilliant correspondent of mine: *"Consequently a cosmic element is introduced in the course of history to achieve it* [a just society]: *The Christ (not as just an ethical guru—but as a spiritual, cosmic, sacramental power). To some, this is mere platitude. Others stake their lives on it and find it true."*

Paul's introduction of an interventionist god into Christianity was, however well-intentioned it might have been, a mistake. Christianity became an arm of the Roman Empire and its inheritors. Paul's changes enabled politicalization of the Most High God such as was evidenced in the Right Honorable Rev. Brown's interpretation of Noah's curse of Ham(bone). Paul's pessimistic view of humanity was an extension of the earlier Judaic view. Recall that "the Lord" intervened *repeatedly* in the *Old Testament*.

Judaism is a philosophy that *professes* free will, but not for all people. One is sorely tested to reconcile free will with "the Lord's" alleged intervention to give the Hebrews "favor in the sight of the Egyptians" such that the Egyptians "loaned" the Hebrews gold and silver—no doubt necessities for the wilderness. Remember *Exodus* 11:2-3? "The Lord" *never* intervened on behalf of anybody but the Hebrews, however. Does that sound strange? Show me a case in the *Old Testament* where "the Lord" intervened on behalf of someone other than the Hebrews. The intervention was, of course, unreal and political. If one dares to ask about this god who favors one man over his brother and brothers over their sisters, well..."Don't question;

some things have to be taken on faith... 'the Lord' works in mysterious ways.'' Sho' nuff! The same type of interventionist god was used to justify Christian and Islamic colonialism and exploitation. "God" authorized all!

Jesus' philosophy was not about literal intervention by "the Father." His philosophy was fundamentally one of rationality. *It is not hard to imagine the historical Jesus as seeing morality as logic viewed over the long term.* Paul had insufficient faith to rely on the progressive philosophy of Jesus. Paul instituted the interventionist Christian god. Many rules, of course, followed the introduction of "the sacramental power." Jesus, however, needed only two rules: Love God and love your neighbor. Paul's philosophy and its extensions have produced what James Baldwin described as "the center of the European horror." Paul could not accept humanity's potential to become Godlike. Jesus, on the other hand, loved his neighbor and had faith in humanity's potential.

The historical record argues against Paul in favor of Jesus. Certainly the society of "the children of the sun" was not perfect. However, everybody was fed. The same can be said of the society of the Taino Indians. Everybody was fed. Those societies were on the right track. Paul, unfortunately, did not see those societies. He spent his ministry in Asia Minor and Europe. He saw the horror that is euphemistically described in Western history books as *"the Pax Romana,"* the peace of Rome. There was no peace in the Roman Empire. There was enslavement, brutality, murder and theft. Similarly, the level of technical achievement in Rome never surpassed that of Greece, and certainly not that of Egypt. Philosophy? The philosophy of Rome is perhaps best revealed by the leading Roman deity, Jove—equivalent in all essentials to the Greek Zeus: a white, male warrior. Moses's god was a god of war, wasn't he? What should one make of the images projected at the end of daily television broadcasting in the United States? Fighter planes? Aircraft carriers? Combat scenes? What god is worshiped here in the USA? Where are the images of classrooms? "Prayer in the schools?" What will the Empire have the children pray for, more fighter planes?

The inventions of Paul were not the end of the corruption of Christianity. Jesus' message was further corrupted. In the 4th century A.D., the Roman Emperor, Constantine, convened the First Council of Nicea. Constantine had a problem. Christianity, in one form or another, was spreading throughout the Roman Empire. Romans no longer considered the Emperor as the last word in all things.

Constantine solved the problem. He convened a council to deal with Christianity. That council dealt with such issues as "the heresy of Arius." Arius argued against the concept of "the Trinity." He suggested that if God was eternal, the son could not be a part of God. To Arius, a son had to have been born of a father at some point in time. Therefore, there must have been a time when the son did not exist. If there was such a time, the son could not be eternal. Consequently, to Arius, the son could not be a part of an eternal God.

The elders of the Church at that time traced their authority to the alleged selection of Peter by Jesus. The authority of the elders was threatened, if Jesus wasn't God. Arius was exiled. Other "heretics" got even worse treatment. Constantine got some niggers, like Augustine, to jury-rig a Christianity that Constantine could control and utilize. Christianity became something that I am sure Jesus would not recognize. Even the identity of Jesus became obscure.

> ...No doubt there will never be complete agreement among experts about a full portrait of Jesus. In general, though, their painstaking work does help us realize the true relevance of Jesus, for all his distance from our day. By recapturing the time of conflict in which he lived—a time of ideological clashes and sectarianism, when great world empires enslaved whole nations in the name of peace, and sincere martyrs and religious charlatans competed for people's allegiance—we can begin to struggle honestly with the question: What does Jesus mean for us today?...
>
> *The Washington Post*, 12/23/84, p. B5.

I have heard nobody speak more knowledgeably on the corruption of Christianity (such as alluded to above by a white Roman Catholic) than Dr. Yosef Ben-Jochannan. Brothers and sisters, if you get a chance to hear "Dr. Ben" speak, do so. According to Dr. Ben's account of the events, the original accounts of the life of Jesus described Jesus' birthplace as a cave in Ethiopia, not in Bethlehem in a "manger." Certainly the Greek word *"katalemna,"* which describes the place where Jesus was born, describes a sheltered place like a cave, not an animal stable. *Think* about the root of the word *katalemna.*

Some fun and games certainly went on with the man's ancestry as evidenced by the *Bible* itself. Jesus' ancestry is traced in two gospels, *Matthew* and *Luke*. In *Matthew* 1:16, Jesus' paternal grandfather is identified as a man named Jacob. In *Luke* 3:23, Jesus' paternal grandfather is identified as a man named Heli. Both cannot be "holy" representations. Both cannot be true. Some "theologians" have attempted to reconcile this obvious contradiction by claiming that the lineage described in *Luke* traces Jesus' maternal ancestry. They claim that Joseph was the son-in-law of Heli, not the son as stated in the scriptures. In attempting to prove that the scriptures are infallible, they have proven the opposite. *Luke* 3:23 clearly states that Joseph was the son—not the son-in-law—of Heli. But that is just a small example of the damage that Constantine and Augustine *et al* did to "the meaning of Christianity."

After that crew got finished with story of Jesus, Jesus became divine; *literally* walked on water; *literally* fed a multitude with a few fishes and such; in some quarters, it came to be held that his mother was *literally* a virgin when he was born (Virgin Birth); in some quarters, his mother was given absolution for "original sin"—an absolution denied to Jesus (Immaculate Conception); Jesus *literally* was raised from the dead and, from age 12 to age 29, there is nothing at all about the man in the *Bible*. But where did he spend his formative years?

Constantine, Augustine and those other so-called theologians robbed the man of his humanity. He was no longer a learned teacher who enjoyed the company of the downtrodden and despised. He no longer was a man who had a workable philosophy for the world to use. He became a part of a three-part god, and his amended message would be used to render people docile—while the "bishops and priests" ran away with the gold. You will not find anything like the following excerpt in the Christian *Bible*:

> ...Jesus may have secretly married Mary Magdelene, the most often mentioned of the women followers. More fuel has been added by the discovery, among the Nag Hammadi hoard, of a 'gospel of Philip' which relates that:
>
>> the companion of the [Savior is] Mary Magdelan. [But Christ loved] her more than [all] the disciples, and asked to kiss her [often] on her [mouth]. The rest of [the disciples were offended]...They said to him, 'Why do you love her more than all of us?' The Savior answered and said to them, 'Why do I not love you as [I love] her.'...
>
> Ian Wilson, *Jesus: The Evidence,* Harper
> & Row, New York, 1984, p. 96.

After the Council of Nicaea, no such information was allowed. Jesus was a god, not a man. He authorized the Popes, who spoke therefore with divine authority. It was a mistake, a bad mistake. Now, after Nicaea, one must be very careful when reading the scriptures to decipher what Jesus was really likely to have said versus what was a political addition or translation. We are asked to believe that the same man said the following:

...Jesus said, "For judgment I came into this world, that those who do not see may see, and that those who see may become blind. Some of the Pharisees near him heard this, and they said to him, "Are we also blind?" Jesus said to them, "If you were blind, you would have no guilt; but now that you say, 'We see,' your guilt remains."...

> *John* 9:39-41

..."Father, forgive them; for they know not what they do."...

> *Luke* 23:34

"Which do I think that Jesus said?" The first passage. The second is out of character and inconsistent with his judgments throughout the gospels. In addition, many versions of the *Bible* have this footnote on *Luke* 23:34:

...Other ancient authorities omit the sentence [*Luke* 23:34]...

Luke 23:34 is the only place in the *Bible* at which that sometimes omitted "quotation" appears. Moreover, I don't believe that Jesus believed in a *literal* "father." I do believe that the Jews and the Romans *knew* exactly what they were doing. They were killing a man who was telling the truth. Josephus Flavius said as much. No, *Luke* 23:34 is just one of the many cases where religion is being used "as a weapon" in an effort to excuse crimes—to make people docile.

After Nicaea, after many translations and *versions* of the *Bible*, one can find absolute claptrap in the scriptures and their interpretations. The differences in the accounts of Jesus' lineage have already been shown. Now consider these passages:

..."And when you pray, you must not be like the hypocrites; for they love to stand and pray in the synagogues and at the street corners, that they may be seen by men. Truly, I say to you, they have their reward. But when you pray, go into your room and shut the door and pray to your Father who is in secret; and your Father who sees in secret will reward you."...

> *Matthew* 6:5

...And they went to a place called Gethsemane; and he said to his disciples, "Sit here while I pray." And he took with him Peter and James and John, and began to be greatly distressed and troubled. And he said to them, "My soul is very sorrowful, even to death; remain here and watch." And going a little farther, he fell on the ground and prayed that, if it were possible, the hour might pass from him. And he said, "Abba, Father, all things are possible to thee; remove this cup from me; yet not what I will, but what thy wilt." And he came and found them sleeping, and he said to Peter, "Simon, are you asleep? Could you not watch one hour?"...

> *Mark* 14:32-37

Mark 14 goes on to describe how Jesus went away twice again, "saying the same thing," and came back twice again only to find Peter, James and John sleeping.

Now in the first passage, Jesus counsels his disciples to meditate (pray) in private. The second passage describes him doing just that. He asked his disciples to keep watch while he went away and prayed in private. When he came back to the detachment of his disciples, they were asleep; not keeping watch. There is a serious problem here. *Who heard what Jesus said in his prayers?* Mark? Obviously liberties were taken with the actual event. The disciples closest to Jesus were asleep. The people who allegedly wrote the gospels, excepting John, were even farther away from Jesus than the people Jesus found sleeping. Jesus admonished us to pray in private. What does the *Bible* say that Jesus said in his prayer at Gethsamane, heard by a person or persons unknown?

"Thy will be done." Yes, God's will be done. God will take care of everything...and the "bishops and priests" will run off with the gold. In exchange, you will get a "soul," just as the Taino Indians did in Puerto Rico. Bullets were issued after the "souls." I heard a radio preacher wax very eloquent on *Mark* 14 a few Sunday's ago. Wealthy man, that radio preacher. Richard Pryor is right on with his joke about the phenomenon:

...‟Have you been touched by God today? If not, send $5.98 for your free touch from God."...

"Religious charlatans?" If you want to do some investigating on your own, find out why a man who was allegedly born in Bethlehem, is called Jesus of Nazareth. The answer is not that Joseph was from Nazareth.

Constantine and Augustine opted for the gold. Jesus became a god. Mary became a virgin. And Adam, by mere "profession" of the faith, "mysterious grace" and a few gunboats, has had quite a run. Does Adam know what was done?

...Only a handful of thinkers have had equivalent influence over such a span of years...Even scholars who find the influence [Augustine's] more bane than blessing grant the point...

Time, 9/29/86, p. 76.

Adam knows or has reason to know. But what is Adam's future?

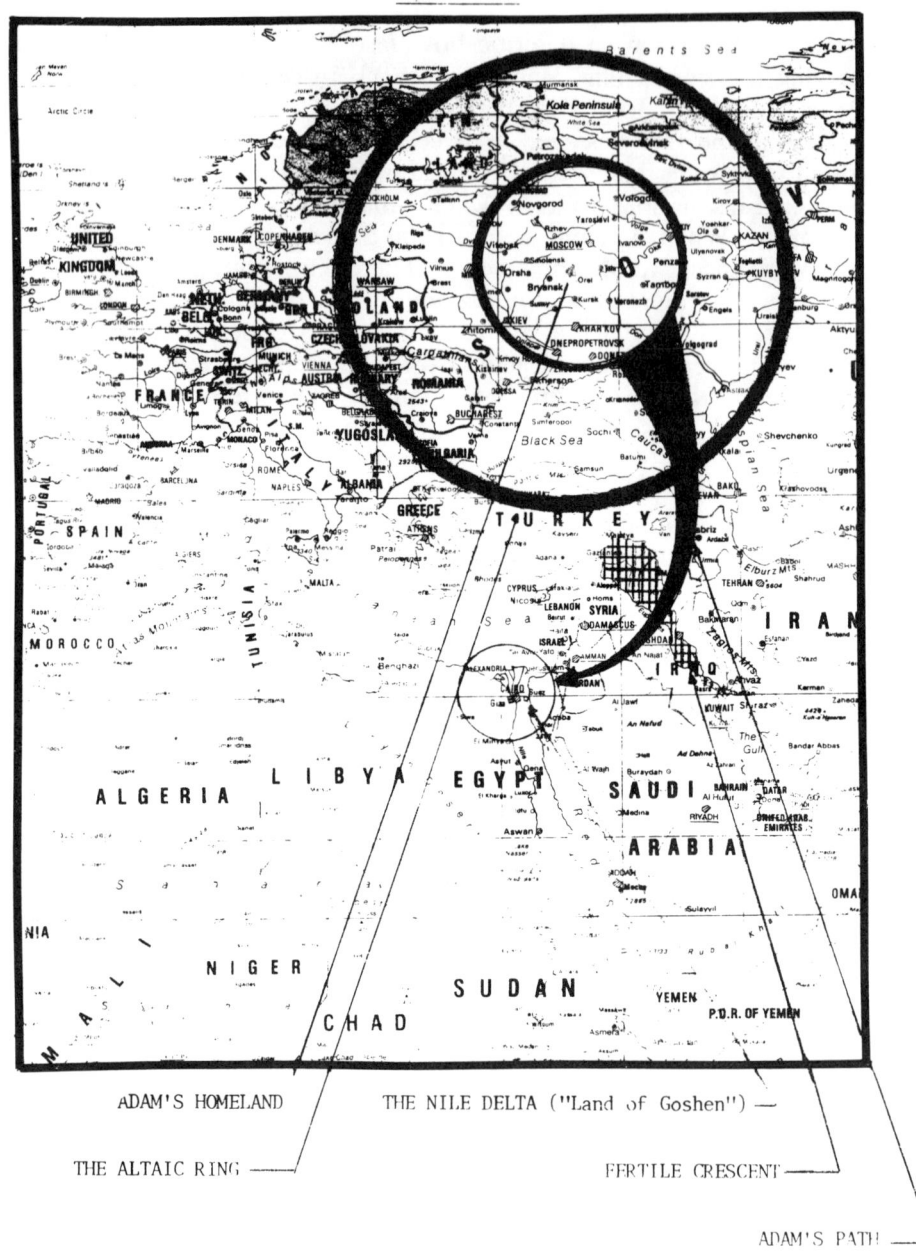

ADAM'S HOMELAND

THE NILE DELTA ("Land of Goshen") —

THE ALTAIC RING ———

FERTILE CRESCENT ——

ADAM'S PATH ——

THE SEQUENCE OF MAJOR EVENTS AND THEIR APPROXIMATE DATES FROM ADAM TO JESUS

Dates (B.C.)	Events
Before 4000	Agrarian-based democracy in *Bilud as Sudan*, Coexistence with Altaics, Adam in the refrigerator.
4000	CATACLYSM—"the Creation." Adam, the Altaics and Arameans invade *Bilud as Sudan*. The beginning of time in the Roman calendar.
3900	The Triple A Alliance occupies the Fertile Crescent and the Nile Delta.
3800	Continuing war.
3700	Continuing war.
3600	Continuing war.
3500	Continuing war.
3400	Continuing war.
3300	Continuing war.
3200	Continuing war.
3100	Menes defeats "the Triple A Alliance," expels the political leadership and founds the Old Kingdom.
3000	Adam returns north; *Bilud as Sudan* enjoys prosperity and peace.
2900	Continuing peace and prosperity in *Bilud as Sudan*.
2800	Continuing peace and prosperity in *Bilud as Sudan*.
2700	Continuing peace and prosperity in *Bilud as Sudan*. The Great Pyramid at Giza and the Sphinx built. Imhotep lives.
2600	Continuing peace and prosperity in *Bilud as Sudan*.
2500	Continuing peace and prosperity in *Bilud as Sudan*.
2400	Continuing peace and prosperity in *Bilud as Sudan*.
2300	CATACLYSM—"the flood of Noah." Old Kingdom ends.
2200	Altaics and Arameans invade *Bilud as Sudan*. Chaos.
2100	Abraham invades Egypt.
2000	Abraham expelled. The Middle Kingdom founded.
1900	Rebuilding effort in *Bilud as Sudan*. Jacob and Esau.
1800	Civil war between "the new breed" and "the children of the sun."
1700	Joseph invades and attempts extirpation of the Egyptian people. Egyptians surrender. Hyksos rule Egypt.
1600	Hyksos expelled.
1500	CATACLYSM—the "plagues of *Exodus*." Moses leaves Egypt with "borrowed" gold and silver.

Dates (B.C.)	Events
1400	Joshua moves into Palestine. Israel founded; ruled by judges. Internal chaos in Egypt. New Kingdom founded.
1300	Relative calm in Egypt; but underlying ethnic and religious turmoil.
1200	Ramses II defeats Greeks and Persians ("the people of the sea").
1100	Saul becomes first king of Israel.
1000	David rules Israel. Solomon rules Israel.
900	Ihknaton lives. Tutankhamen lives.
800	CATACLYSM—"commotion of Uzziah." *Iliad* created; Greek pantheon developed. Pianki and Shabaka free Egypt —the 25th dynasty.
700	Assyrians invade Israel and Egypt.
600	Assyrians rule Egypt. Israel in Babylonian Captivity.
500	"Age of Pericles" in Greece. Socrates lives.
400	Alexander of Macedon invades Egypt; founds Ptolemaic Dynasties. Plato lives.
300	Greece in decline; Rome ascendant.
200	Romans war with Carthage.
100	Romans war with Celts, Teutons, Picts and Egyptians. Julius Caesar lives. Augustus becomes first Roman Emperor.
0	Jesus born.

Chapter 5

ADAM'S FATE

During 1987, the Arts and Entertainment Cable Network ran a series called *"The Triumph of the West."* That series alleged that never before in history has a civilization imposed its values more widely than European civilization. It's very hard to argue with that assertion. Adam's path has been long, wide...and bloody.

Rather than a "triumph," however, I think that Adam's path must be viewed objectively as a curse, for Adam—and for all the niggers, aborigines, "little brown people" and whoever was in Adam's way. Although the earth has cooled since before Adam came out of the refrigerator, Adam has not found salvation. His children must look forward to less, not more. There is little gold associated with "extirpating" the remaining Indians. There is little gold and silver left to "borrow." The world is on to Adam's *version* of "Christianity," and the "bishops and priests" will be met with, at the very least, a healthy skepticism. Adam's last few wars (Afghanistan, Korea, Lebanon, and Viet Nam) have not been overwhelming successes. The Arts and Entertainment Network's proclamation was perhaps a century too late.

Adam's Empire:

Adam's Empire today is very similar to the late Roman Empire. Fundamentally, there are two sections and three classes in the Empire. The divisions are political, with very few real ideological differences. Adam's current Empire can be viewed on the next page.

The terms used to describe the structure are Orwellian. "Why?" Because Adam's Empire *is* Orwellian. There are no significant ideological differences between the Soviet Bloc and the Western Alliance. They are two halves of a whole, sharing a common outlook on the world and its people. But what then of "the Cold War?" That war is *very* cold:

> ...The war, therefore, if we judge it by the standard of previous wars, is an imposture. It is like the battles between certain ruminant animals whose horns are set at such an angle that they are incapable of hurting one another. But though it is unreal it is not meaningless. It eats up the surplus goods, and

```
                    ADAM'S EMPIRE

        WEST                      EAST
┌─────────────────────────────────────────┐
│                      |                    │
│  INNER PARTY (2%)    |   INNER PARTY (2%) │
│                      |                    │
├─────────────────────────────────────────┤
│                      |                    │
│  OUTER PARTY         |   OUTER PARTY      │
│                      |                    │
├─────────────────────────────────────────┤
│                      |                    │
│  PROLETARIAT         |   PROLETARIAT      │
│                      |                    │
│                      |                    │
└─────────────────────────────────────────┘
```

helps preserve the special mental atmosphere that a hierarchical society needs. War, it will be seen, is now a purely internal affair... The war is waged by each ruling group against its own subjects, and the object of the war is not to make or prevent conquests of territory, but to keep the [hierarchical] structure of society intact...

George Orwell, *1984*, New American Library, New York, p. 164. Originally published in 1949.

Note carefully that the line separating the left and right factions in the preceding diagram of Adam's Empire is a broken line. There is a line between the two factions, however. Minor differences in techniques and professions exist. Given an opportunity for a bloodless coup, one side would definitely take the possessions of the other side. Such is Adam's culture. He is still a "gold-worshipper." However, in the steady or at least shaky state, there is much more to encourage private cooperation and public bluster between the ruling elites on both sides of the Iron Curtain. The lines separating the classes within each society are solid lines. Those divisions are much more tangible—on both sides of the Iron Curtain.

Chancellor Williams made the same observation that George Orwell made about the structure of Adam's current Empire:

> ...Those who have been so brainwashed into ideological blindness that they cannot see that the actual political, economic and social structures of capitalism and communism are substantially the same, same upper ruling classes, same elite classes, and the same controlled and exploited masses—those unable to see this operating over the world before their very eyes, will, of course, be unable to see what is presented here...

> Chancellor Williams, *The Destruction of Black Civilization,* Third World Press, Chicago, 1976, p. 352.

The observation about the similarities on the two sides of Adam's Empire is not confined to learned teachers like Chancellor Williams. You will recall the testimony of Specialist 4 Charles Strong who observed that, "They be telling us to fight the spread of Communism, but they be helping the Communist economy. I don't walk around blind anymore." That observation of Orwell, Williams and Strong is not rare among black Americans:

> ..."When this man [Uncle Sam] asks me to go to the army he insults me. He thinks I'm a fool. We got a war here. He talks about Communism. What does he think this is?

> This is hell. It's a bitch."...

> "Roy" quoted in *The Choice: The Issue of Black Survival in America* by Samuel F. Yette, Cottage Books, Silver Spring, Md., 1971, p. 31.

George Orwell and black Americans are not the only people who have expressed the aforementioned view of Adam's Empire:

...The U.N. is not a tool of Soviet diplomacy. The Soviet Union is as suspicious of the U.N. as the U.S. is. Whatever their disagreements the two superpowers agree that a strong and vigorous U.N. led, say by an aggressive personality like the late Dag Hammarskjold, is not in the interest of either party...

Kishore Mahbubani, Singapore's Ambassador to the U.N., Letter-to-the-Editor, *The Wall Street Journal,* 10/30/86, p. 32.

What happened to Dag Hammarskjold?

..."To me, both the Declaration of Independence and the Communist Manifesto contain undying truths, but the West doesn't permit a middle road. They manipulate you so you're no longer able to stay independent. To President Roosevelt's four freedom's I add a fifth: the freedom to be free! The West keeps threatening, 'Do you want to be dominated by the Communists?' We answer, 'No...but neither do we want to be dominated by you!' At least Russia and China don't call you names when we smile sweetly at America. A nation engaged in surviving must take help from all sides, accept whatever is useful and throw away the rest."...

Sukarno, Former President of Indonesia.

The ideologically blind are now screaming, "What about the Gulags, the planned economy and the denial of civil liberties in the Soviet Union?" Well, those things exist here too. Can the Gulags really be worse than Attica or Soledad? Read *Soledad Brother* by George Jackson. Alexander Solzhenitsyn survived the Gulags. George Jackson was murdered in Soledad. Is the method that another country uses to produce and distribute goods and services really our business? If their method doesn't work, and they are our enemies, what is *our* problem? Before *any* American starts screaming about civil liberties in the Soviet Union, he or she should read the *McCarran Act* to understand just what civil liberties Americans have or don't have. What civil liberties did the Japanese-Americans have during World War II? What were the Palmer Raids all about? How did all of those Black Panthers get shot in the back—asleep? One's religion is what one practices, and all the beautiful words on a piece of parchment in the National Archives don't mean a thing when the rubber meets the road.

Oh, oh. The blind are now saying something about "inhumane experiments on people, hideous mental institutions and people trying to escape from Communist countries." Those things are certainly deplorable, but they also exist here. Who would want to go to an American mental institution? Weren't the Tuskegee Experiments, the

Ohio State Penitentiary Experiments, MK Ultra and all of the other hideous experiments carried out by the CIA every bit as hideous as whatever is going on in the Soviet Union? Could AIDS be a genetically engineered virus? Why is that almost 70% of the victims worldwide are black? *CONSIDER* what Dr. Francis C. Welsing is trying to tell us, brothers and sisters. AIDS could very well be a genetically engineered virus. Read *The Survey of Chemical and Biological Warfare* by John Cookson and Judith Nottingham. Don't millions of Americans attempt chemical escapes every day of the year? Yes, the Russians drink vodka to excess. Here it's cocaine, crack or sterno—and vodka. So? Was Jonestown an illusion?

The blind are now saying, "The Soviets are sending arms to Nicaragua, and we are sending arms to Afghanistan." Sure those things are happening, but the ruling elites are not dying in those places. The ruling elites use those charades to sap more money from "naive, young, dumb-ass niggers" of all complexions. They are used to create an external enemy to hate (seemingly a requirement in Adam's "civilization") and to induce niggers to "die for strangers." Evans and Novak, the "conservative" columnists, wrote that using political connections to avoid combat is acceptable in America. The ruling elites laugh all the way to their respective dachas—and sleep well. The purpose of these skirmishes is "to keep the structure of society intact"—to keep the respective hierarchical societies on both sides of the Iron Curtain intact. There might be differences in professed dogma and technique, but Afghanistan, Nicaragua and Viet Nam are identical in function.

The histories of the two superpowers are even very similar. Russia engaged in colonialism during the 15th, 16th, 17th, 18th and 19th centuries, subjugating brown people to the south and east of European Russia. Holy Mother Church authorized it. The Communists came to power early in the twentieth century, preaching a people's democracy. That quickly changed into a dictatorship of the proletariat—without the proletariat having the slightest power whatsoever.

In any case, the Russian proletariat didn't include the Kazaks and Mongols who had been colonized. Whatever democracy Russia professed, it did not include those people. Not an acre was given back to them after the October Revolution.

British subjects colonized the United States, all but "extirpated" the "Red Indians" and enslaved Africans to build the country. There was a "revolution" in the United States also. It did not include "Red

Indians," women or blacks, whom the U.S. defined as 3/5ths human. The American Revolution didn't even include poor whites. There was nary a peasant at the table in Philadelphia. FIND ONE! The purpose of the poor whites was what it always was in Adam's Empires and revolutions—cannon fodder.

Today, the Soviet Union is controlled by the Communist Party which comprises about 2% of the Soviet population. Find a woman or a Kazak in the inner circle of the Communist Party in the Soviet Union.

The blind are now saying, "America's different! There are women and blacks in Congress." Sure there are. *So what*? Can you, Joe Blow Citizen, actually meet your Congressman or Senators today? How many millions of dollars does it cost to run for a seat in the U.S. Senate? How much does a U.S. Senator make? Who makes up the difference? Donations from Joe Sixpack?

...."The masters of Government in the U.S. are the combined capitalists and manufacturers.".....

President Woodrow Wilson, 1913.

Has anything changed since Woodrow Wilson?

...."They tell me I'm the most powerful man in the world. I don't believe that. Over there in the White House someplace, there's a fellow that puts a piece of paper on my desk every day that tells me what I'm going to be doing every 15 minutes. He's the most powerful man in the world.".....

President Ronald Reagan, 1984.

...."The most single important legacy of the war [WW II] is what Eisenhower warned us about in his farewell speech: the military-industrial complex. In the past, there were business representatives in Washington, but now they *are* Washington. And with the military buildup beyond all our imaginations, we have a new fusion of power. It has become a permanent feature of American life."

Joe Marcus, quoted in *"The Good War"—An Oral History of World War Two,* by Studs Terkel, Pantheon Books, New York, 1984, p. 328.

Yes, things have changed since Woodrow Wilson. Senate seats have gotten much *more* expensive. The result: The MIC rules more tightly now than when Wilson was in office. Today, 2% of America's families own over 50% of the common stocks and real estate. Two percent is approximately the percentage of Russians who are members of the Communist Party. The ruling elites are the same size on both sides of the Iron Curtain. The ruling elites are the same people on both sides of the Iron Curtain: Adam. If you still doubt, look at the descriptions of the *Helsinki Accord*. That treaty is not described as one aimed at bringing peace on earth. It is described as "an agreement for the preservation of European civilization." Damn peace on earth! The Soviets supplied Viet Nam and Korea during both wars. Why didn't the U.S. bomb Moscow? Soviet bullets were killing Joe Sixpack. Didn't it matter?

The proles on both sides of the Iron Curtain attempted revolts. The proles in Russia attempted to revolt during the 1920s and 1930s. Stalin, an ex-seminarian, would not have it. He purged the General Staff of the Red Army and killed about thirty million Soviet citizens. No problem, at least not right away.

Stalin ran into a problem when Hitler tried to define the Slavs as niggers. Then Stalin had a *big* problem. He had purged the leadership of the army. He had not endeared himself to the Russian people. The Nazis were initially welcomed by the Soviet people, especially in the Ukraine where Stalin's slaughter was heaviest. But the Nazis didn't realize the opportunity. They were bent on playing "monster's filled with joy" as per Herr Nietzsche. The Nazis killed Russians by the millions. Stalin was saved.

He was not saved by the ideological commitment of the Russian people to communism. He didn't even *try* to appeal to the Russian people on the basis of communism. Instead, Old Joe urged defense of Holy Mother Russia: "Fight for your children, your wives and your lives!" The Russian proles had two options: fight Stalin or fight Hitler. As Hitler made no bones about killing them right away; and Stalin would simply enslave them, the Russian people took Hobson's choice. They defeated Hitler. They are perhaps more advanced than the proles in the West. They are more advanced because they *know* that they have no shot, while Western proles still are largely deluded by "noble causes."

The proles in the USA attempted to revolt in the last quarter of the 19th century and the first quarter of the 20th century. Child labor, subhuman working conditions in general, at least two financial panics, poison food and corrupt government led to the formation of very militant labor unions and the growth in socialism, populism and "utopian" societies seeking escape. This Second American Revolution succeeded in engendering some moderate reforms, but the reforms were more cosmetic than substantive. Are the labor laws observed today? Do you really know what's in the food you eat? Be serious:

> ...In 1961, the U.S. government banned DES in poultry after dogs that ate food from discarded chicken parts and men who ate chicken necks developed feminine traits. The implants were banned in cattle in 1979, but illegal sales and use continued for months and years after...
>
> *The Washington Post,* 9/16/84, p. A1.

The Second American Revolution was largely defeated by shooting people, deporting people (*e.g.* the Palmer Raids), the unwillingness of the Labor Movement to include black people (*e.g.* the Industrial Workers of the World), the patriotism ploy ("Remember the Maine!") and the general cold-bloodedness of the American Inner Party:

> ..."I can hire one half of the working class to kill the other half."...
>
> Jay Gould, 1886.

> ...The Austrian Emperor rules securely, because he can play off race against race, the Serf against the Magyar, the Bohemian against the Lombard; occupying Italy with Hungarian regiments, and garrisoning Vienna with Italians. Much upon the same principle does the slave holder administer his principality; crushing the poor whites by the labor of his slaves, and yet having in these same poor whites a standing force, costing nothing to maintain it, wherewithal to put down any attempted rebellion of the blacks...
>
> George M. Weston, *The Progress of Slavery in the United States,* published by the author, Washington, 1857, p. 41.

Both of the phenomena described in the preceding excerpts came true. Jay Gould, in a strike against his railroad, *did* hire one half of the working class to kill the other half. During and immediately after World War I, niggers were lynched by the scores. Recall the time frame of Leila Amos Pendleton's poem. *Who* did the lynching? Right: poor whites. The Inner Party made it a terrible thing to be a nigger. The poor whites, who were in many cases every bit as poor as the blacks, were fed an illusion that somehow they were not niggers —*anything* but a nigger. So they stayed poor, and the niggers got hanged. Niggers hanged them. In fact, the poor white niggers hanged and shot each other. Any honest miner from Pennsylvania, Colorado or West Virginia will tell you that it happened. Despite all of that, Joe Sixpack, given his "education" and religion, was quite happy to do the bidding of the Inner Party. As it was in the Third Reich, it was fun for Adam to murder people. That's right, "fun." I didn't stutter or slip. Murdering people gave Joe relief from his "life of quiet desperation," adventure and an illusion of importance.

> ...A volunteer from the state of Washington [in the American conquest of the Philippines] wrote: "Our fighting blood was up, and we all wanted to kill 'niggers.'...This shooting human beings beats rabbit hunting all to pieces."...
>
> Howard Zinn, *A People's History of the United States,* Perennial Library, New York, 1980, p. 307.

I ask you readers, "WHAT COULD BE MORE SAVAGE?" The "volunteer" *knew* that he was killing human beings for fun. Is not *"Rambo"* an extension of the same mentality? America, dig y-o-s-e-l-f!

Adam's history books on both sides of the Iron Curtain now tell many lies. The A&E Network has proclaimed "the triumph." The proles on both sides of the Iron Curtain seem to be well under control, yet Adam is haunted by the wisdom of Ricardo: *"All* empires must fall." Will Adam's Empire last forever?

Adam's Fate:

No, Adam's current Empire will fall just as the many before did. Ricardo was right. Adam knows it, and he knows that the end is not far away:

> ..."The meaning of World War Two for me was being victorious. That was what the war movies taught us, what John Wayne taught us. We conquered the world. We were riding it, taking it for everything it was worth. We were the giants. We could do what we wanted to do...
>
> The economics have changed. People are grabbing what they can grab before the bottom falls out."...
>
> Steve McConnell, quoted in *"The Good War"* *—An Oral History of World War Two,* by Studs Terkel, Pantheon Books, New York, 1984, p. 583.

How could this be true? Could the bottom really be about to fall out? Yes, the bottom could be about to fall out. In fact, I would go so far as to say that it is *likely*—and soon. "Why?"

Fundamentally, Adam told himself lies about himself and about other people. It worked for a while, but Adam was not capable of any more savagery than he could engender in other people. His conquests were largely achieved with surrogates. The Roman Empire was built that way. The British Empire was certainly built that way. England used African troops to fight Africans and Asian troops to fight Asians. Englishmen took the credit and the gold for the victories. *"Ng'enda thi ndeagaga motegi!"*

In the late 19th century, an English general under Cecil Rhodes said of the black people whose surrender he was accepting, *"HIS PAST IS GONE AND HE HAS NO FUTURE!"* With that arrogant proclamation, Rhodesia was born—another nation for Her Majesty to bleed unto death. There is no Rhodesia today. Yes, there is much to do to bring prosperity and justice to the people in Zimbabwe, but there is no Rhodesia. There was a time when the sun never set on the British Empire. Today, the British Empire gets plenty of shade as it tries to bleed a little more time from its former slaves by controlling their markets:

> ...South Africa is run by two forces which, although they are not overtly hostile, have elements of bitter antagonism. South Africa, uniquely among nations, is run by an unwritten alliance between two groups which hate each other. One is the National Party, *i.e.*, Afrikaner nationalism, which includes such factors as the Broederbond, the Dutch Reformed church, the universities of Stellenbosch and Potchefstroom, and personalities such as Mr. Strijdom. The other is the Chamber of Mines, *i.e.*, financial interests concentrated largely in the City of London...
>
> John Gunther, *Inside Africa*, Harper & Brothers, New York, 1955, p. 560.

The neocolonialism will pass also. Britain has an unemployment rate of about 12% today. What happens when she loses the remaining jobs associated with her neocolonial Empire? What happens to a society with prolonged, high unemployment? How could this happen?

It happened because God never was an Englishman. England got fat the same way that Moses got fat—from "borrowed" gold and silver:

> ...Empire was at a sunset too [c.1913]. In the great days of her unchallenged industrial supremacy, Britain had a healthy contempt for her colonies, regarding them as liabilities to be liquidated rather than possessions to be cherished. It was only as competition became sharper on the world market that Britain retired into her empire as an old-age home, finding there a quiet shelter where it was no longer necessary to bustle about for business, to keep improving the product and refining the process...

D.J. Goodspeed, *The German Wars 1914-1945,*
Bonanza Books, 1985 edition of the original
published in 1977 by Houghton Mifflin
Company, Boston, p. 71.

"Healthy contempt" or not, the colonialism was fundamentally flawed. The problem that it presented was Moses' dilemma: Internal order could be kept only by making nonsensical rules. In order to rationalize the external exploitation, it was necessary to create racist theories about almost everything—false premises. Consequently, Englishmen could not "inquire too closely about what was going on." The English started with false premises and taught themselves ignorant:

> ...The second great tragedy is in the nature of what is called "education." It is mainly rote learning, the ability to memorize phrases, concepts and other required data. *Thinking* is neither required nor expected...
>
> > Chancellor Williams, *The Destruction of Black Civilization,* Third World Press, Chicago, 1976, p. 26.
>
> ...The characteristic British and French leaders of this [interwar] period were capable rather than intelligent, well educated only in terms of an education system designed to produce mere custodians, suspicious of and so ill equipped to understand new ideas and forces...
>
> > Peter Calvocoressi and Guy Wint, *Total War,* Ballantine Books, New York, 1973, Vol. 1 p. 28.
>
> ..."When such men [Adam] come to write on the subject [black people], without technical training, without breadth of view, and in some cases without a deep sense of the sanctity of scientific truth, their testimony, however interesting as opinion, must of necessity be worthless as science."...
>
> > W.E.B. Du Bois, 1898, quoted in *W.E.B. Du Bois Speaks,* edited by Dr. Philip S. Foner, Pathfinder Press, New York, 1970. p. 115.

Given the dynamics of Moses' dilemma, it is not hard to see how the British Empire gets plenty of shade these days. It is not hard to see how a ridiculous theory, like Darwin's, gains prominence. But what does the British Empire have to do with Adam's current Empire?

Everything! The process was repeated. The truth has been politicized on both sides of the Iron Curtain. Both Americans and Russians have been taught ignorant. Russians are taught about the glories of the October Revolution. Those lies whistle past the graves of the thirty million or so Russians killed by Stalin. In America, the children are being taught about "Manifest Destiny." *HOW CAN AMERICAN SCHOOLCHILDREN BE EXPECTED TO THINK?* They are asked to condemn Hitler, condemn Stalin and praise Ben Franklin, Moses and Columbus. It is a ridiculous scenario. It certainly isn't a formula for success.

Both Russia and the United States have failing economies. Both have poisoned their nests and the nests of most of the rest of the world. Even animals have more sense than to do that. Nevertheless, Chernobyl, Three Mile Island, dying rain forests and who knows how many "Love Canals" have been bequeathed to the world's children.

The leadership in Adam's Empire is a tragicomedy. Ronald Reagan? A man who doesn't know that one can sink a submarine? A man who doesn't know that nuclear missiles can't be recalled? A man who has confessed to not being able to operate a pocket calculator? He is a sorry joke on humanity's future:

..."I believe that the future is far nearer than most of us would dare hope."...

President Ronald Reagan, 1984.

American proles voted for the man who made the above statement—twice! It didn't matter that he gave them the highest unemployment in 40 years in his first term. It didn't matter that he doesn't know that a submarine can be sunk. "Archimedes who?" What mattered was that he would stop "reverse discrimination," put the niggers in their place and reinstitute "merit." Can you beat that? Ronald Reagan talking about "merit?" Move over British Lion; the American Eagle is about to join you!

While the white American proles were electing and reelecting Ronald Reagan, their high-paying jobs in the steel mills, electronics factories and what used to be called the auto industry were being shipped overseas. Well how did the white American proles get those high-paying jobs in the first place? Did American industry ever work? Did the proles get the jobs on merit?

No, American industry never worked. No, the proles did not get their jobs on merit. The scenario is a lot more complicated. Recall the excerpt from Mr. Weston's book. "America was built by negroes from Africa." During the 1850s, slaves represented the single largest "financial" asset of the United States of America. Cotton, planted and picked by those "financial" assets, represented 60 to 70% of

U.S. exports. The Northern States could not yet compete on the world market for manufactured goods. In view of that non-competitiveness, the North wanted high tariffs to protect its fledgling manufacturing industries. The South wanted low tariffs to enable continuation of the Triangular Slave Trade. The American Civil War was about money, just as all other American wars were about money. The North won. The North got to write the history books. The Civil War became a war about slavery, but it wasn't that at all. Niggers (white) were lynching niggers (black) in New York during the Civil War. Where was the anti-slavery sentiment? Yes, there were a few sincere voices; but the war was about money.

The North, protected by high tariffs and enjoying the spoils of victory in the South, acquired a manufacturing base over time. It wasn't any more efficient than the manufacturing base in France or Germany at the time, but it had some things going for it. For one thing, the genocide of the Indians freed up a lot of land. However inefficient her agricultural efforts, America could feed itself with the "borrowed" land. America didn't always feed itself despite the vast territory, however.

In addition to the land, there was a cheap labor force. It was cheaper to hire an Irishman than it was to buy an African. If the Irishman got sick, so what? If he died, so what? No investment to protect, and there were more Irishmen on the next boat; or Italians, or Jews, or Germans, or whatever. As long as they were told that they weren't niggers, they would work cheap and the Inner Party (Jay Gould et al) didn't give a damn whether they lived or died. "Just keep the boats coming!"

European wars provided a market for American agricultural products. American manufacturing got a boost from cheap raw materials. America took over a bankrupt Spanish Empire. Puerto Rico? Uncle Sam just walked in uninvited. Cuba? Same thing. The Philippines? A few promises in the dark, murder a half million (or so) people, and the Philippines were American. No problem. An American military commander in the Philippines ordered his troops to kill "anything over ten." Americans, people from "the land of the free and the home of the brave," did just that. Remember *Numbers* 31, Moses' genocide against the Midianites? The nominally independent nations of Latin America were largely co-opted by purchasing the leadership. If the peasants revolted, "Send in the Marines!"

...[Tip] O'Neill said that when he was a teen-ager in Cambridge, Mass., "a 17-year-old kid, Eddie Kelly, a dear friend of mine, went down to Nicaragua [as part of the U.S. Marine contingent that occupied Nicaragua to protect U.S. interests from 1912 to 1933] and got stabbed down there. When he came back I said, 'Eddie, what are we doing down there?' "He said, 'We're taking care of the property and the rights of United Fruit. I got stabbed for United Fruit,' " O'Niell recalled. "That always stuck in my head. We kept that nation in servitude for years, we exploited them.''...

The Washington Post, 6/5/85, p. A29.

Via the initially naive efforts of people like Eddie Kelly, American Inner Party members gained access to even cheaper labor than was available in the USA, next to free raw materials and captive markets. But along with the booty came a price. The Eddie Kelly's of the nation were not going to get stabbed forever for somebody else's "Trojan plunder." They made demands. Labor unions. Labor unions meant higher wages. The Eddie Kellys were purchased by higher wages.

World War I came along. America initially sat on the sidelines. She was the "arsenal of democracy." Riiight. American plutocrats made cash money. The European manufacturers saw their plants either blown up or drained of capital. The capital came to the USA for guns and bullets. There was no technology advantage here at that time. The French, Germans and even the English had better weapons. What were the outstanding fighter aircraft of the war? Where were they made? But the U.S. came out of the war as a creditor nation.

The 1920s saw this nation and Europe go on a binge. They (" the lost generation") were trying to forget the horror of watching the cream of their youth ("the real lost generation") march stupidly into machine gun fire. "The roaring 20s!" Flappers, bathtub and bootleg gin, gangsters...Nobody was watching when the economy that never worked without slavery or war or both collapsed. The Great Depression!

World War II was a chance to square things away. American history books tell how our free-market system produced the material that brought victory. The usual lies! There weren't any "free markets." There were material allocations and price controls. Victory was ensured in Russia, almost a year before D-Day. American supplies to the Soviets amounted to roughly 10% of the Soviet war production. Allied strategic bombing of Germany was anything but decisive. Germany's peak production in aircraft was in 1944. Yes, cities were made into rubble. No, production in Germany didn't stop until the country was overrun.

The Battle of Kursk was the single largest armored battle of World War II. Most *real* military historians consider it THE decisive battle of the war. The Nazis never were able to undertake a strategic offensive on the Eastern Front after that huge battle, although they did manage one in the West. Try to find Kursk in an American high school history book. *The largest battle of history's largest war is largely missing from what Americans are taught is history.* False premises...

The European industrial plant was largely destroyed. Peacetime brought no real market for Panther tanks, Spitfires and T-34s. The American economy, which had failed prior to World War II, was given new life. It ran by default for about forty years. Today, the USA is the world's largest debtor. Show me a period in American history when the "free market" economy worked without war or slavery or both.

There was no technology advantage in the U.S. after World War II either. The Germans had operational jet aircraft during World War II. We didn't. The Russians and Germans had better tanks than the U.S. The German rocket program was years ahead of the American program. What about the bomb?

Where were the people who conceived and built the bomb educated?

So the U.S. didn't educate its people. The Eddie Kelly's of the nation never earned their high-paying factory jobs on merit. The Inner Party in America became pressed for profits once the world's industrial base was rebuilt. Eddie Kelly became too expensive as a common laborer. Solution? Hire Latins and Asians to do the manufacturing. No problem. The balance sheets and profit and loss statements of the *Fortune* 500 would improve for a while. Lower labor costs, you see. Higher profits are good for the country? Who was equipped to contradict the traditional dogma? Eddie Kellys?

The Eddie Kellys were not a big problem. Since they had been trained and not educated, the Kellys could easily be given a bill of goods. There were always the "real" niggers to fall back on—always worked before. The Inner Party would use the ploy again. Nixon would keep 'em down. Well, that didn't work out too well. "Eggheads talking about the Constitution and such—Watergate."

Eddie didn't like Gerald Ford. He pardoned Nixon. Whether Nixon did anything wrong or not, that pardon said to Eddie: "Eddie, you are a nigger. You can't get a pardon. That's for Inner Party members." Eddie should have listened to Nixon speak about him, in-

138

stead of listening to what Nixon was saying in code about the "real" niggers:

...[The average American is like] "a child in the family."

President Richard Nixon, 1973

Enough Eddies were angry enough to narrowly put a man—portrayed as an "outsider"—in the White House: Jimmy Carter. Carter was *not* an outsider. He was inexorably linked to the Inner Party, the Rockefellers *et al.* Carter's Administration worked even less than Nixon's. Carter was unable to come to grips with the collapse of the economy, and he wasn't skillful (or perhaps deceitful) enough to reestablish the American hegemony in Iran, a thoroughly evil country according to the Inner Party. The Inner Party told Eddie that the evil Khomeini was holding innocent American diplomats hostage. Couldn't really use the "real" American niggers on that one. Call up number two—"patriotism." The Inner Party didn't tell Eddie that the Inner Party had engineered the overthrow of a democratic government in Iran and put the Shah on the throne. They didn't tell Eddie that the Shah killed about 10,000 Iranians in his last year on the throne. They didn't tell Eddie that the hostage crisis and Khomeini were precipitated by the American actions. Eddie wasn't educated, and besides, *he didn't want to know.* Fundamentally, Eddie is "a good German." Get rid of Carter!

Bring on Reagan. Reagan gave Eddie a temporary job at a hamburger stand. The job is temporary because somebody has to make something in order to buy hamburgers. Does the Inner Party give a damn? Be serious:

...Mr. Teeley, challenged on the veracity of something Mr. Bush had claimed in his televised exchange with Geraldine Ferraro two Thursdays ago, gave the following revealing explanation of the vice president's position on the matter: " 'You can say anything you want during a debate, and 80 million people hear it,' he continued. If reporters then document that a candidate spoke untruthfully, 'so what?' He said, 'Maybe 200 people read it or 2,000 or 20,000.' "...

The Washington Post, 10/20/84, p. A18.

No, the Inner Party has no more respect for Eddie now than when they sent him to get "stabbed for United Fruit," or when he was hired to kill the other Eddie Kellys.

But now the Inner Party is having problems. The off-shore manufacturing plants don't need or want American managers. They have their own people. Why do they need American managers? Did American managers earn their jobs on merit? Do they have exceptional knowledge?

...''The problem is that inside a corporation everything is subjective. The marketplace is not truly competitive. They don't promote the best talent, they promote their friends. The competition promotes its in group, and so you don't have the best rising to the top. You have the mediocre competing with the mediocre.''...

An ''intense,'' black, Summa graduate of Stanford.

Quoted in *Black Life in Corporate America,* by George Davis and Glegg Watson, Anchor Press, New York, 1982, p. 30.

...Pennsylvania used to symbolize America's sinews. America's first oil was found here. Pennsylvania was the Saudi Arabia of coal. Pennsylvania was synonymous with steel. But by 1985, steel-industry employment nationwide had plummeted 58 percent from its 1953 peak of 726,000. ...360,000 of Pennsylvania's ground-water wells are contaminated...at the Hilton in Scranton you find a bottle of Perrier next to your sink to use when brushing your teeth...

The Washington Post, 10/30/86, p. A27.

The world could poison its own wells—no Americans required. American managers are experiencing shriveling demand for their services. Top management has even gotten predatory with each other. ''If I can't run my company, I'll take over yours!'' The mergermania makes nobody rich but the lawyers. There is no real increase in output as a result of the top level wars. America's industrial sector faces complete and total bankruptcy. Then what?

The same scenario can be seen on the other side of the Iron Curtain. A failing Soviet economy is looking to the West for a solution. The West can't save itself. Why are they looking here? America's economy has never worked without war or slavery:

...The House Democrats have put out a paper needling the Reagan administration for a growth rate that falls far short of its consistently (and groundlessly) optimistic forecasts.

The Democrats' memories are short...

Both parties continue to inflict damage on the economy, and on themselves, by trying to believe that 4 percent growth is the normal growth rate for the economy—a rate that can be maintained simply by competent policy. Since the beginning of this century the country's economy has expanded at a rate that averages 3 percent a year. There was one long cycle of fast growth—the years from 1939 to 1969, when the average was 4.1 percent a year. But that included three wars that accelerated the economy at a cost that no sane person would pay merely for economic advancement...

The Washington Post, 10/23/86, p. A22.

WHOA! We need to think about this for a minute. The Reagan 4% forecasts have the purpose of projecting constant employment levels. The proles cannot be told that they are going to be out of their jobs. They can't be told that their steel jobs are now in South Africa. No way. Tell the proles that we're going to grow at 4%, a growth level capable of sustaining "full employment."

But what happens when the statistics show that we're not growing? No problem. Employment is usually expressed as a percentage of the labor force. The labor force includes all of those people actively seeking employment. If we just say that Joe Sixpack numbers 352 through 7,000 are no longer actively seeking employment, we will reduce the labor force. The percentage of unemployment will therefore not rise. As for the number of employed, well...The statistics don't differentiate between Joe's temporary job at the hamburger stand and his former job at the steel mill.

Ahh, we have per capita income. But if the managers are getting fatter, won't per capita income be distorted? Are the managers getting fatter?

...Year after year, corporate management gets higher percentage pay increases than the labor force in general...The dollar gap between the bosses and the rest grows steadily wider every year...

Newsweek, 6/27/83, p. 13C Executive Ed.

Joe Sixpack or Eddie Kelly, whatever name we want to give the people who call themselves "working Americans," are working less and less these days. Plant closings aren't really "news" now—too common. Joe survives the best way he can. It is frequently said that, "We are going to have a service economy." Who is going to buy the services? Who will buy the hamburgers from Joe's hamburger stand? There are very few factory jobs such as existed when Joe moved to the suburbs to get away from the niggers. As the factory jobs continue to decline in number and pay scale, there will be fewer and fewer customers for Joe's hamburgers. "But isn't unemployment down?"

In short, "liars figure and figures lie." Joe Sixpack is not trained to evaluate things like economic statistics. He is trained to believe that "Columbus discovered America."

But back to the *Post's* assertion that the American economy has grown at a rate that averages only three percent since the beginning of this century. *If one takes out the periods of war, the economy has grown at less than three percent.* Did the economy ever work? For Joe Sixpack? For Eddie Kelly? For United Fruit, the CIA retirement home?

Adam's economic empire is a shambles. The West has a slight advantage because it has stolen more. The East has a slight advantage because its Joe Sixpacks expect less. But the thefts of the West give it a geopolitical disadvantage. Most of the niggers in the world see the West as these men did:

..."A Nazi is a Yanqui carried to its logical conclusion."...

> Don Pedro Albizu Campos,
> Puerto Rican Patriot, imprisoned and
> tortured by "Yanquis."

..."It is better to go to hell without America, than to go to heaven with her."...

> Don Manuel Quezon,
> Philippino Patriot.

..."[the U.S. Government] is the greatest purveyor of violence in the world."

> Rev. Martin Luther King, Jr.
> Murdered American Nobel Peace Laureate.

...Kwitny [Jonathan Kwitny in his book *Endless Enemies: The Making of an Unfriendly World*] has the courage to say that "except in areas contiguous to the Soviet borders, where the might of Soviet ground forces can be brought to bear...It stacks up as less threatening than the U.S. record." He also grasps the nettle of the U.S. obsession with Cuba by saying, and producing evidence to back up his statements, that the average Cuban lives very well by Third World standards and is happier and more supportive of his government's policies than most citizens of the governments which the U.S. defends in Central and South America...

> *The Washington Post*, Book World, 6/24/84,
> p. 9.

...In the late 1920's, the U.S. created the National Guard to defeat nationalistic rebels led by Augustino Sandino. With U.S. help, the National Guard seized power, and its leader—Anastasio Somoza—began a 45-year family dynasty that was one of the bloodiest and most corrupt in Latin America.

The Nicaraguan people—deeply conscious of their own history—show no signs of falling for the same trick twice.

> Edgar Chamorro, Key Biscayne, Fla.
> Dec. 30, 1985
>
> The writer is a member of the Commission on U.S.-Central American Relations a non-profit organization based in Washington.
>
> *The New York Times,* 1/9/86, p. A22.

Joe Sixpack doesn't want to believe what Kwitny and the others have written and said. He sees the well-publicized "mercy missions" after this earthquake or that flood. He doesn't see when the CIA runs the guns in, blows up the hospital or "terminates with extreme prejudice" some "Communist," like Salvador Allende or Patrice Lumumba.

> ...In a radio interview with Metromedia reporter Dan Blackburn on June 5, 1970, AID [Agency for International Development] administrator, Dr. John A. Hannah, was forced to admit that AID was a cover operation for the Central Intelligence Agency (CIA) in Laos under the guise of assisting Laotians with development of agriculture, hospitals and other benefits. AID's pacification programs in Vietnam and Cambodia were similarly implicated in the interview...
>
> Samuel F. Yette, *The Choice: The Issue of Black Survival in America,* Cottage Books, Silver Spring, 1971, p. 38.

THE PENTAGON *says that the U.S. has used military force over two hundred times since World War II.* Joe Sixpack doesn't want to hear that. If it's true, anybody killed was a "Godless Communist." Joe has been well trained, but not educated. He will continue to get stabbed for United Fruit—for somebody else's "Trojan plunder."

Adam has *not* had an uninterrupted run in the geopolitical arena for thousands of years. Greece ascended and fell over a period of about 500 years. The Romans did the same thing. After Rome, Adam went back to sleep. He believed for centuries that the earth is flat. The more Holy Mother Church ruled in the academic arena, the less education Adam got. Obedience was the rule, not learning. It has always been Adam's rule. "Leave the damn snake alone!"

Learning was only reinvigorated when Adam made contact with the outside world again. In the 13th century A.D., Marco Polo took no treasures *to* China. He returned with a knowledge of gunpowder.

Adam learned about steel from the Arabs, from whom he also got a number system. These things did not happen in prehistory. They happened A.D., in the current era. At the time of the previously quoted testimony of the Arab traveler in West Africa, there was nothing in Europe to compare with the West African universities at Timbuktu and elsewhere. European "scholarship" was largely centered in monastaries under the control of Holy Mother Church, where scholarship was inevitably in trouble. There were too many questions that couldn't be asked. Consequently, most of the mental energies in the monastaries were focused on debating such burning issues as how many angels could fit on the head of a pin. Africans could have walked through Europe like Sherman through Georgia. Why didn't they? For the same reasons that they didn't do it when Menes kicked Adam out of *Bilud as Sudan*.

With gunpowder, steel, a number system and a malignant philosophy, Adam began to move about in the world again. Europe began to "colonize" aborigines and such. Europe brought us "rum," Christianity and souls...and death. These gifts were brought in the 15th through 19th centuries, leading to the arrogant Englishman's proclamation: *"HIS PAST IS GONE AND HE HAS NO FUTURE!"* The Englishman was *wrong*.

The homeland of Nietzsche and Goethe has been split in two. The Spanish Empire is gone, and Spain has yet to recover from its fratricidal war in the 1930s. Portugal's Empire is gone, and Portugal is now the rump of Europe that it always was with a national illiteracy rate of about 30%. Is there a French Indo-China? Where is Italy's African Empire that was acquired so nobly by soldiers blessed by the Pope? One can hear the death rattles in the chest of the neocolonial Empire of the British Lion without a stethoscope. Britain's colonial Empire, the one that she had when she had "a healthy disdain" for her colonies, has long gone. But all of these recent events just bring us down the river of history to the present. What is the U.S. foreign policy?

The "diplomats" have already answered the question. U.S. foreign policy is simply "to knock off little brown people on the cheap." "Why?" The Inner Party thinks that it can acquire gold that way—"American interests." The U.S. has to do it on the cheap because her proles are not happy about the reception that they got twice in Asia—Korea and Viet Nam. Therefore, in the tradition of Rome and Britain, the U.S. attempts to use surrogates—"Contras" and such:

...The most heated exchanges came over Washington's stand in the Third World. Deng attacked Reagan for depending too heavily on "your four aircraft carriers"—Taiwan, South Korea, South Africa and Israel...

Newsweek, 5/7/84, p. 30.

I wonder what Reagan was told to say in response? In any case, for the sake of history, it is necessary to look at the seaworthiness of the "four aircraft carriers."

TAIWAN, now there's a democracy. Taiwan has just put an as yet nominal end to thirty-eight years of marshal law. Her policies are so bankrupt that Taiwan found it necessary to assassinate a U.S. citizen here in America to keep him from telling the real deal.

SOUTH KOREA is getting ready for the Olympics, maybe. Daily her youth are protesting about the oppression. Opposition leaders get arrested on arrival from abroad.

SOUTH AFRICA, another stellar democracy. Democracy in South Africa, of course, means one man, one bullet. Soon the democratic forces in South Africa are going to say, "TODAY!"

ISRAEL? Well, the war with the Canaanites has been going on for a long time. Basic arithmetic dictates that the Canaanites will win eventually. Israel is bankrupt and depends on aid from the U.S. for its existence. But the U.S. is the world's largest debtor. What can Israel's future be?

The fleet is in sad shape, and the port is decaying rapidly. The East and West wings of Adam's Empire suffer from open borders. America's borders to the south are certainly open. Despite the efforts of increased patrols, "little brown people" flood in daily seeking food. All the trillions of dollars spent in recent years for weapons have not been able to keep the dope planes out of American airspace. That which was intended for the niggers got there, but it ended up in the veins of Adam's children also. America could build a wall, like the Great Wall of China, and the "barbarians" would still get into the Empire—just as they did in China and Rome:

... "there is turmoil in your country, and it will increase. America will be invaded by the Hispanics—Mexicans and others. I think that you can't build a fence." ...

Wally Jumblatt, quoted in *Playboy,* 7/84, p. 53.

Some readers are saying that, "The military expenditures were meant for the military. Dope planes are a domestic problem." Since when? The U.S. and European nations forced dope into China. What goes around comes around. But let's assume that the dope planes are "domestic," and not military. How would you know if one of them had a few pounds of plutonium on it or not? Will "Star Wars" (SDI) solve that problem? Or will it just put more money into the pockets of the military-industrial complex?

But aren't the Soviet borders closed? Not on a bet. Russia's colonial conquests were annexed to Mother Russia. Kazakstan, Tadzhikistan *et al* are nominally part of the Soviet Union. They don't have any people in the Inner Party, but they are already within the Soviet borders. Russia fears Islamic fundamentalism. That political force could serve to make restive the Soviets' captive nations. The weapons favor the Soviets. The numbers favor the Altaics. In the long run, numbers are going to win. *It is apparent that an end to the current world order is in sight:*

> ...Greece declined because men came to distrust reason and Rome fell because it tried to maintain an exclusively privileged society wherein the rich were enervated and the poor alienated...
>
> Peter Calvocoressi and Guy Wint, *Total War*,
> Ballantine Books, New York, 1973, Vol. 1,
> p. 633.

Adam keeps making *the same mistake*.

Does Adam have any options? Sure he does. He's not powerless. Option one is always to do nothing—pretend the problems away. Option one won't change anything for Adam. He will end up ignorant and powerless.

Option two is to destroy the world. "Nuke the bastards!" Adam can do that. The issue is: Will he do it? There's no gold in it for him. What did the *Post* write? "No *sane* person." But *is* Adam sane?

It is generally conceded that Nietzsche died crazy as a June bug. But what is not generally conceded is that he was *always* crazy. The *Post* can find the sanity to write about the sanity of peace; but the *Post* also supported building more MX missiles. It didn't matter that a single MX missile carries the equivalent of 800 Hiroshimas in its nose. The *Post* editorialized that building a few more MXs was an appropriate thing to do. [See *The Washington Post*, 5/6/84, p. A22] Adam's sanity is *really* an issue. The gold that he would lose is a brake on his rush to put radioactive roaches on rubble thrones. However, Adam has not educated his people. The Inner Party doesn't actually run the war machine; surrogates do. These surrogates are necessarily trained to believe that the threat from the other side is real. Accidentally, Adam could ignite the world. A flock of geese, a strayed airliner...anything:

> ...The early-warning system on which the country relies for notice of Soviet attack is only partly alert at any time; it cannot provide information about the size of an attack, and its links to the Pentagon and the president are unreliable, unduly complex and under-rehearsed. In an unsettling incident recounted at the beginning of the book, Ford [Daniel Ford, author of *The Button*] describes the inability of the brigadier general at NORAD (North American Aerospace Defense Command) in charge of combat operations, the man who is supposed to alert the president in case of Soviet attack, to get through to the White House in a demonstration of the 24-hour connecting phone link (NORAD fact sheet: "When we pick up a telephone, we expect to talk to someone at the other end—right now."). Later, the general explains to Ford that he has been in charge of NORAD combat operations for only a few months, and "I didn't know that I have to dial '0' to get the operator."
>
> The U.S. military...are determined to "go first" during a deepening crisis with the Soviet Union, for fear that if they wait, they will not be able to launch their nuclear weapons...
>
> *The Washington Post,* Book World, 6/2/85,
> p. 5.

The general "didn't know?" What can the world do about that kind of insanity? The only thing that we can do is to fulfill our moral responsibility to say loud and clear: "YO' MAMA!" The world cannot be intimidated by that sickness. The world has Hobson's choice.

Neither of the aforementioned options brings salvation for Adam, but there is an option that will do that. All that Adam really has to do is to go through the drill that Jesus tried to teach him, if Adam wants salvation. Adam, confess your sins before it's too late, rewrite the history books and make amends. The amends are not a few hurried and mumbled "Hail Marys." The amends are to contribute to rectifying the destruction that you have brought to the world. Adam will not listen. A hard head makes a soft ---.

Adam's social order is increasingly disorderly. The lies upon lies made conditions whereby it became difficult for one generation to speak to the next. The only thing that Adam could rely on to keep his hierarchical society in repair was racism. The Inner Party would tell the proles over and over that they are not niggers. The proles would be sold down the river at every turn in exchange for their souls. A few tidbits from the hoard of "borrowed" gold and silver and the proles were under control. Many learned the word "nigger" shortly after arrival in the USA. "Foreigners" ranked ahead of "niggers" on the social ladder according to the following testimony from Carl Rowan:

> ..."When I grew up in McMinnville, Tenn., Jews, 'foreigners, and Catholics were way down on the social ladder, and blacks didn't even count.". . .
>
> *The Washington Post,* 7/19/84, p. A21.

The ravings of a disenchanted black man?

> ..."Since the war [WW II], Italo-Americans have undergone this amazing transformation. They're now the most right-wing. There was a general black dislike before the war, like you disliked Jews. We had Jews in our apartment building, but that's different. That's my Jew. Keep your hands off him or you get killed. (Laughs) But blacks didn't exist. We had two black guys in school and they were nice. There was never a threat. They didn't threaten us on the employment level. But after the war...
>
> There were riots in Harlem in '45. I remember standing on a corner, a guy would throw the door open and say, "Come on down." They were goin' to Harlem to get in the riot. They'd say, "Let's beat up some niggers." It was wonderful. It was new. The Italo-Americans stopped being Italo and started becoming Americans. We joined the group. Now we're like you guys, right?...
>
> Everybody started to get a piece of the rock. Everybody wanted to have a house away from the niggers. Now guys were talking about niggers: I gotta move out or my kids...The whole sense was to make money. We became respectable. We lost class...
>
> Suddenly we looked up, we owned property. Italians could buy. The GI Bill, the American Dream. Guys my age really became Americanized. They moved to the suburbs. I think American suburbs are bound by their antiblack sentiments. That's the common denominator. They're into it very easily, it seems. They feel they've achieved.
>
> But they're worse off than they were before. That's the part they don't understand...The war bred the culture out of us...My friends in the suburbs know nothing about opera, nothing about jazz. Just making money.
>
> It [the war] obliterated our culture and made us Americans. That's no fun."
>
> Paul Pisicano, quoted in *"The Good War"*— *An Oral History of World War Two,* Studs Terkel, Pantheon Books, New York, 1984, p. 140.

Mr. Pisicano, a noble heir to Sacco and Vanzetti, is an observant and honest man: "the common denominator." The scenario he described was pertinent to many "ethnics." Fresh from a war in which they had put their lives on the line, the "ethnics" demanded and got a small piece of the pie. The Inner Party, however, did not pay for the GI Bill from its share of the pie. Instead, it was paid for out of Joe Sixpack's wages and some unholy arrangements overseas. The higher wages told Joe that he wasn't a nigger.

But since the Inner Party wasn't any more gifted than people elsewhere in the world, the United States could not afford to pay Joe Sixpack higher wages, give 50% off the top to 2% of the population and remain competitive. The solution was, of course, to maintain the 50% share for the Inner Party, ship Joe Sixpack's job to Taiwan or someplace and trot out the thinly veiled racist candidacies of Richard Nixon and Ronald Reagan. "Joe Sixpack?" He got a temporary job at the hamburger stand. When did the previously quoted excerpt say that peak employment in the steel industry was achieved? 1953? About eight years after the war? About eight years after the war, the devil came to begin collecting his due from Joe Sixpack. Joe is now bewildered again.

Each generation seems to become more estranged from its parents than the last. The early 50s saw "the rebels without a cause." They knew that something was wrong, but they couldn't or wouldn't consider just what it was—especially with Senator Joseph R. McCarthy lurking about. The Korean Conflict had to be fought to stop "Communist aggression." America bled and lost the war, but more people sold their souls for the Korean GI Bill. Later in the same decade, "the beat generation" evolved. They waxed philosophical, leaned left, and, by age thirty, they were voting Republican. They also sold their souls, with a few noble exceptions.

The sixties were tumultuous times in the USA. Almost daily demonstrations for this and that. Nationally televised political assassinations. Woodstock. Viet Nam was brought into our homes by the lobotomizing device called television. The infant self-awareness movements in black America were *simply shot down*. Malcolm, King, George Jackson, the Panthers; all opposed the war. All were murdered. That was okay. Just niggers, you see. And then...Kent State. Everybody became a nigger on that day. Joe Sixpack was really confused. But he got the message: OBEY! He didn't listen to the words that came about a year before Kent State. He enjoyed it when "the niggers" were shot and hosed. But when the Inner Party started firing bullets at Joe, he listened.

...MAY [1969] Assistant Attorney General Richard Kleindienst called for the repression of "ideological criminals."...Five years later, on May 16, 1974, Kleindienst became the 1st Attorney General in American history to plead Guilty to a crime. For having testified dishonestly during his Senate confirmation, he was sentenced to one month in jail and fined $100, both suspended, which drew much fire from proponents of equal justice for all citizens...

> David Wallechinsky and Irving Wallace, *The People's Almanac,* Doubleday & Company, Inc. New York, 1975. p. 254

Corporate America moved people around the country with recklessness. Any ethnic roots that survived the post-World War II flight to the suburbs (remember the Levittowns that sprang up?) were crushed with the shuffle of middle managers and their dependents. "There's an opening in Omaha, Joe." "Omaha?" "You want to get ahead, don't you? We need you out there, but if you don't want to go...Eddie Kelly's been waiting..." The scenario was repeated over and over and over. The nation became more cosmopolitan, but lost the check on outrageousness that was provided by the social brake of roots. Of course Joe went to Omaha; don't be silly.

The division of generations has climaxed with Yuppies. Gold is now unabashedly "in." Gold, after all, was what Yuppies were taught. The old, the sick, the poor..."Losers." "The poor are poor because they want to be. All they have to do is go to Stanford and meet the right people." Riiight.

The Yuppie generation is not trained or inclined to take care of its parents. Do *not* get old in Adam's Empire! We have cream x, lotion y, exercise device number 307 and almost anything else that one can think of to keep an illusion of youth. Wisdom still doesn't matter. Adam still disdains the snake. Get the gold, like Moses and Columbus. Become a "winner." Don't forget the survivalist training on weekends.

Thus Adam faces the future. He has the three options previously described:

1.) Do nothing,
2.) Nuke 'em, and
3.) Make amends.

Which will Adam pick? It's between number one and number two. Number three would be the choice of a rational society:

...You were the dead; theirs was the future. But you could share in that future if you kept alive the mind as they kept alive the body, and passed on the secret doctrine that two plus two make four...

George Orwell, *1984*, New American Library,
New York, p. 182. Originally published in
1949.

Seems easy for a rational society. But Adam has a religion that says .that the snake is evil. He has chosen to define himself by his possessions. He has not cultivated a workable philosophy on which rational decisions can be made. "The Lord is a man of war." Approximately six thousand years of history argue very strongly against Adam selecting option three, the rational option. The history books have been politicized. Therefore, not only is Adam missing a religious or philosophical base on which to make a rational decision, Adam has no real light over his shoulder—no real history to guide him. Those conditions imply an irrational decision: False premises yield false policy. The nuclear option gives Adam no gold. For that reason, and the fact that there is nothing to plan for should it happen, I choose to believe that Adam will delude himself until the end of his current Empire. He taught himself ignorant. The ravings of a disenchanted black man?

..."For.him Art has no marvel, and Beauty no meaning, and the Past no message."...

Oscar Wilde, 1882
on "The Average American."

..."American life is a powerful solvent. It seems to neutralize every intellectual element, however tough an alien it might be, and to fuse it in the native good will, complacency, thoughtlessness and optimism."...

George Santayana, 1920

...What opinions the masses hold or don't hold is looked on as a matter of indifference. They can be granted intellectual liberty because they have no intellect...

George Orwell, *1984*, New American Library,
New York, p. 173. Originally published in
1949.

..."Because I hate to say it, the average American does not know the difference between a Contra and a caterpillar. He does not know the difference between a Sandinista and a sardine."...

U.S. Sen. John East (R.-N.C.), 1984.

Only time will tell whether my pick is correct. What *is* certain is that the world is getting warmer again, and there's going to be some excitement. There's just gotta be excitement. Ronnie said so. Would he lie?

...“You ain't seen nothing yet.”...

President Ronald Reagan, 1984.

What it iz, Adam? What it iz?

Chapter 6

THE FATE OF "THE CHILDREN OF THE SUN"

The last time "the children of the sun" were mentioned in this book, Benin was described as "a city of blood." This description was made in the 19th century, after several hundred years of the European slave trade. The Arabs, Adam's erstwhile "Semitic" brothers, also were heavily involved in a dehumanizing slavery of African people at that time *and into the 20th century.*

Following the overt slavery was the period of European colonialism over the whole continent of Africa. During this period, the Arabs also became niggers ("sand niggers" according to some in the Reagan Administration). Italy, England, France, Holland, Germany, Portugal, Belgium and Spain all sent their priests to give us souls. Somewhere between 30 and 115 million of Africa's sons and daughters were shackled from the European slave trade alone. We have truly been dragged along Adam's bloody path.

Most of Africa has nominal political independence at this time. Adam still holds the purse strings, however; and until such time as "the children of the sun" regain the control of the tribe's treasury, the political independence will remain nominal:

> ...Here [in *Endless Enemies: The Making of an Unfriendly World*], in great detail, and using new material obtained through the Freedom of Information Act, he [Jonathan Kwitny] reveals the tie-up between the U.S. government, the International Monetary Fund, the World Bank, the New York banks, and the multinational mining firms, who use the government of President Mobutu as a way of earning high profits both on the cobalt and copper which they extract and the loans they provide...
>
> *The Washington Post,* Book World, 6/24/84, p. 9.

The above scenario is being played in far too many countries in *Bilud as Sudan.* The corruption of the leadership is not a new story, is it? The people are put in the situation of the Russian proles during World War II: fight Hitler or fight Stalin. The situation will not last forever. The oppression of the people is too great, and the power behind the thrones is dying. The new Hyksos will be thrown out again.

154

Between thirty and forty million people of African descent live in the United States, and several tens of millions live elsewhere in the Western Hemisphere as a result of the European slave trade. The Africans in the United States have the highest number of trained people among the groups of black people in the Western Hemisphere. Proportionately, however, the training level is relatively low.

We have a 44% functional illiteracy rate in black America. That disgrace exists because some want it to be so. It has absolutely *nothing* to do with genetics. Trinidad and Cuba have higher literacy rates than white America.

... "It would surprise you if I tell you that in proportion to the total populations, there are more illiterates and semi-illiterates in the United States than in Cuba."...

Fidel Castro, 1984.

There must be a message here. Trinidad has a higher literacy rate than white America. So does Cuba. Both are largely black nations. Why is it that blacks in the United States are *genetically* inferior, according to the doctrines of Jensen and William Bradford Shockley? We must have mutated or something. *"OR SOMETHING"* is, of course, the correct answer. It was never intended that we read. There used to be laws against teaching black niggers to read and write. White niggers were prevented by circumstances and seduction. The circumstances included 14-hour days. The seduction was the right to lynch black niggers. Television is a pernicious seduction today for niggers of all complexions.

The Inner Party became more progressive. It repealed the laws which prevented us from learning to read and write. We became controlled by circumstances instead of "law." In a fit of liberalism, the Inner Party conceded, with feigned tenacity, the right of all Americans to read and write. The IP was not conceding a thing. They had taught some Joe Sixpacks to read, and it wasn't a problem. If the IP controlled what was in the books, and Joe wasn't taught to think, Joe would be more effective cannon fodder. The same thing would work with the black niggers. If any survived their training with an education, buy them. If they couldn't be bought, send Joe after them. "Hang there, O my murdered brothers, sons of Ethiopia,"...

"The Movement:"

The real tragedy of the educational developments was that many in black America handed the rope to the hangman. We engaged in a misguided exercise called the Civil Rights Movement, hereinafter referred to as "the movement," that set back development and progress in black America several generations. The focus was to integrate the schools. It was a tragedy of a very high order.

Fundamentally, the error was a failure of the black leadership to "know the enemy." The essence of the error was Rev. King's misreading of the developments in India between the British and Mr. Gandhi. To Dr. King's credit, he recognized the error and sought to change it before he was murdered. Dr. King said that we must develop new tactics that do not count on the good intentions of our oppressors.

What developments were misread in India? To understand the misreading, one has to understand the popular mythology about the Indian independence movement. The popular mythology states that Mohandas Gandhi, through nonviolent protests, caused the British to realize the inhumanity of their occupation of India and concede independence. That was *not* the real deal.

To begin, the British *knew* that their Empire was immoral. The British Empire was simply Rome enhanced with machine guns, steamships and airplanes. There was never any mystery about that. The world knew that it was immoral when Britain, the U.S. and European powers forced dope into China. The world knew that it was immoral for Britain to impose laws that prevented Indians from picking up salt off their own beaches in order to preserve price levels for a royal salt monopoly. Morality was not the issue. Money was the issue. All parties knew that.

Gandhi felt the pain of his people, and it became apparent to him that independence was necessary for progress. The issue was how could it be achieved without a blood bath. The popular mythology says that Gandhi read the Christian scriptures and was motivated by the allegedly nonviolent politics of Jesus. Gandhi may or may not have read the scriptures. But if he did read them, it would have been very hard for him to have found a nonviolent Jesus. Jesus beat the moneychangers in the temple with a whip, according to all four gospels. Is *that* nonviolence? Yes, Jesus is alleged to have said "turn the other cheek." Yes, that is a solution for minor injustices and low stakes. If European Christians believe that it is a universal solution to injustice, why do they spend so much money for weapons of war?

Building on the Jesus myth was the popularized version of the events in India which portrayed the British as filled with Christian repentence. They were leaving India as an act of Christian spiritual resurrection. The real deal began in earnest about 15 years before Indian independence, in 1942.

In 1942, the Japanese, "an inferior yellow race," conquered all of the French, U.S., Dutch and British colonies in the Far East. Included in those conquests was the fortress of Singapore. The British said it was an impregnable fortress. Outnumbered Japanese took Singapore with very little problem and sank two British capital ships—to add insult to injury.

The world said, "Wait...a...minute...Yellow folks just whupped on white folks. Maybe God is not an Englishman. Maybe all this invincibility is as phoney as the English god." Yes, the Japanese lost the combat; but they most certainly won the war. The Japanese ended up as the world's largest creditor. Great Britain became not so great. Uncle Sam bled too. Within forty years, Uncle Sam would be the world's largest debtor. Europe and the U.S. were effectively denied a large host, Asia, from whom blood could be sucked. The awe of the exploited was significantly diminished. Without awe, Adam was naked to arithmetic.

The Indian People had been demonstrating for decades against the British injustices. Britain, rather than feeling the compulsion of Christianity to leave, held on as long as possible before her time ran out.

Gandhi's demonstrations were not nonviolent. They were nonbelligerent. The English and their lackeys had enough violence to go around, as they tried to intimidate the Indians by enforcing "Rule .303." "Rule .303" stated that Englishmen were allowed to shoot Indians with their .303 calibre rifles, because God was an Englishman.

Gandhi told the British, "One hundred thousand Englishmen cannot control three hundred million Indians, if the Indians do not want to be controlled." Gandhi organized the nonbelligerent protests. Those protests had two effects. First, the weapon of Christianity (the "mysterious grace" form of Christianity) was defeated up front. Indians, standing or sitting in their native land, were bloodied and killed by people whom Jesus wouldn't have spoken to on a bet. Gandhi exposed the Englishmen to themselves as savages. The second great impact of the nonbelligerent demonstrations was that they demonstrated to the British that a large number of Indians were committed enough to die for independence. With that commitment demonstrated, Britain faced a reality that precluded continued direct occupation of India. If Britain had sent in more troops, hundreds of thousands of Indians would have been killed. But tens, perhaps hundreds of thousands of Englishmen would have been killed also. In the end, because of the very simple arithmetic problem that Gandhi presented to the Englishmen, Britain was going to lose. Britain could have nuked India, but that wouldn't have provided any gold. Therefore Britain withdrew from direct occupation and fomented dissension between Hindus and Moslems as she was leaving. The idea was to keep control of the marketplace while relinquishing nominal control of Government House. There obviously was no Christian renaissance. If there was, why did Britain agitate the trouble in India? What was Winston Churchill's opinion of Gandhi? Answer: "A HALF-NAKED FAKIR!" Why didn't Britain grant immediate independence to Africa? Why doesn't she speak out against South Africa today? Money!

Britain walked out of India, just as Gandhi said would happen. The time factor was Gandhi's life. The English put the man in jail, but they didn't dare kill him directly. Why? The arithmetic would have still been the same, and the next Indian general might not have been as artistic as Gandhi. Gandhi fought his war and won. He minimized his own casualties, and he minimized the casualties of the British. A remarkable man. He doesn't need any myths. Gandhi's assessment of Churchill, Mr. Hyena *et al* was that he (Gandhi) had never met a single Christian. It would seem that Baldwin's identification of "the center of the European horror" put him in good company.

King's attempt to transplant Gandhi's tactics to the U.S. ended with failure. "Why?" For the simple reason that the mathematics of India did not apply in the United States. White America has about 160 million people. Black America has between 30 and 40 million. There was no compulsion to change. Gold, however, was a compulsion to keep the *status quo*.

...*Mar 3* [1968] FBI director J. Edgar Hoover issued a memo to FBI offices concerning the goals of a "Counter-Intelligence Program" against "Black Nationalist Hate Groups":

1. Prevent the coalition of militant black nationalist groups. In unity there is strength; a truism that is no less valid for its triteness. An effective *coalition* of black nationalist groups might be the 1st step toward a real "Mau Mau" in America, the beginning of a true black revolution.

2. Prevent the *rise of a "messiah"* who could unify, and electrify the militant black nationalist movement. Malcolm X might have been such a "messiah"; he is the martyr of the movement today...King could be a very real contender for this position should he abandon his supposed

"obedience" to "white, liberal doctrines" (nonviolence) and embrace black nationalism...

David Wallechinsky and Irving Wallace, *The People's Almanac,* Doubleday and Company, Inc., New York, 1975, p. 253.

Most of black America didn't believe in King's tactics. Of course we wanted an end to oppression, but the support for King's tactics was never more than lukewarm—and that support was waning severely when King was murdered.

..."It [King's murder] killed a lot of hopes," said Spanky, raising his shades to look at the reporter.with his natural eyes. "Don't get me wrong," he went on, readjusting his shades, "I don't necessarily say that I would have been in one of them nonviolent marches with him, but everybody knows that he was out there trying to work this thing out the right way."...

Roy admitted that he was not a pacifist. Nor even nonviolent. But would he have marched with Dr. King?

"Yes, I would have marched with him. And I would have been nonviolent, for a while—until some white man did something I didn't appreciate. I admired the man. I didn't dig his ways, because I don't want to wait another 400 years for my rights."...

The testimony of "Spanky" and "Roy"

Samuel F. Yette, *The Choice: The Issue of Black Survival in America,* Cottage Books, Silver Spring, 1971, p. 27 & 31.

King never argued for political independence. He only wanted civil rights and economic opportunity within the American system. Those demands were too dangerous for the Inner Party. If the blacks got equal access, white proles could not be fooled with the racist gambit. Competition would be engendered, and, of course, that could not be allowed. How could the Inner Party insure its jobs with competition? No, no, no. Delay. Engender a little more race hatred with Nixon and Reagan. Make sure the schools are geared to teaching people stupid, then allow the blacks to trickle into the hostile environments. If they survive that, let a few of them pay on BMWs—for a while.

Was Hoover really afraid of a *"Mau Mau"* insurgency?

...*Mau Mau* is beyond doubt an anti-white, anti-European movement, but one striking thing about it is, as I have already mentioned, that the terrorists have killed extremely few white men—only fifty-three in more than two years...

John Gunther, *Inside Africa,* Harper & Brothers, New York, 1955, p. 358.

Sometimes Adam's mind just amazes me. How could John Gunther expect the Kenyans to like Europeans when the Europeans stole their land? They most certainly did not *like* the Europeans, but they loved them. Just as Gandhi did in India, the *Mau Mau* limited casualties on both sides in Kenya. This was done despite the callous disregard for African lives that was expressed in the regrets of the white hunter who *ordered* "the Kuke" to halt. The violence of the *Mau Mau* was largely directed at the black collaborators. The intention was to punish traitors, engender unity and demonstrate to the British, "We are ready to die." The British got the message, but John Gunther evidently did not. Were the American Founding Fathers "anti-white" and "anti-European" as John Gunther portrayed the *Mau Mau*? Or were the Founding Fathers just against the *policies* of white Europeans—policies that were much more benign than those in Kenya where white hunters could order "Kukes" to halt and shoot them with impunity? Gunther preferred his myths.

In any case, there was no Christian concern for human life on Hoover's part. A *Mau Mau* uprising in the U.S. was not a possibility at that time. Hoover was only interested in maintaining power for his masters. The racism that Hoover used was just a tool. King was murdered. The movement failed.

Some readers are now saying, "It didn't fail!" Oh? The movement was not without victories, but, on the whole, it was a retrogressive step. Yes, we got some jobs that were closed to us before the movement, but how many CEOs, CFOs and COOs in the *Fortune* 500 are black? "We're not qualified?" *WE* did not make Pennsylvania what it is today. Yes, a few us got to live in that alien world called "the suburbs." Yes, a few of us got to wear neckties to choke off the flow of blood to our brains. Yes, we got to ride in the front of Adam's bus; but it is still Adam's bus. *We own next to nothing.* Those who have a little something are in harm's way just like everybody else. Consider the data on the next page which I compiled from my high school yearbook and a list of deceased classmates distributed at the recent twenty-five year reunion of my class.

Included in the faceless statistics of deceased black classmates is a boy named Eddie Ross. He signed my high school yearbook, "We fight and die together." His reference was to the mock wars (rites of passage) that took place in the locker room after gym class. Our lockers were next to each other's. He would watch my back; I would watch his. He was one of my many brothers who died in Viet Nam—for someone else's Trojan plunder.

THE MORTALITY OF THE CLASS OF 1962
TRENTON CENTRAL HIGH SCHOOL,
TRENTON, NEW JERSEY
BY RACE AND SEX

	Black			Non-black			Total		
	Male	Female	Total	Male	Female	Total	Male	Female	Total
TOTAL CLASS (from photos in yearbook)									
- Number	90	101	191	269	293	562	359	394	753
- % of total	12.0%	13.4%	25.4%	35.7%	38.9%	74.6%	47.7%	52.3%	100.0%
KNOWN DEATHS (per list distributed at Twenty-fifth Reunion: 11/28/87)									
- Number	6	2	8	8	1	9	14	3	17
- % of total	35.3%	11.8%	47.1%	47.1%	5.8%	52.9%	82.4%	17.6%	100.0%
PERCENTAGE OF POPULATION DECEASED									
- Percentage	6.7%	2.0%	4.2%	3.0%	0.3%	1.6%	3.9%	0.8%	2.3%

blacks 2.6x others

I still have your back, Eddie. No, these handkerchief heads are not going to tell me that the movement didn't fail; not when my black classmates are dying at 2.6 times the rate of my non-black classmates. Yeah, I'll put the word out that Muhammad Ali, Stokely Carmichael and the others were right about the war. Don't even worry about it. Say hi to James Baldwin, Lady Day and Frankie Lyman for me. You're right, the old town *does* look like Berlin in 1945. Be talkin' to ya. . .

The greatest tragedy, however, was the integration of the schools. That was a mistake that will cost us generations of progress. It is not so much that most of us actually go to a racially integrated school. We don't. The problem is that the black administrations in the formerly segregated school systems were destroyed. As long as Adam is picking the teachers, issuing the administrative posts, selecting the text books and approving the curricula, we will be taught stupid.

"The public schools aren't equipped to deal with the learning disabilities of ghetto youth!" Marva Collins seems to teach us quite well. Her students can read. Why can't the black youths in the "public" schools read? If you buy the lie that our youth are disabled, you might as well roll over and die. The only disability that ghetto youth have is the lack of the commitment of the leadership to teach them. Yes, they suffer from malnutrition. No, their fathers cannot teach them about insider stock trading. But the disability is really poverty, and has absolutely nothing to do with genetics. Gandhi described poverty as "the worst form of violence." It is, and the Kerner Commission told us why poverty exists.

We traded away the administration of our schools for the privilege of sitting next to someone who *welcomed* being taught that "Columbus discovered America." We doomed our youth to learn that "Manifest Destiny" was part of "mysterious grace" instead of the genocide that it was. My youngest daughter came home recently and asked me to test her on her "history" lesson. Question: "Why did the French come to the New World?" The answer expected by her teacher was: "For furs and fishing." I could *not* let that go. I said, "Now wait a minute, Michele, let's go to the map on the wall. Find France." She did. "What is that north, west and south of France?" She answered, "Water." I moved in for the *coup de grace:* "If the French had water around their country, and you will also note the rivers inside France, why did they have to come over here for fish? Didn't they have fish at home?" I was foiled. Her ten year-old mind was already programmed: "Yes, but their fish weren't as good as ours." That small incident depicts the legacy of the integrated schools. Our children will very shortly be taught to the same degree of ignorance as Joe Sixpack's children. The development *must be* considered a failure. The only way that we can make it a victory is to have the mistake serve the only useful purpose of mistakes: Learn from it.

If King had attended so-called integrated schools in his youth, he might not have been so anxious to integrate. Yes, the white schools had shiny facilities. Yes, they had the best equipment. But they were teaching Darwinism. They were teaching about "Manifest Destiny." They were teaching racism. Even the maps are racist maps. "Hyperbole?" Look at a Mercator projection of the world, the kind frequently used in American classrooms. Where is the equator on a

Mercator projection? Is it in the middle of the map, where it belongs? Take a long look before you accuse me of hyperbole. The projection is designed to enlarge the Northern Hemisphere, at the expense of the Southern Hemisphere. If you use a Mercator projection to navigate, you might end up believing that the earth is flat.

With a generation of teachers who went to "integrated schools" now teaching the children, we in black America are getting exponentially more stupid. *"Thinking is neither required nor expected."* My daughter can only get an "A," if she memorizes the claptrap about Frenchmen coming to America for fish. The same is generally true of sons and daughters in black America. Even the black teachers are disappearing. We are projected to be about 5% of the public school teachers in the next fifty years. When I hear that so and so's child finished this or that prestigious university, my immediate reaction is: "I wonder if the child survived?" What about black colleges?

Black colleges are a dying breed, thanks to integration. According to statistics presented in *Of Foxes and Hen Houses* by Stanley J. Gross, 0.9 percent of America's physicians were black in 1890. In 1920, 2.7 percent were black. By 1969, when the movement was essentially over, 1.4 percent were black. But some say that the movement didn't fail. During the same time frame, the number of black medical schools went from seven to two. The number is now three, less than half the number that we had in 1920.

But traditionally black schools by themselves don't mean anything, if the only thing black about the schools is the complexion of the students and faculty. If these schools exist only as low-cost imitations of white schools, instead of institutions that engender learning, the black schools have little purpose except the physical safety of the students. Physical safety of black students in white universities is a problem. It's a small problem, because all that we have to do to correct the problem is leave.

The movement also destroyed the small economic base that was so painfully acquired in black America. After the movement, a few blacks were given lower level jobs in American industry; no CEO's, mind you, but a few jobs. "Only the land of the priests he did not buy." Remember *Genesis* 47? The time came when the priests were landless too. Generally, the priests have jobs in American industry in which they never get to see the big picture. A great many of the black management employees are "niggers in charge of niggers." The priests administer this equal employment project and that, but they do not see the real deal when it's made. They are just like their white co-workers: compartmentalized. The executive committees of the boards of directors? You might as well be in Cape Town. Ham(bone) could now wear a tie. He might even have some responsibility—to execute. Plan? "Mind your business, boy." The small economic state in black America was destroyed as a result of the movement.

The destruction of the education system and the fledgling economic state were two of the conspicuous developments from the movement. There was another development that tied into an external factor—drugs. The drugs showed up in black America in quantities during the early 50s. Harlemites of the time said it was like "a plague." The street gangs, which had some positive things to teach adolescents, went away. You could not depend on somebody who would steal from his mother to watch your back in a street fight. The gangs, which would call recesses to their fights when somebody's mother came down the street, were blown away by the dope. The crime to support thousands of two hundred dollar a day habits became rampant. The priests, as a result of the movement, could now move to the suburbs. They didn't have to stay with ignorant niggers any longer and solve the problems. It was a mistake.

It was mistake because the priests knew where the dope was coming from: Adam. Adam should have been confronted. Now the priests and Adam get to watch the tragedy of the ghettos replayed in the suburbs. The problem is getting larger. Adam's philosopy has predictably resulted in the involvement of the U.S. Government in the drug trade. The hypocrisy of prosecuting drug peddlers (especially petty, black drug peddlers) in this environment is *the same* hypocrisy practiced by Moses in his attempt to promulgate rules in the absence of religion. The USA *et al* are, of course, simply repeating Moses' error:

> ..."Wherever I looked, I ran into old Nazis, arms dealers, East European agents, and various secret services. I appointed a police team to investigate this, and the politicians emasculated it."...
>
> French magistrate Germain Sangelin, 1984, commenting on his four-year investigation of contraband smuggling.
>
> ..."Substantial evidence links drugs, money and arms networks in Central America. The fact is, if you want to go into the subversion business, collect intelligence, and move arms, you deal with the drug movers."...
>
> General Paul F. Gorman, head of U.S. Southern Command, 1984.
>
> Quoted in *The City Paper* (Wash., D.C.), 11/13/87, p. 12.

Orwell named his book well, didn't he? What a year, 1984!

One result of the movement was that we did get the right to vote in some areas where we didn't have the right before the movement. In some cases we have been able to elect officials, especially mayors:

> ...It is a concession masking the face of power, which remains White. The presence of these beleaguered Black men—some of whom, after all, putting it brutally, may or may not be for sale—threatens the power of the Republic far less than would their absence...
>
> James Baldwin, *The Evidence of Things Not Seen*, Holt, Rinehart and Winston, New York, 1985, p. 26.

Was James Baldwin lying? Well, one black mayor, evidently to prove his mettle, decided to drop a firebomb on his city to burn out some black "malcontents." Another has stated that the 9 to 10-minute response time for ambulance service in his city compares unfavorably to the 4 to 5-minute response time in a neighboring city because the poor people in his city are abusing the service. Priests!

In fact, since King was murdered, the leadership in black America has been increasingly composed of priests. The black masses have Hobson's choice again, and pray for some leadership. In 1984, Rev. Jesse Jackson had the temerity to run for the Presidential nomination of the Democratic Party. Most in black America knew that Jesse had a snowball's chance in hell of winning the nomination—or becoming President. Yet, most black people had the mother wit to understand that holding office was not the important factor. The masses were crying for someone to tell our story and to negotiate on our behalf without compromising our humanity; for someone who wouldn't sell us down the river for a Mercedes or a BMW. Seventy to eighty percent of the black electorate supported Rev. Jackson's relatively progressive 1984 program. It was an impressive display of solidarity in the face of overwhelming odds. *Where was the rest of the so-called black leadership?*

The priests were playing Mobutu or Savimbi. Most of the prominent black people spent the 1984 campaign trying to convince black people that we should support a candidate who advocated increasing the defense budget, first use of nuclear weapons and some kind of sanctions against Nicaragua—a candidate who could not bring himself to say "quota" in any positive way, and who wouldn't even address the Black Caucus in San Francisco. Even former associates of Rev. King endorsed a man who advocated first use of nuclear weapons. It was shameful, despicable—and there has been no plausible explanation offered by the priests.

The only thing that even approached an explanation was, "We want to establish a link to a future president!" The priests could have kept that offering to themselves. If the man didn't listen to us when he needed us, why did the priests think that he would listen when he didn't need us? What were the priests going to do if the man dishonored his hypothetical political obligation for black support? Poke out their lips, act hurt and drive home, past the ghetto, to whimper—in a BMW?

> ...Mondale added to unhappiness among some blacks, especially for his own supporters, when he alone among the candidates failed to appear before the black caucus. In addition his choice for his running mate, Rep. Geraldine A. Ferraro, who had been expected to appear in his stead, did not attend...
>
> Rep. Mickey Leland (D-Tex.) Caucus chairman and a Mondale supporter, said Mondale would appear tomorrow. An intense chorus of boos followed. Later when told that Ferraro would not appear today, Leland told reporters, "I'm p-----."
>
> "I happen to be a Mondale supporter," he said. "I'm trying to do all I can to make sure that blacks feel they are treated fairly and equitably. It's a personal affront to me."...
>
> *The Washington Post,* 7/18/84, p. A10

Note very carefully that the concern of the priest in the preceding excerpt was that black people *"feel"* that they are treated fairly. Note also the real cause of his pout: "a *personal* affront." Why was the priest surprised when his master had no respect for him?

It was disgraceful. In fact, Mondale, the man whom the priests supported, had *no chance* of winning the Presidency. It was an ideal time for stating principles. Principles were cheap. Socrates, Jesus, Gandhi and King all influenced events at least as much as their contemporaries. None of those men held any office. The mass of black Americans could make the necessary analysis. The priests? Well...maybe they had too much integrated education. The integration movement died with King. It's up to the living to learn from the mistakes. We must learn and never forget that Western "civilization" murdered, or caused to be murdered, all four of the previously mentioned humanitarian leaders: Socrates, Jesus, Gandhi and King. The Romans, creators of one of the West's two "classic" civilizations, burned what was the world's greatest library at Alexandria in Egypt. The other "classic" Western "civilization," Greece, sentenced

Socrates to death. Do you remember why? "The children of the sun" made Imhotep a god. He was one of two people of non-royal birth to be so honored. Both of these non-royal gods were philosophers. Neither was a warrior. *Never* forget! History tells us in no uncretain terms that *there are cultural norms of behavior.* "Experience is a great school, and fools will learn in no other."

Unfortunately, the so-called leadership in black America have been promoting solutions to "the black problem" since King's death that are doomed to failure before they start. *It certainly cannot be realistically argued that the proposed solutions have worked.* Most of these proposals include, to a greater or lesser degree, the false assumption of the mythical Gandhism. That is, the proposed solutions seek relief from the person from whom relief is sought. It is perhaps appropriate that a few of these proposals receive a brief examination.

The Media Cure:

This proposal essentially states that the need is to focus media attention on various aspects of "the black problem." With attention so focused, Adam will either have a spiritual renaissance or be embarassed such that the problem will be corrected. *Don't* count on it!

A silly proposal like "the media cure" could only be proposed by sincere people who don't know the enemy or insincere people who know the enemy too well. The media know the problems. They read the Kerner Commission report, just like we did. The media are owned by the same people who cause the problems, as specified by the Kerner Commission. Here is more testimony:

> ..."There is no such thing in America as an independent press, unless it is the small towns...We are the tools and vassals of rich men behind the scenes. We are the jumping jacks; they pull the strings and we dance. Our talents, our possibilities and our lives are all the property of other men. We are intellectual prostitutes."...

> John Swinton, U.S. Journalist, 1880.

...10 BEST CENSORED STORIES OF RECENT YEARS

Project Censored is a nationwide research project begun at Sonoma State University in California in 1976. Significant news stories that have been ignored by the mass media are located, evaluated, and submitted to a panel of prominent judges, who rank them annually. The Sonoma State researchers stress that the suppression of these stories is not so much the result of a "conspiracy" as the media's lack of perception, its drive for profits, its common interest with big business, and a general desire not to rock the boat.

1. CANCER, INC...
2. AMERICA'S SECRET POLICE NETWORK...
3. BANNED IN THE U.S.—SAFE FOR THE THIRD WORLD...
4. CORPORATE CONTROL OF DNA...
5. THE MYTH OF BLACK PROGRESS

In an article in the *Progressive*, author Joel Dreyfuss wrote that most of the indices of poverty, unemployment, and drug abuse in the black population—conditions that were considered a scandal in the 1960's—have actually become worse. For example, only 3% of all professional jobs are held by blacks, a statistic that has not changed since 1969. In addition, the number of black youths under 16 who are arrested today is almost 10 times what it was in 1950. Dreyfuss, who warns that the 1980s could be a decade of racial unrest, says that his article was rejected by major publications because the article was not considered "exciting" enough.

6. WAR ON SCIENTISTS...
7. THE REAL IRANIAN STORY...
8. U.S. GUILTY OF HUMAN RIGHTS VIOLATIONS

In 1979, a panel of seven international jurists came to the U.S. to conduct a nationwide investigation of prison conditions and the judicial system. They found the U.S. guilty of systematic violations of human rights. Their findings were submitted to the U.N. but not reported by the mass media. When U.S. media representatives were asked why the story was not covered, they said, "The big black story now is Andy Young and fallout from his resignation." There was only room for one sizeable "black story" at a time, the media people explained.

9. WORST NUCLEAR SPILL...
10. THE TRAGEDY IN EAST TIMOR...

> Irving Wallace, David Wallechinsky, Amy
> Wallace and Sylvia Wallace, *The Book of
> Lists #2,* Bantam Books, New York, 1980,
> p. 158.

A media establishment that can argue against employment quotas, while imposing a quota of one on "black stories," cannot rationally be expected to bring a balanced perspective to reporting. We are not a significant source of the media's advertising revenue, and, in America, one must, *"Follow the money!"*

The American media, on the whole, did not report the first years of the African famine, even though 100 million people faced starvation. The American media, on the whole, have given Reagan a free ride. The media are big businesses. Can anyone think of a rational reason why bombers should be advertised in the newspapers?

The media will not produce an awareness leading to amends by Adam's Empire. It is an institutional impossibility. The media, despite the disclaimer in the prior excerpt, *are* engaged in a conspiracy. Here is an example:

> ...When WTOP [radio/TV station once owned by The Washington Post Company] vice-president John Hayes joined a secret CIA task force which considered the practicality of broadcasting propaganda into China, no one mentioned it to Katherine Graham, though the action committed the *Post* to support of the project. If she had known that she had been ignored she would not have complained.
>
> "I didn't feel discriminated against," she told a reporter. "How can someone at the top of the company be discriminated against?"

> Tom Kelly, *The Imperial Post,* William
> Morrow and Company, Inc., New York, 1983,
> p. 131.

If the American media are involved with the CIA in attempts to compromise other nations, where is "the free press?" Doesn't the above excerpt describe a conspiracy? The media *are* big business.

Any positive benefits that black America will derive from the media will be from black controlled media with the purpose of informing black America. The CIA already knows what it is doing. *The Washington Post* already knows what it is doing. Nobody has to tell them. The rest of the United States either knows or doesn't want to know. We have limited resources, and we cannot waste those limited resources trying to make pigs sing:

> ..."And if any house will not receive you or listen to your words, shake off the dust from your feet as you leave that house or town."...

> *Matthew* 10:14

The Work Ethic Cure:

Another proposal that is frequently put forward is "the work ethic" proposal. This proposal states that the root of "the black problem" is our lack of work ethic.

Black people are in America because Adam lacked a work ethic. We built the nation. Adam does not have his (dying) Empire because he had the work ethic and "the children of the sun" lacked a work ethic. Adam has his Empire because he had gunboats and no real problems with "extirpation" and inhumane slavery.

It is true that we are not as industrious as we once were. There are three primary factors causing that lack of industry. First, as a group, we are not healthy. Medical care delivery is getting worse, in part as a result of the loss of the black doctors from closed black medical schools. Another factor affecting medical care is the general decline in medical care in the USA. Approximately half of the nation cannot afford to get sick. Second, lack of industry was a survival tool under slavery. In order to survive, blacks had to maim themselves, feign ignorance, feign illness, do whatever was necessary to avoid the killing labor imposed upon us by the people with the work ethic. Slaves were generally financed over seven years during the 19th century. Such was the life expectancy for people who were expected to work "from see to can't see." Finally, the lack of opportunity engenders a lack of industriousness. We were *legally* kept from learning to read or write for most of the history of this country. The sons and daughters of the illiterate people, when finally given half a chance to learn, were rewarded for learning that "Columbus discovered America." The leadership, the priests, were induced to believe that their brothers and sisters were poor because they wanted to be poor. *Are white women poor for the same reason?* A leadership so corrupted necessarily did not pursue plans in the appropriate direction or on the scale required to yield equal opportunity to the community as a whole. The consequent lack of real opportunity is a barrier to industriousness. Success breeds success. Failure breeds failure. "I got mine, get yours."

The Political Cure:

"Get out and vote; that will solve our problems!" The black vote, especially on the local level, can be a tool for progress. It is not a panacea, however. To participate in politics-as-usual is not a formula for success.

In the 1984 Presidential election, *both* of the candidates from the major parties advocated increasing the defense budget, building more nuclear weapons, first use of nuclear weapons and some type of sanctions against Nicaragua. Neither candidate supported quotas. Neither supported a jobs program.

The differences between the Democratic Party and the Republican Party are fleeting at best:

> ...As a participant in the Hunt Commission, I saw the Democratic Party bigwigs push through "reforms" that pushed out the minorities (particularly blacks and Hispanics) by changing the way delegates were selected. Although the party had been opening its doors, at least in some measure to minority representation, the new rules closed the doors to any real representation...
>
> Lilia Molina,
> Letter-to-the-Editor, *Newsweek,* 5/21/84, p. 4.

There is no real difference between the two parties. Priests, however, have chosen to promulgate the myth that there is a difference. This mythology does not benefit the black community. Myths do not benefit anybody. Myths are false premises which necessarily lead to false policy. Nevertheless, the mythical difference between the two parties continues to be promulgated with such nonsense as: "We have got to make sure that Reagan doesn't appoint any more judges."

That justification was a false policy on two counts. First, of course, is the simple fact that Mondale had absolutely no chance of winning the general election. If the priests couldn't see that, then their political acumen must be called into question. Moreover, Walter Mondale's "New Reality" was simply an extension of old ignorance: interventionist foreign policy, first use of nuclear weapons lunacy, increased funding for the military-industrial complex ...an agenda designed to pander to Joe Sixpack's warped view of the world. Why should anyone have expected that Mondale's judges would have been significantly different from Reagan's? The second count is much more generic. The second count is that judges tend to make rulings based on the political climate at the time of the ruling, rather than on the political orientation of their patrons. The American judicial system is intrinsically conservative. If the priests had done their homework, they would have known that.

The priests have proposed political alliances with strong groups as a means to salvation. Another false policy. Politics is often described as "the art of the possible" and "the science of advantage." Under both definitions, the proposed alliances with the power groups in the Democratic Party are flawed for black Americans. The proposed alliances most frequently have been with Jewish-Americans and labor. There is currently no basis for an alliance with either group.

In 1980, the labor vote went overwhelmingly *against* the Democratic Party's candidate, Jimmy Carter. More Jewish-Americans voted *against* Carter and Mondale than voted for them. Blacks supported the Democratic candidates. Yet in 1984, Walter Mondale couldn't even find the time to address the Black Caucus at the convention in San Francisco. In view of his platform, it was perhaps the best thing. Jewish leaders and labor leaders could see Mr. Mondale, but Mondale could not find the time to hear Ham(bone)'s case. Why? We voted for Mondale in 1980, didn't we? Yes, we did. But that was only part of the dynamic.

The Democratic leadership perceives a reality in which black people have no place else to go. They are quite correct that we cannot go stampeding to the Republican Party. That is not the same, however, as saying that we have no place else to go. Given that the Democratic leadership counts our votes in any case, and black leadership has not yet found the wherewithal to figure out that we will always be taken for granted unless we demonstrate that our concerns and agenda must be given a fair hearing, our numbers are next to meaningless. Democracy does not exist under such conditions. Dinerocracy does, and black America, lacking *dinero*, cannot hope to be heard where gold rules:

...The study [by the American Jewish Committee] found that American support of Israel is at its most secure level and anti-Semitism at its lowest point in the century.

It also reported that Jews contribute to political parties disproportionately to their numbers in the U.S. population: they give more than half the money collected by the Democratic Party and up to a quarter of the Republican funds.

The Washington Post, 3/6/85, p. A5.

...Despite the praise won by Democratic National Chairman Paul Kirk for subduing "interest group" factions in the party at its recent meeting in Washington, one special interest still managed to get its way: organized labor. Southern and moderate Democrats had been fighting to reduce Big Labor's influence on the Democratic National Committee by cutting the union's share of the 25 at-large DNC members from 15 to just 5. But several top labor officials told Kirk that they would cut back their generous financial contributions to the party if that happened. Kirk yielded to the threat, agreeing to seat 15 labor members—and the full DNC went along...

Newsweek, 7/15/85, p. 17.

Who were the "interest group" factions that Kirk "subdued?" It most certainly wasn't Jewish-America who, with 3% of the population, donate over half of the Democratic Party's funds. Obviously, it wasn't labor. Who could it be? Until such time as black leadership gets its collective act together and says to Mr. Kirk and his ilk, "We don't think it's in our interest (or yours) to support a candidate who advocates what Walter Mondale advocated, and we will pursue our agenda—alone, if necessary—until such time as we have a realistic basis for discussion," black Americans will be second class citizens in the Democratic Party and everywhere else in American life.

At one time, there might have been a basis for political alliances with Jewish-Americans and labor. But the conditions have changed, and the basis for the alliances went away with the old conditions. Jewish-Americans came to the USA as a labor-oriented, reform-minded group. They suffered from discrimination and exhibited all the same symptoms of poverty that black Americans exhibit today:

> ...It was little more than half a century ago that American Jews scored below the national average on mental tests. They were also over-represented in basketball before the 1950's...
>
> *The Washington Post,* 8/12/84, p. B1.

What changed? Surely nobody mutated in the last fifty years. We didn't. The changes were that Jews dropped a syllable here and there, sneaked one of their own through the employment office here and there, acted cohesively, worked hard and moved into the American mainstream. A Jewish gangster (coincidently named "Hymie") describes the process in *The Autobiography of Malcolm X.* It was the same process described by Mr. Pisicano that was experienced by Italo-Americans. The result was the same for Jews as it was for the Italo-Americans: (temporary) prosperity, "the American Dream:"

> ..."In almost every field they have entered," he [Charles E. Silberman, author of *A Certain People: American Jews and Their Lives Today*] writes, "be it crime or medicine, scientific research or real estate development, journalism or commodities trading, Jews have gravitated to the top."...
>
> *Newsweek,* 9/23/85, p. 77.

With the new prosperity came a new perspective. Principles became lost in the pursuit of the sacred and once almighty dollar. Injustice became obscure, and Jews, like the Italo-Americans, "lost class"—for a "dream." It was a bad trade for both groups, and all the other groups that made the same deal.

Given the new Jewish prosperity and perspective, several issues came to the surface between blacks and Jews in the 1984 campaign. Basically these issues fell into four catagories: (1) foreign policy, (2) quotas/"merit," (3) crime, and (4) "anti-semitism."

The foreign policy issue was fundamentally an issue about the proper U.S. role in the Mideast. Jewish-America, as a group, wanted continuation of the American largesse and military backing to Israel. Black Americans supported Rev. Jackson's position on the Middle East:

..."I have been a supporter of Israel's right to exist, but I'm also a human rights activist. I support Palestinian's right to exist also."...

Newsweek, 3/5/84, p.26

Black America knows that the American/Israeli policy in the Middle East is bankrupt. So do many Jews, as evidenced by the testimony of Joseph Eger:

...We may find, if it isn't too late, that what is good for the Arabs—and for all peoples—is also good for the Jews.

Newsweek, 9/15/80, p. 17.

Black Americans had just seen the U.S. Government approve billions of dollars in aid to support the Israeli war machine and, in the same time frame, propose to count ketchup as a vegetable for needy and malnourished children here in America. Black Americans had just seen Lt. Goodman shot down in Lebanon, and the President's special envoy, Donald Rumsfeld, never even asked about that "naive, young, dumb-ass nigger." Black Americans know that any rational definition of "terrorism" must include Israeli and American actions. So we reached an impasse on foreign policy. Black people could not figure out why it was morally (logically) or politically in our interest, the interest of Jews or the interest of the United States as a whole to continue to pursue the invisible Arab policy of the United States and Israel:

..."It is not as though there was a Palestinian people and we came and threw them out and took their country away from them. They did not exist."...

Golda Meir, 1969.

..."In Palestine we do not propose even to go through the form of consulting the wishes of the present inhabitants of the country. Zionism, be it right or wrong, good or bad is rooted in age-old traditions, in present needs, in future hopes of far profounder import than the desires and prejudices of the 700,000 Arabs who now inhabit the land."...

Lord Balfour, 1917.

Black America, knowing the real deal about the Middle East and aware of the Israeli "arrangements" with South Africa and Zaire, saw no reason to send our sons to fight a losing battle for, at best, dubious morality. There is an impasse on foreign policy that no amount of pretending by priests is going to dissolve. Our perspectives

174

and interests are diametrically opposed on the foreign policy issues. In fact, the foreign policy issues reach to the level of *values*.

The second significant issue between the two communities in 1984 was quotas versus "merit." From the Jewish community, positions such as the following have been offered:

> ...Once race is the starting point, educators and courts are immediately embroiled in competing claims of different racial and ethnic groups that would make difficult manageable standards consistent with the equal protection clause.

> The progress of the law from status to contract and freedom has been temporarily detoured. But we should at least keep the signposts honest.

> MORRIS B. ABRAM, a practicing attorney, is a former president of Brandeis University and served as United States Representative to the United Nations Commission on Human Rights from 1965 to 1968. He is also past president of the American Jewish Committee.

> *Commentary*, 1/80, p. 16.

Black Americans understand that we should "keep the signposts honest." What we cannot understand is how an attorney and former college president can write about race being a new development in American law? *Race and sex have always been elements of American law.* Read *In the Matter of Color—Race & The American Legal Process: The Colonial Period* by A. Leon Higginbotham. Did the U.S. Constitution define black people as people, or were we counted as 3/5ths human? Were there laws that made it illegal for us to learn to read and write? Could women vote in 1789? What was Brown v. Board of Education about? Who is being fooled?

The economic progress of the Jewish-American community since the time when they were over-represented in basketball is remarkable. But the progress was not made on "merit." We were not in the competition, so it could not have been done on anything that could rationally be called "merit." The avenues available to Jews were not (and still are not) available to black people. We cannot drop a syllable from our names and sneak one of our own through the employment office. Our ethnicity is displayed for all to see. In the absence of justice, we proposed quotas. As the nation has said "no justice and no quotas," we will do something else; but please do not ask us to believe in American "merit." "Merit" in the USA means money, gold:

> ...Unfortunately all the verbage from the high court ignored much more important factors that figure in medical school admissions: economic and political payola...

Several officials at Davis ruefully note that Bakke would have been accepted with no historic appeal to the Supreme Court, had not at least five other less qualified white applicants been accepted ahead of him because of their family clout. . .

subpoened records. . .showed the parents of 270 of the 349 applicants accepted at the Chicago [medical] school from 1970 through 1974 had coughed up almost $11 million in contributions. This averaged out to approximately $40,000 per student.

A subsequent federal audit discovered that 25 of those who gained entry after their parents had made sizeable donations later received federal loans and scholarships on grounds they were needy students. . .

The Washington Post, 7/6/78, p. DC9.

The corruption that passes for "merit" is a bankrupt policy *for everybody.* The best doctors do not get trained. The number of doctors is artificially limited. The doctors, who do gain admittance to medical school and eventually practice medicine, start out in heavy debt. The result: Medical care delivery for everybody has suffered. Doctors themselves are being forced out of practice by the cost of insurance. Who benefits?

Crime was an issue in 1984 also:

. . .Every time I [Carl Rowan] open a bag of mail from my syndicate I am reminded of the distance black people have to go to reach an equality beyond automatic scapegoating. I always find several letters containing torn-out newspaper stories about some black looters, or rapist, or a murderer, with a notation, usually in red ink, that I should "stop bleating about equality until you stop this."...

The Washington Post, 8/6/84, p. A11.

Yes, there is crime in black America. But there is not any more crime in black America than there is anyplace else where one finds people living in depressed conditions. The black people who suffer most from black crime deplore the criminal actions, but there is a degree of understanding. We know that we are no more criminal than anybody else.

. . .What white Americans have never fully understood—but what Negroes can never forget—is that white society is deeply implicated in the ghetto. White institutions created it, white institutions maintain it, and white society condones it. . .

Report of the National Advisory Commission on Civil Disorders; Washington, D.C.; U.S.G.P.O., 1968, p. 1.

It is very difficult to teach a child that it is wrong to steal or murder, when any objective analysis of the history of the United States of America reveals stolen land, labor and "extirpation." If there is a genuine concern for crime on moral grounds, why isn't that same concern reflected in American high school history books? And if there is a genuine concern for crime in the Jewish community and elsewhere in America, then people in those communities must speak equally against insider stock trades, political corruption (at home and abroad) and gangsterism. Howard Beach, New York cannot logically kowtow to a gangster and accuse black people of being criminals. Americans are confronted with Moses' dilemma: trying to administer rules in the absence of a workable philosophy. Moses failed. The USA will fail.

But let's do the impossible and forget the past for a moment. Does anybody *seriously* suggest that black Americans are the heads of the crime syndicates in this country? We don't even own our own crime. As long as the dual standard on crime continues, the fingers pointing at crimes by black people will belong to hypocrites. The crime in black America will go away when the leadership in black America manages to feed the people in black America. The world's greatest criminals wear three-piece suits.

"Anti-semitism" was an accusation in 1984. That accusation was so ridiculous that it is tempting not to comment. However, ridiculous or not, it is *dangerous,* and comments are appropriate. Fundamentally, the accusations of anti-Semitism were red-herrings used to discredit Rev. Jackson. It was deemed by some to be "anti-Semitic" just because Rev. Jackson supported a more even-handed policy in the Middle East. When Rev. Jackson used the term "Hymie" to describe Jewish people, that, of course, was proof.

"Hymie," in black slang, is not necessarily a derogatory term, however. It is a term used to describe a group of people, Jews. Any connotation other than the defined group depends on the context of the usage. Similar terms, which are more comic than anything else, are used to describe black men (Sam), black women (Sapphire), white men (Chuck) and white women (Miss Anne). *In the same conversation* that Rev. Jackson used the term "Hymie," the terms "nigger" and "Ay-rab" were used by different people including the reporter, "the prostitute," who wrote the story about Rev. Jackson using the term "Hymie."

Jewish people use the terms "Bubba and Zadie" as characterizations of Jews. Somehow "Hymie" was a defamation. Rev. Jackson apologized, nevertheless. In mock and/or misguided displays of outrage, Rev. Jackson's apology was largely refused. So be it. However, we in black America are perplexed by a community crying "anti-Semitism" about "Hymie," when no similar cry of "anti-Semitism" was evoked by these events:

...In a letter to Mondale, James Zogby, executive director of the [Arab-American, Anti-Discrimination] league, said "five Arab-Americans who previously had contributed $1,000 each to you personally, following a meeting with you in Chicago on May 22, have had their checks returned to them."...

The Washington Post, 7/28/84, p. A4.

...Last year his [Gary Hart's] campaign borrowed more than $700,000 from First American Bank in Washington, where the senator had been doing his personal banking for many years. Only later did it dawn on campaign aides that someone might make an issue of the fact that in 1982 the bank was sold to a group of Middle Eastern investors.

"We didn't know it was an Arab bank," said Kenneth Guido, special counsel to the Hart campaign. "We got him (Hart) out of it as soon as we knew."...

The Wall St. Journal, 3/23/84, p. 60.

Any *genuine* concern with "anti-Semitism" must exhibit equal concern with the actions described in the preceding excerpts as was exhibited over "Hymie." And how can a community that has promulgated the idea that black people are "thieves, fornicators and liars"—in its "religious" literature—accuse *anybody* of bigotry? The Jewish community, with a few appreciated exceptions, called on Rev. Jackson to "denounce" Rev. Farrakhan for remarks that were *construed* as anti-Semitic. Did we ask them to "denounce" Moses? Did Rev. Farrakhan kill women and children? By what standard was Rev. Farrakhan judged? The call to "denounce" Rev. Farrakhan and the threats against and harassment of Rev. Jackson were miscalculations that will have repercussions for generations. Perhaps the disrespect is a manifestation of the teachings in the *Babylonian Talmud* and *Genesis* 9 and 10. Perhaps the disrespect is due to association with easily influenced black priests. In any case, the actions by the Jewish community in 1984 are viewed by the mass of black Americans as the *lowest* form of hypocrisy.

Are we supposed to be ignorant of the memo circulated by the "Anti-Defamation" League about Rev. Jackson *BEFORE* Jesse became a candidate? The masses in black America are going to insist that these issues be raised, even if the priests are reluctant to do so. It was a *profound* insult to us to be portrayed as bigots, and we know that there can be no meaningful dialogue unless real issues are addressed. As for the present, there is no basis for an alliance. The once allies are better off, with reference to their respective goals, going their separate ways. We certainly are.

Labor has also been promulgated as a potential ally for black America. The idea is a joke. Big labor is a big business. The labor leadership also supported a first use of nuclear weapons candidate in 1984. How did that help the working man? Walter Mondale wanted to build more nuclear missiles. How did that help the working man whose real need was for competitive steel and auto industries?

Labor is, in fact, a mirage. There are large labor unions which, as previously shown, exhibit considerable clout on Democratic Party politics. But their constituency is not deliverable in general elections. Labor did *not* deliver "the labor vote" in 1980 or 1984. The voters backed Reagan to the hilt both times. The labor leadership (priests) kept their seats on the DNC, but they have no constituency to speak of.

The labor masses vote not to benefit the working man, but to keep from becoming niggers. It is the white workers' abiding fear: "Please leave us enough such that we are not niggers." Anybody who mouths the right code words can get the labor vote. It doesn't matter if the workers' factories are closed. They closed in large numbers during Reagan's first term. The rank and file voted for Reagan again in 1984. It's "the common denominator" that Mr. Pisicano observed. Always worked before. It will work for the foreseeable future. We in black America cannot wait for good intentions.

When confronted with that reality, labor leadership waxes mealymouthed and states that blacks have to understand the political realities. The real political reality is that blacks cannot and will not negotiate our humanity away. It is not even a point of discussion. If labor management wants to have some power in the future, they had best start an education campaign to teach their charges which way is up. Closed plants mean no labor force. No labor force means no labor leadership. Who benefits by pandering to bigotry?

The image of labor as an ally of black America is new, dating back not much before the 1950s. Labor, at its most strident, banned black people from joining the labor movement. The Industrial Workers of the World did not accept black members. What world? The same unions that have ballot by murder today have memberships who accuse blacks of being characteristically criminal. Nothing significant has changed since the time of the I.W.W.

As labor is dying in influence, the political attraction is also dying. There is currently no basis for a political alliance with labor. Logically, poor blacks and poor whites are a political match. Racism, however, is not logical. As the poor whites seem to think that our color differences are more important than our economic similarities, there is no basis for an alliance.

Political alliances are transient things. Only alliances on principle are really meaningful, and with such an alliance one doesn't need to negotiate very much. In order for political alliances to be meaningful (albeit for the short-term), power must be wielded effectively. However, black leadership includes few people who have any experience whatsoever in effectively wielding power. An Adam Clayton Powell comes along all too infrequently. We need to "shake off the dust." The Democrats cannot win a national election without us, but we can win local elections without them. What is the big deal? Let's be Christians and "shake off the dust." We can't love anybody, if we don't love ourselves. Politics-as-usual will not yield salvation, and creative politics are only part of the answer.

The Black Capitalism Cure:

This absurd proposal is closely allied to the work ethic proposal. In summary, the proposal states that we should become capitalists in order to participate fully in the American Dream. Why is the proposal absurd?

This proposal is absurd because for all the talk of "free-market capitalism," there is not a single capitalist, of any complexion, who can point to a "free" market—a market that is not regulated or subsidized either directly or indirectly. Free markets are a myth. Free markets did not build this country, as shown in the brief economic history in the last chapter.

In 1980, Ronald Reagan's revolution was heralded as a return to a more pure form of free enterprise. Laissez-faire, trickle-down, Reagonomics, "blue smoke and mirrors," "voodoo economics," "a riverboat gamble,"...collapse. After becoming more pure six years ago, we have gone from the world's largest creditor nation to the world's largest debtor nation. Why? *Capitalism never worked,* and becoming more pure just exacerbated the problems. Without "extirpation," war and slavery there would be no American economy. The nation has survived its wars, to date, reasonably well. It's peace that the USA can't handle. Twenty years of peace are all that it takes to kill the American economy. Look at the historical record. You're going to have a problem finding twenty years of peace.

Americans were not educated to understand the stark reality that America's economy cannot exist for long periods of peace. We were "educated" to believe that we are "guardians of the Free World," made great by "the miracle of free markets."

> ..."Our books as a nation are wildly dangerously, intractably out of balance, a condition that is fundamentally threatening to our economic and political health at home and our leadership and strength abroad."...
>
> David Stockman, 1985.
>
> ..."with the tolerance of the press, Mr. Reagan is placing a mask of fantasy and deception over the true state of the economy and it's portents for the future," [Ralph] Nader said. He asserted that in private conversations, Federal Reserve Board Chairman Paul Volcker and New York banker Felix Rohatyn say "they are scared out of their minds on the course of the economy."...
>
> *The Washington Post,* 10 30/86, p. A27.

Still not convinced? As I write this book, the stock market has experienced its largest drop in history—shades of 1929. *Per se,* that drop has next to no impact on the economy. Fundamentally, the commodities being exchanged in the stock markets are hope and pieces of paper. The drop is, however a bellwether of the future of the economy in Adam's Empire. It means that the devil deficits that Reagan created in 1981 are coming to collect souls. Take a look at the charts on the next page. Note the year, 1981 on the second chart. See what happened after "the Reagan Revolution." Can you see your job and your childrens' jobs in the first chart?

"Why has capitalism never worked?" It has never worked because the theory is *fundamentally flawed.* The theory seeks to rationalize exploitation rather than explain reality. Don't believe it? Consider the diagram on the page after the next page.

The diagram is an illustration of a market (in this case the food market) drawn according to capitalist economic theory. The vertical axis is the price of food. The horizontal axis is the quantity of food. The dotted horizontal line represents the cost to produce the food, a portion of the price. The curved line drawn from northwest to southeast represents the demand curve. The demand curve serves to illustrate how much food will be purchased at a given price.

The curved line drawn from southwest to northeast represents the supply curve. The supply curve serves to illustrate how much food will be provided for sale at a particular price.

ADAM'S DYING ECONOMIC EMPIRE

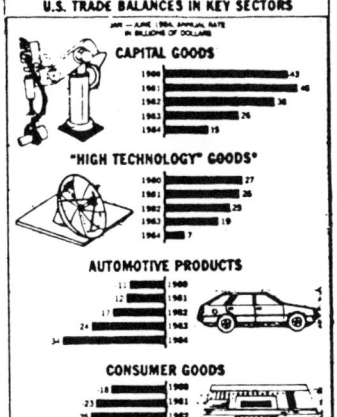

- The Washington Post, 11/18/84, p. Fl.

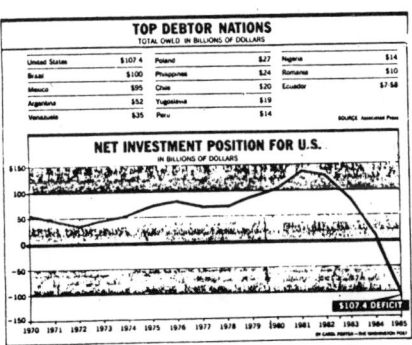

U.S. Replaces Brazil as No. 1 Debtor

- The Washington Post, 6/25/86, p. G2.

Now that you have studied the diagram, here's the question: How much demand for food does a hungry person with no money, no credit and existing in a world with insufficient charity have?

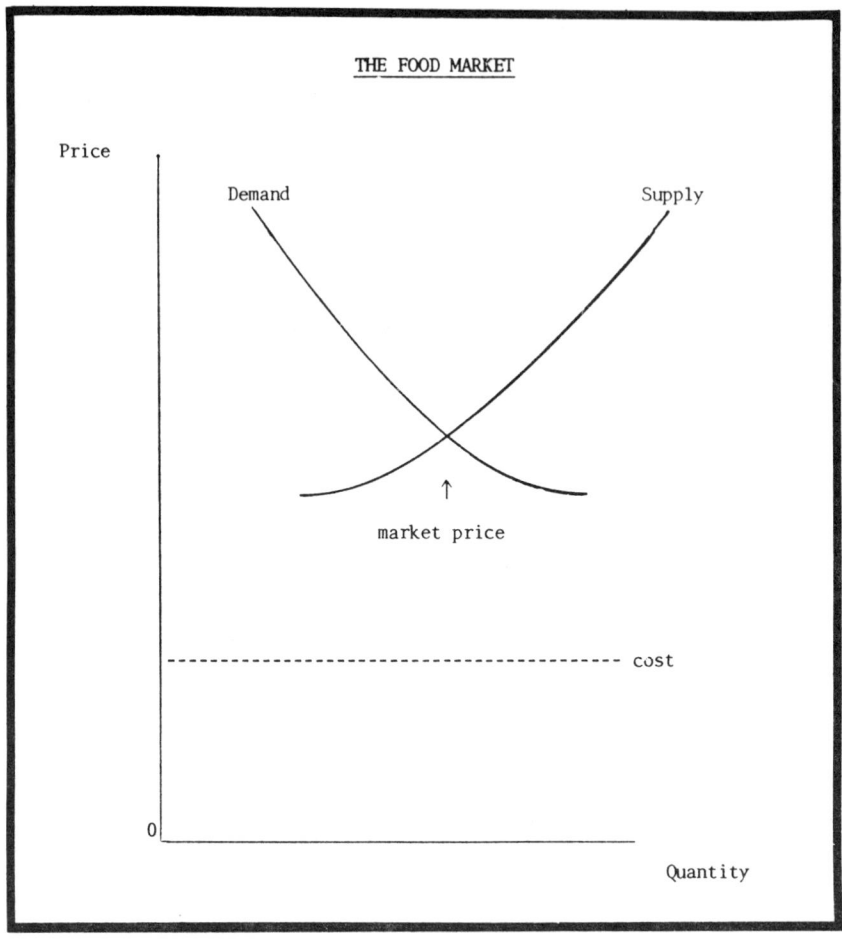

The correct answer is *zero*. *The free enterprise model of the food market shows that a hungry man with no resources has zero demand for food.* Why? Because economic demand is how much of a particular product will be purchased at a given price. Given that the hungry person in our example has no resources, obviously the person cannot purchase food unless the food is free. Since food is not free (free is below the cost of production), the hungry person will have zero demand for food. *The concept of demand in the capitalist model of markets does not recognize needs—at all.*

If one studies Adam's economics, one is taught that wealth is produced by combining the factors of production: land, labor and capital. That assertion, when combined with a review of the historical record, should give a serious student a reason to question the viability of capitalism as an economic system capable of sustaining a society of freedom, justice and equality. "Why?"

The capital that came to this country was initially British capital. The British acquired the capital from the Spanish, other Europeans, like the Irish and Greeks, and bleeding their African and Asian colonies. Recall that England had "a healthy contempt for her colonies." The threat of the withdrawal of British capital was a significant factor in the political decisions of the young United States. Indeed, British capital largely underwrote the construction of the railroads in this nation, so British capital was a factor well into the 19th century. The land? The land was simply stolen. "Extirpate" the savages; take their land. Labor? God forbid that Japheth should work. Enslave Africans. No, don't give a damn how many die; clean it up in the history books. So, capitalism in American economic history had little to do with "the miracle of free markets." Capitalism had everything to do with murder and theft. The capital was borrowed from murderers and thieves. The land and the labor were stolen via murder. The "miracle of free markets" is that people actually believe the baloney (you know that's a euphemism) about "free markets." Economics is called *"the dismal science"* for a reason: As taught, it contains precious little science.

And yet, some in black America tell their brothers and sisters, "We've got to pursue black capitalism." Dear black capitalists, why should black people pursue an economic system that (1) has never worked and really doesn't exist as professed, (2) is failing rapidly for those for whom it was designed to work, and (3) assumes that a hungry, resourceless person has zero demand for food? Speak up, black capitalists. Don't be ashamed. Speak up! Whom do you propose that we "extirpate?"

The Gawd Cure:

This cure is a variation on a smaller scale of the "mysterious grace" form of Christianity, or Islam, or Judaism or whatever. In view of the previous chapters, not a lot will be said about this proposed cure. *The fact is that we have never prospered as a people with anybody's religion except our own.* Facing Canterbury, Rome, Mecca or Jerusalem has *nothing* to do with our salvation. None of the religions with earthly bases in those capitals are operated for the salvation of black people.

Most Judeo-Christians call us "cursed by God." Some Moslems call us "brothers," but that never stopped our enslavement. Saudi Arabia has given sanctuary to Idi Amin and consistently votes against loans to black nations in the IMF. Col. Gadhafi calls us "brothers," loans a few dollars to Rev. Farrakhan and attacks Chad. We can do without that form of brotherhood.

We have a workable, progressive religion of our own. We do not need to be blessed by anybody. Gawd ain't gonna' do it for us. Our God works through eternal laws, and we better begin very quickly to relearn the laws of our God. *The reality is that there is nobody at home but us lions.* When we are able to throw off the mental shackles of slavery and figure out that *us lions are sufficient,* we will be free, healthy, prosperous people. That is all that is required: the ability to think and have the courage of our convictions.

The Options:

Like Adam, we have several options for the future. Also, like Adam's, our first option is to do nothing. In view of the retrogression that has taken place in black America as a result of the bad intentions of others and our own mistakes, the do nothing option means continued retrogression—with all that entails. There is a generation growing up in black America who have the eyes of sharks.

Our second option is to continue the senseless and historically unjustified attempt to bring Adam to his senses. Adam will not save himself. If he saved himself, we wouldn't have a problem. Many of the black people who advocate the senseless integration strategy point to the white people with good intentions as evidence that the strategy can work. They are poor evidence.

If the powers that be in the United States did not want black America to have a 44% functional illiteracy rate or Hispanic America to have a 56% functional illiteracy rate, those things would not exist. We can be trained to go prop up this dictator and that, but we can't be trained to read and hold jobs with liveable wages at home. The people in Adam's community with good intentions are exceptions, not the rule. If they are the rule, then why don't they control their savages? That is the area where the people in Adam's family with good intentions can demonstrate their religion.

The fact is that the savages are not being controlled. Howard Beach can kowtow to a gangster and murder a black man who didn't do anything. Then they tell us about "law and order." All of the sit-ins, swim-ins, ride-ins and other-ins did not produce equal opportunity. If learning that "Columbus discovered America" is the price of equal opportunity, we can do without it.

We have two priorities in black America. The first is to regain control of our children's education. This must be done *quickly*. The longer it is undone, the harder it will be to do it. The second priority is creation of an economic state in black America such that we have the capability to produce necessities for ourselves.

Both of these priority tasks are difficult, but both can be done. We have the resources to make these changes, but neither can be done with other people's religions, financial institutions or charity. Creative solutions are in order. The questionable ingredient is leadership, and that is true in the Motherland and here in the Western Hemisphere. Priests like Idi Amin must be called to account:

> ...Amin's faction of the army had in fact been trained and backed up by the Israelis, during and after the coup [that brought Amin to power]. In the midst of the Entebbe Raid in 1976, the Israeli Colonel Bar-Lev, chief of the Israeli military team in Uganda in 1971, boasted to the New York Times about the Israeli role in the overthrow of Obote, because he had 'turned anti-Israeli and intended to expel the Israeli delegation from Uganda'. The Israeli paper *Ha'aretz* reported:
>
> > Col. Bar-Lev, who headed the delegation and is still on good terms with Amin, said that Amin had approached him saying that his loyal supporters were outside Kampala and that the President would be able to arrest him and kill him before they could rescue him. Bar-Lev advised Amin to bring to Kampaia those soldiers who were from the same tribe as Amin, and to make sure he had paratroopers, tanks and jeeps. So equipped, explained Bar-Lev, 600 men could overpower 5,000. These forces, which had been trained by the Israelis, played a key role in the defeat of Obote's army.*...

> *Ha'aretz, 7/18/86
> Mahmood Mamdani, *Imperialism and Fascism in Uganda,* African World Press, Trenton, 1984, p. 31.

The Amin scenario should demonstrate for one and all that *THERE'S NOBODY AT HOME BUT US LIONS.* Amin was a member of the King's African Rifles, meaning British King. He fought with the British against the liberation movements in Kenya and Uganda. He was supported initially by the West (especially the British and the Israelis), and then by the Soviets. He is a Muslim who is currently in sanctuary in Saudi Arabia, a fact that should give a serious pause for thought to those who advocate Islam for black people. How would the Islamic world react to a black nation giving sanctuary to a mass murderer of Muslims? All parties to the conflict in the Middle East benefited from Idi Amin's reign, *except black people*. The Amin phenomenon cannot continue, if we are to survive and progress. Priests must be measured by their accomplishments for the community. If a priest doesn't produce, "Next priest!"

> ..."Next to the Jewish members of Congress, no group supports Israel as strongly as the black caucus—even those like me," said [Rep. Mervyn M.] Dymally [D-Ca.], who has been critical of U.S. policy in the Mideast. "...The only troubling issue is Israel's relationship with South Africa."

> Freshman Rep. John Lewis (D-Ga.) a prominent civil rights leader, is among Israel's staunchest supporters within the caucus—a position that occasionally has put him at odds with other members.

> "As our closest ally in the region, we must do what we can to protect Israel," Lewis said last week, after returning from an eight-day official visit to Israel...

> *The Washington Post*, 9/23/87, p. A16.

Congressman Dymally, is the Israeli arming of South Africa the *only* issue? If it is the only issue, is it a trifle? What of the Israeli support of Amin? What of the support to the dictator in Zaire? What of the Israeli war policy, in general, that takes bread and opportunity from Americans *and* Israelis? Why should Americans die for Israeli adventures in Lebanon (*e.g.*)? The Lebanon adventure was described by a member of the Israeli Knesset as *"the final solution to the Palestinian problem."* Is support of such adventures in the interests of black Americans? Israelis? Anybody? South Africa is the *only* issue? Explain yourself, Congressman.

Congressman Lewis, have you asked yourself *why* the USA has few allies in the Mideast? Who paid for your trip? The American taxpayer? The same PAC that sent interns from Rep. Leland's district to Israel? Did you visit the progressive forces in Israel, Matti Peled and the Peace Now movement? Do allies spy on one another? Nobody needs allies like that, and neither black Americans nor most white Americans have a nickel in investments in the Mideast to protect. We do have dire needs here at home. Why do you gentlemen call yourselves "the BLACK Caucus?" The black tuxedos at the annual gala? Explain yourself, Congressman.

Option three, then, is to *build on our own institutions* with the dual priorities of reclaiming the education of our children and creating an economic state in black America.

Which option will we take? The smart money's on number one. Doing nothing (option one) has the same result as number two, the integration strategy. Our "leadership" is the limiting factor. I only know of one person, for sure, who is going to go for number three. How many do you know? In any case, we in America are about out of time:

> ...But a dreadful day is upon us, and as nobody's going to give us any straw—Ireland was raped and the Irish were allowed to starve *to death*, in order to protect the profits of British merchants—people, we best make ourselves ready...
>
> James Baldwin, *The Evidence of Things Not Seen,* Holt, Rinehart and Winston, New York, 1985, p. 91.

Amen, James. "We best make ourselves ready."

Chapter 7

CONCLUSIONS

What has been proposed in this book? Essentially what has been proposed is an overlay of megahistory, a history of races, on a generally ignored, cataclysmic natural history. Documentation of the events has been offered from many sources, especially various *versions* of the Judeo-Christian *Bible*. Several summary conclusions can be drawn from the construct:

1.) There *are* cultural norms of behavior.
2.) The cultural norms of behavior can be traced to early physical environmental conditions of various cultural (and coincidently, racial) groups.
3.) The principles underlying the cultural norms of behavior are specified in the philosophies of various cultural groups. These are the *"more or less vividly conceived ideals of life"* that W.E.B. DuBois spoke about in 1897.
4.) Much of the data supporting the above conclusions has been *deliberately* suppressed for political reasons.

Is it fact or fiction?

Pros and Cons:

This deliberately abbreviated presentation of the construct is neither fact nor fiction. *It is a theory offered for examination by others.* There are documents and analyses supporting and contradicting the construct. However, I believe that the data supporting the construct far outweigh the data which contradict it. The opinions, both pro and con, are simply opinions. As the construct is new, naturally there is a body of accepted wisdom which contradicts the theory. Many historians, including black historians, have published contradictory information. However, I think that the differences between the construct offered here and the theories of other black historians are minor as compared to the similarities.

For example, Cheikh Anta Diop has constructed a chronological table of the evolution of humanity. His early work placed the origin of Adam's family approximately where it is identified in this work—east central Europe. Later, Diop moved the origin of Indo-Europeans westward. In Diop's revised construct, racial differentiation begins about 20,000 B.C. with the appearance of Cro-Magnon man in France. Cro-Magnon man is identified as the prototype of Adam's family, as he is so identified by many white historians. Approximately 5,000 years later, Chancelade Man appears in France, and Diop (*et al*) tentatively identified Chancelade man as the the prototype of the so-called "yellow" races. Prior to that time, Diop states that Europe was peopled by Grimaldian (black) people. He states in his book *Precolonial Black Africa* that the Sahara dried *circa* 7000 B.C. Diop states that Semites first appeared about 2700 B.C., when Sargon I moved into Akkad in the Fertile Crescent. What are the similarities and differences between Diop's construct and the one offered in this book?

In terms of similarities, Diop and I agree that the original inhabitants of western Europe were black people. We agree that the first member of the species Homo sapiens sapiens was Ham(bone)—black people, the original people on this planet. The wisdom from the reggae tune, *"Third World People,"* comes to mind: *"Life did not start in a refrigerator; it had to have been in an incubator."* We agree that the Sahara was not always the Sahara. We agree on the divine nature of gold in Adam's civilization. We agree that the known African civilizations originated in Central Africa, although Diop's site is slightly east of my site. We agree that culture follows nature:

> ...To the extent that African collectivism and European individualism grow out of the material conditions of existence, the preceding considerations are founded upon an objective basis...
>
> Cheikh Anta Diop, *Precolonial Black Africa,* Lawrence Hill & Company, Westport, Connecticut, 1987, p. 160.

We agree that European individualism relates to economic institutions, not to freedom of thinking. Diop brilliantly contrasted the relatively benign constraints of the Pharoahs on their people with the requirements in Spartan society for mothers and other relatives to display joy at the death of their loved ones in lost battles and anger at their survival. Therefore, while Europeans practice individualism in terms of economic survival, there are European institutions which control individuals to the point of specifying what to feel. We agree that Homer (Homer means "hostage") lived in the 8th century B.C.

However, I do have some problems with Diop's construct. I believe that nature does not waste anything. I think it is probable that racial differentiation developed before 20,000 B.C. There might be trials of species which ultimately expire because they are unable to adapt to changed environments, but, in the final analysis, the surviving species are suited to their environments. This suitability is true with respect to all aspects of creation, including skin pigmentation. Accordingly, I think that it is much more probable that white people inhabited (got caught in—like the mammoths) a very cold and overcast region. Adam lost pigmentation. Narrow-nosed and hairy people then had survival advantages over wide-nosed, smooth people in Adam's home environment. The offspring of the hairy people became more numerous because that type was more adapted to the cold environment. People who remained black, of course, inhabited a torrid region, and people who came to be brown people (called "yellow" or "red") inhabited a region between the blacks and whites. All of these races were once one black race, with the minor differentiations (acquired mutations) caused by changed environmental conditions that I can only account for with a cataclysmic natural history. There were *no* genetic changes producing different species of Homo sapiens sapiens. Blacks and whites can mate and produce biologically viable offspring. How could there have been a new species produced? By definition, it could not have happened.

SPECIES: the basic category of biological classification, composed of related individuals that resemble one another and can breed among themselves but not with members of another species.

Today's cultural behavior patterns grew out of the original environmental conditions of the races. To have the white and "yellow" races both originating in France within 5,000 years of each other presents several problems. For example:

1.) What were the agents of mutation?
2.) How can one reconcile the origin of white people in western Europe with the many, many legends of western Europeans that they migrated from the east?
3.) How does one reconcile Diop's construct with the geographic pattern of the Altaic Ring? The Altaic Ring *exists*. Should we ignore it?

4.) Were Cro-Magnon Man and Chancelade Man capable of pro-creation with modern man? If not, they are likely to have been dead ends of human development. If so, then where did the "fair-haired Achaeans" come from? How did all of the Mongols get into China—from France?

On the issue of Semites first appearing in 2700 B.C., I also differ with Diop. As presented earlier in this book, the original "Semites" were Afro-Asians of mixed black and Oriental (Altaic) ancestry. They inhabited the border areas between the homeland of black people and "yellow" people. Didn't Menes defeat "Semites" in 3100 B.C.? Were "Semites" not around before that time? Later invasions of Indo-Europeans created today's "Semites," including both Arabs and Jews. Chancellor Williams wondered how the colonies of black people in southern China came to be. The Altaic Ring, cataclysms, "ethnic migrations"...

Diop suggested that the Sahara dried *circa* 7000 B.C. I have accepted Velikovsky's dating of the event as *circa* 1500 B.C. Which is correct? Those who support Diop's dating will have to produce their evidence. Only the date is offered by Diop. To the best of my knowledge, Diop offered no agent for the change, and, in tracing the migration patterns of West Africans, the Sahara is carefully avoided by all groups in Diop's construct.

However, cities have been discovered in the Sahara. Chancellor Williams was "puzzled." As previously discussed, poor farming methods could not have been the agent of change.

...It was likewise observed that on the drawings [in the Sahara] discovered by Barth the cattle wore discs between their horns, just as the Egyptian drawings. Also, the Egyptian god Set was found pictured on the rocks. And there are rock paintings of war chariots drawn by horses "in an area where these animals could not survive two days without extraordinary precautions."*...

* P. LeCler, *Sahara* (1954), p. 46

Immanuel Velikovsky, *Earth in Upheaval,*
Pocket Books, New York, 1977, p. 87.
Originally published in 1955.

How did the referenced drawings, which were apparently contemporary to Egyptian civilization, manage to get in the Sahara? Why would anybody build a city in a desert? How and when did horses disappear from Africa (and the Americas)? When and how did horses reappear? How did white people come to be known as "Caucasians?"

Was Random House wrong in identifying east central Europe as the homeland of Indo-Europeans? How did the Black Sea get its name? I believe that the construct offered in this book offers a credible explanation for all of these issues. Give these issues some thought, brothers and sisters. Show me something.

> ...In the second book of his history, Herodotus relates his conversations with Egyptian priests...The priests asserted that within historical ages and since Egypt became a kingdom, "four times in this period (so they told me) the sun rose contrary to his wont; twice he rose where he now sets, and twice he set where he now rises."*...
>
> *Herodotus, *Bk. ii,* 142 (trans. A.D. Godley, 1921).
>
>> Immanuel Velikovsky, *Worlds in Collision,*
>> Pocket Books, New York, 1977, p. 118.
>> Originally published in 1950.

If the construct presented in this book is true, then why isn't it widely known and accepted? There are three primary reasons. First is, of course, the fact that some did not want it known. Recall the difference in the account of "the plague of darkness" in the Judeo-Christian *Bible* (for public consumption) and the account from the rabbinical tradition (for private consumption). Recall "the Velikovsky affair."

A second reason for the lack of knowledge and acceptance is offered by the brothers from the past. An Egyptian priest speaking to Solon suggested:

> ..."for many generations the survivors died with no power to express themselves in writing."*...
>
> *J.G. Frazer, "Ancient Stories of a Great Flood," *Journal of the Royal Anthropological Institute,* XLVI (1916).
>
>> Immanuel Velikovsky, *Worlds in Collision,*
>> Pocket Books, New York, 1977, p. 160.
>> Originally published in 1950.

The third reason is, of course, the whole syndrome in Western civilization which promotes soap operas as the standard fare for its children. Once you believe—or stop trying to fight—such nonsense as "Columbus discovered America," you have become "a beast of Atlantis." A slave by any other name...

The Lessons for Today:

The whole point of history is to provide guidance for today. Some, like Henry Kissinger, have a different opinion. Kissinger views history

194

as "the memory of states." In that assertion is the implicit admission that Henry Kissinger's version of history is a tool for control, rather than nourishment, of minds. Kissinger's history is the unfortunate reality in Adam's Empire, however. In view of that fact, Adam's Empire is doomed. There are only two issues about the Empire: (1) Who goes down with Adam? and (2) What comes next?

> ...By the end of the nineteenth century the realism of Judeo-Christian teleology was rapidly running out and was leaving the Western world with a condition presumed to be ideal by Claude-Henri de Saint-Simon: science had replaced religion and all scientific conviction was now sacred and absolute. The culmination of this Positivist ethos, at least in regard to the human condition, was what anthropologist Marvin Harris (1977) has very aptly called the "biologization of history." Science has elaborated upon the logical extremes of race in order to produce an "objective" racism...

> Jamake Highwater, *The Primal Mind,* New American Library, New York, 1981, p. 32.

The corrupted history results in Gulfs of Tonkin. It enables Adam to try to tell the people in Nicaragua what kind of government they can have. The U.S. can support "democracy" in Central America, and support the most blatantly anti-democratic government in the world in South Africa. It enables Adam to attempt to tell Iranians what kinds of weapons they can have on their own soil. "The memory of states" creates Ollie Norths, who can talk about the "democratic resistance" in Central America, and—in the same "testimony"—describe those forces as always outnumbered in their encounters with the Sandinistas. How does the little colonel define "democracy?" What should be made of a nation that thinks that Ollie is a hero? They are people who live "lives of quiet desperation," much too timid to think and brave enough to die—"O men of little faith."

In Chapters 5 and 6, the river of history was traced down to the present time. The *same* cultural patterns of behavior can be seen today that were exhibited 6,000 years ago. Diop and others have pointed out that there is nothing new in the essentials of Western culture. Following is an excerpt from an article, "A Nigerian Looks at America," by T. Obinkaram Echewa, that I think summarizes the developments, or lack of same:

> ...In temperament, America is young and hyperactive, unwilling and unable to ponder deeply or at length. Americans apprehend rather than comprehend ideas. They do not have the discipline or the endurance to wrap their minds around a thought. Instead they prefer to grab, snatch or make a stab at it.

Their mental energies are usually exerted as pulses rather than as continuously flowing force...

Living successfully in modern America no matter how or where one chooses to live, can be like trying to hail a cab in Times Square after the theater on a rainy Saturday night. It demands more than a little Philistinism. The "American way of life" is not founded on the interplay of human virtues supporting and encouraging one another, but rather on competing human appetites keeping one another in check...

Newsweek, 7/5/82, p. 13.

The preceding excerpt from Mr. Echewa's article is a pretty good summary of the situation. Adam still does not have a workable philosophy with which to apply his many rules. He still judges "prey or predator" quickly. The hypocrisy, frequently offered as "history" or "religion," has prevented rather than encouraged Adam from developing a workable philosophy such as described in the following quotation:

...."The Sudanese are not volatile as a people. They don't see individuals of other racial and ethnic groups as abstractions, they see them only as people."...

Alexander Horan, U.S. Ambassador to the Sudan, 1986.

Implicit in Ambassador Horan's observation is that *SOMEBODY* must view "individuals of other racial and ethnic groups as abstractions." *SOMEBODY* must not view people as people. *SOMBODY* must be "volatile." If these things were not implicit, why would Horan cite the opposite tendencies as characteristics of the Sudanese? Who could somebody be?

Of course, it is Adam, "the chosen," "the master,"..."the rude and barbarous." The most learned in Adam's family, "diplomats" and doctors of philosophy, still view people as "little brown people" and "aborigines." That racism is certainly going to cause more problems than it already has caused, but it is not the ultimate problem for Adam. Given an instantaneous "extirpation" of all the races in the world except Adam's family, Adam's first task in the new world (after rewriting the history books, of course) would be to decide: "WHO WILL BE THE NEXT NIGGERS?"

That assertion is not speculative. There are many historical precedents. Irishmen were and are niggers to the English. The peasants of Europe, in general, were left to starve for centuries while European royalty lived high on the hog: "Let them eat cake!" We also have several historical precedents which suggest that Adam would develop a new religion in an all vanilla world. Some of Adam's family would, no doubt, be cursed by God according to this "new" religion.

Adam's mindset is still that of a carnivorous "beast of prey." His philosophy is bankrupt. The philosophy was engendered by Adam's original environment. It is maintained by the Faustian (conscious) trade of his soul for gold. (Columbus was unabashed about his absent soul, wasn't he?) Adam has defined himself by his possessions, and he will shortly be without possessions or soul. The rape, murder and enslavement of people around the world has been proclaimed as "The Triumph of the West." But the devil will have his due.

People trained, that is diseducated, in schools that tout "Manifest Destiny" will, no doubt, say that even the events cited in this book never happened—just like Hitler's holocaust "never happened," according to some people. However, as Orwell pointed out, "Whatever was true now was true from everlasting to everlasting." Denials do not change the historical reality. One does not honor one's father and mother by lying about them. One only dooms one's children by such a course.

Many readers will reject the cataclysmic cause of the initial migrations of Europeans that has been identified here. No problem. Present your evidence. But can you really believe in "religious" stories about "the Creation," "the Deluge," "plagues" and a "commotion," and divorce those stories from the secular historical record?

> ...As concerning the fighting by the persea tree near him in Annu [a city just southeast of the Nile delta, called Heliopolis by the Greeks and On in Biblical references], [with] the children of impotent revolt, it is done when there is justice for what they have done. Now concerning that night of battle, [when] they enter it is into the eastern part of the sky, there straightaway taketh place a battle in heaven [and] on the earth to its whole extent...
>
> *The Egyptian Book of the Dead,* plate X.

Remember what Orwell wrote about the truth? There cannot be *two* historical realities that lead to the instant present. Either the Red Sea parted, or it didn't. But if it did part, then it had to have happened at a point in time which can be related to contemporaneous natural and social history.

I happen to believe that the cataclysms happened. I think the reader can view a great deal of evidence by reading Velikovsky's works. Here are three tidbits from other sources to ponder:

> ...The greatest part of [Arab] Chronologers agree, he which built the Pyramids was Saurid Ibn Salhouk, King of Egypt, who lived three hundred years before the flood. The occasion of this was because he saw in his sleep, that the whole earth was turned over, with the inhabitants of it, the men lying upon their faces, and the stars falling down...
>
> > John Greaves, Professor of Astronomy at Oxford, *Pyramidographia,* 1646, quoted in *The Pyramids and the Sphinx* by Desmond Stewart, Newsweek Book Division, New York, 1971, p. 156.

> ...His Majesty does these works to last a million years, and his Majesty knows that they will dwell beneath the earth...
>
> > Inscription on some epic statues ordered by Ramses II.

> ...The scientists report in today's issue of Science magazine that in eight widely separated places around the world they have found some of the bits of rock flung out by the impact [of a large comet or asteroid thought to have hit the earth 65 million years ago ending the Age of Reptiles] and that the rock grains show the fracturing effects of having sustained a cataclysmic impact...
>
> The discovery lends significant support to a controversial theory advanced in 1980 by the father-son team of Walter and Luis Alvarez of the University of California at Berkeley that blamed the mass extinctions on a meteorite.
>
> The Alvarezes examined the layer of sediment that formed at the end of the Cretaceous period, just when the mass extinctions occurred, and found that it was unusually high in the element iridium—rare in earthly minerals, but far more abundant in meteorites and other extraterrestial objects.
>
> The Alvarezes speculated that the iridium-rich layer could have formed only if a large asteroid or comet hit the Earth with enough force to vaporize the object, sending its iridium into the atmosphere, eventually to settle as sediment...
>
> In the years since the Alvarezes' theory was propounded, the same iridium-rich layer has been found at many places around the world, in exactly the right stratum. But critics of the theory also have emerged, pointing out that lesser iridium-rich layers can be found above and below...
>
> > *The Washington Post,* 5/8/87, p. A16.

Well, sports fans, we've been talking about four (or five) of those "lesser iridium-rich layers above" the layer that saw all the dinosaurs bite the dust. Why do those layers argue *against* a cataclysmic natural history? How did His Majesty "know?" Still not convinced?

...In reporting his results, [University of Michigan researcher, Wesley] Brown suggested that perhaps the human species had "passed through a severe population constriction ('bottleneck') relatively recently."...Brown also wrote that there were other population dynamic processes that might produce this pattern, but the caveat fell to the editor's pen and never saw the printed page. As a result the bottleneck idea became the focus of considerable discussion, reverberations of which linger on...

Science, Vol. 238, 10/2/87, p. 25.

"A severe population constriction relatively recently?" In one form or another, "the Velikovsky affair" continues. The cataclysmic natural history will, nevertheless, be beyond the credibility thresholds of some readers. But so too will the history of accomplishments by "the children of the sun." In view of Western "education" and the sorry circumstances in which the descendants of "the children of the sun" find ourselves today, that is understandable. However, if you can look at the Sphinx and not see a black man, then you need your eyes examined. If you can look at King Tut's deathmask, which was on the cover of many national magazines during the recent tour of his relics, and not see a black man, well, brothers and sisters, you have become blind in a way that is much more serious than physical blindness.

Europeans who have had contact with Africans seem to sense the real deal, even if their "educations" prevent them from making two plus two equal four:

...Africans may not be "primitive" but were, until recently, in a state of degeneration from a former high culture...

E.G. Parrinder, *African Traditional Religion,* Hutchinson's University Library, London, 2nd revised edition 1962, p. 19.

We sons and daughters of Ham(bone) must prepare for the coming catastrophe in Adam's Empire. We cannot prepare using Adam's myths or anybody's myths. Many of the sons and daughters of Shem and Japheth seem bent on trying "to grab what they can grab before the bottom falls out." *"Dat's DEY biznezz!"*

Sacred Cows:

In this book, I have touched a lot of sacred cows. Some say that you shouldn't do that. I disagree. You do that, if you want beef. Some of Adam's "religious" myths have been examined. So? Anybody's assertion that I am less favored by the Most High God will certainly get examined. Remember the wisdom from James Baldwin: "At the center of the European horror is their religion." Remember the lesson of the historical record: There is no such thing as a "moderate abolitionist." *"If my course was wholly different, if I distilled nectar from my lips and discoursed sweet music,"* what could be expected but continuation of the downward spiral in socioeconomic conditions in black America?

I come from a long line of lions. I have millions of brothers and sisters whose mothers did not raise us to be slaves. Our God made us each the equal of every other person; different, but equal. If others choose to ignore that simple truth, they have to walk blind in their ignorance. We *have to* move on. A pox on any god who would will us to be slaves—and on the horse that that god rode in on. I make no apologies for touching Adam's sacred cows. Nor do I apologize for not admiring Adam's Empire. Given a real choice, most in Adam's family would not choose European "civilization" either. Jamake Highwater, a Native American, made the same observation:

> ...That Zuni [Native American tribe] parable reminds me of another fiction, *Through the Looking Glass* by Lewis Carroll, one of the first books to help me understand that my alienation was both precious and interchangeable with the experience of children of the dominant culture...
>
> "What—is—this?" the Unicorn asked.
>
> "This is a child!" Haigha replied eagerly, coming in front of Alice to introduce her.
>
> "I always thought they were fabulous monsters!" said the Unicorn. "Is it alive?"
>
> "It can talk," said Haigha solemnly.
>
> "The Unicorn looked dreamily at Alice, and said: "Talk, child."
>
> Alice said: "Do you know, I always thought Unicorns were fabulous monsters, too. I never saw one alive before!"
>
> "Well now that we *have* seen each other," said the Unicorn, "if you'll believe in me, I'll believe in you. Is that a bargain?"...
>
> Jamake Highwater, *The Primal Mind,* New
> American Library, New York, 1981, p. 211.

> ...Hector St. Jean Crevecoeur, the Frenchman who lived in America for almost twenty years, told, in *Letters from an American Farmer,* how children captured during the Seven Years' War and found by their parents, grown up and living with the Indians, would refuse to leave their new families. "There must be in their social bond," he said, "something singularly captivating,

and far superior to anything to be boasted among us; for thousands of Europeans are Indians, and we have no examples of even one of the Aborigines having from choice become Europeans."...

Howard Zinn, *A People's History of the United States,* Perennial Library, New York, 1980, p. 54.

If Mr. Zinn's book became the standard history textbook in American high schools, the United States would be well on the road to a beautiful future. The reality is unfortunately that the United States at this time has a President who reportedly believes in a purifying nuclear war possibly during his term—to fulfill biblical prophecy. His actions certainly support the macabre reports, and James Baldwin was ever so correct about "the center of the European horror." Unless the dangerously fuzzy thinking of the Prez and his ilk is corrected, the times must get much worse before things can possibly get any better. Far too many of us have severely malignant philosophies.

Who voted for this man, this interpreter of prophecies? Adam? "The children of the sun?" Let the record show (and I hope there is somebody to read it) that the descendants of "the children of the sun" did not vote for the man. It was Adam's children, searching for truth in "heroes." Truth is not in such "heroes" or the Empire's history books. One has to dig very deep to find truth in Adam's *Bibles.* Adam's children who lived with the Indians evidently found truth. It is time for us in black America to move on. I must repeat myself: *The cultural norms of 6,000 years ago still exist today. "The Lord is* [still] *a man of war."*

Step one in our continuing trek could be to examine the assertions presented in this book. The presentation has been deliberately abbreviated. This was done to enhance readablity. My concern is that the pattern of the events be offered for examination by others. However, there are many references given in this book for your use. Read them. Peel the onion, think and "judge for yourselves what is right." "Accept whatever is useful, and throw away the rest."

I hope that, at a minimum, all readers of this book have learned that there are alternative possibilities to the accepted dogma on history. I hope also that readers understand that this book is not directed at any person or group of people. If *any* person starts with false premises, that person must necessarily end, in the final analysis, with false policy. Therefore, it is necessary for us to begin with true premises about ourselves and others. We must acknowledge the historical realities in order to have "a light over our shoulders." If that light is obscured by lies, all suffer. Call the Most High God what you will, the essence of God is truth. Without God's grace, which is real but neither "amazing" or "mysterious," we all face inquisitions, wars and rumors of war:

> ...There had been Amu in the midst of the Delta and in Hauar [Auaris], and the foreign hordes of their number had destroyed the ancient works; they reigned ignorant of the god Ra.*...
>
> *Petrie, *History of Egypt*, II, 19
>
>> Quoted in *Ages in Chaos* by Immanuel Velikovsky, Doubleday & Co., Inc., Garden City, New York, 1952, p. 65.
>
> ...This is the sacred god, the lord of all the gods, Amen-Ra, the lord of the throne of the world who liveth by right and truth, the first ennead which gave birth unto the other two enneads, the being in whom every god existeth, the One of One, the creator of the things which came into being when the earth took form in the beginning, whose births are hidden, whose forms are manifold, and whose growth cannot be known. The sacred Form, beloved, terrible and mighty in his two risings (?) [sic]...
>
>> An extract from a papyrus written for Princess Nesi-Khonsu (XVIII dynasty) quoted in *The Egyptian Book of the Dead -(The Papyrus of Ani),* Translation and Transliteration by E. A. Wallis Budge, Dover Publications, Inc., New York, 1967, p. xcv. Originally published in 1895.

The sacred "form" is the sun. But how can the sun be "beloved, terrible and mighty in his TWO risings???" Could the "enneads" referenced above possibly represent world ages? So that we don't "reign ignorant of the God," please: *FIND THE ERRORS!* If you would dismiss my assertions in their entirety, logic dictates that you must have in hand a credible chronology of the alleged 400-year period of oppressed Hebrews in Egypt. If you have such a chronology, let the world see it. If you don't have such a chronology, maybe you should rethink your position about rejecting my assertions in their entirety.

Peace.

SELECTED BIBLIOGRAPHY

This bibliography is by no means comprehensive. It is intended to point the reader to key sources of information, most of which have additional bibliographies. Asterisks (*) indicate works directly quoted in *Adam, The Altaic Ring & "The Children of the Sun."*

Books:

Allegro, John M.; *The Chosen People,* Doubleday & Co., Inc., Garden City, New York, 1972.*

The American Heritage Dictionary of the English Language, William Morris, Editor, American Heritage Publishing Co., Inc. and Houghton Mifflin Co., Boston, 1975.

Baldwin, James; *The Evidence of Things Not Seen,* Holt, Rinehart and Winston, New York, 1985.*

Ben-Jochannan, Yosef; *The Black Man of The Nile And His Family,* Alkebu-Lan Books, New York, 1972.

The Judeo-Christian Bible, various versions.*

Bradley, Michael; *The Black Discovery of America,* Personal Library, Toronto, 1981.*

Calvocoressi, Peter and Wint, Guy; *Total War,* Ballantine Books, New York, 1973, Vol. 1.*

Cookson, John and Nottingham, Judith; *The Survey of Chemical and Biological Warfare,* Monthly Review Press, New York, 1969.

Darwin, Charles; *The Origin of Species By Means of Natural Selection or the Preservation of Favored Races in the Struggle for Life,* New American Library, New York, 1958, originally published in 1859.

Davidson, Basil; *A History of Western Africa to the Nineteenth Century,* Anchor Books, New York, 1966.

Davidson, Basil; *The Lost Cities of Africa,* Rev. Ed., Little, Brown & Co., Boston, 1970.

Davis, George and Watson, Glegg; *Black Life in Corporate America,* Anchor Press, New York, 1982.*

Diop, Cheikh Anta; *The African Origin of Civilization,* Lawrence Hill & Co., Westport, Connecticut, 1974.

Diop, Cheikh Anta; *Precolonial Black Africa,* Lawrence Hill & Company, Westport, Connecticut, 1987.*

W.E.B. Du Bois Speaks, edited by Philip S. Foner, Pathfinder Press, New York, 1970.*

The Egyptian Book of the Dead—(The Papyrus of Ani), Translation and Transliteration by E.A. Wallis Budge, Dover Publications, Inc., New York, 1967. Originally published in 1895.*

Fanon, Frantz; *The Wretched of the Earth*, trans. Constance Farrington, Grove Press, New York, 1965.

Funk & Wagnall's New Encyclopedia, Funk & Wagnall's, Inc., New York, 1979, Vol. 2.*

Funk & Wagnall's New Encyclopedia, Funk & Wagnall's, Inc., New York, 1979, Vol. 11.*

Funk & Wagnall's New Encyclopedia, Funk & Wagnall's, Inc., New York, 1979, Vol. 12.*

Funk & Wagnall's New Encyclopedia, Funk & Wagnall's, Inc., New York, 1979, Vol. 13.*

Funk & Wagnall's New Encyclopedia, Funk & Wagnall's, Inc., New York, 1979, Vol. 22.*

Goodspeed, D.J.; *The German Wars 1914-1945,* Bonanza Books, 1985 Edition of the original published by Houghton Mifflin Company, Boston, 1977.*

Gross, Stanley J.; *Of Foxes and Hen Houses,* Quorum Books, Westport, Connecticut, 1984.

Gunther, John; *Inside Africa,* Harper & Brothers, New York, 1955.*

Hargreaves, John D.; *West Africa: The Former French States,* Prentice-Hall, Inc., Englewood Cliffs, N.J., 1967.*

Harris, Joseph E.; *Africans and Their History,* New American Library, New York, 1972.*

Higginbotham, A. Leon; *In the Matter of Color—Race & The American Legal Process: The Colonial Period,* Oxford University Press, New York, 1978.

Highwater, Jamake; *The Primal Mind—Vision and Reality in Indian America,* New American Library, New York, 1981.*

Hoffman, Michael A.; *Egypt Before the Pharoahs,* Alfred A. Knopf, New York, 1979.

Jackson, George; *Soledad Brother,* Coward, McCann & Geohegan, New York, 1971.

Jantzen, Steven; *Hooray For Peace, Hurrah For War: A History of World War I,* A Borzoi Book, New York, 1971.*

Kelly, Tom; *The Imperial Post,* William Morrow and Company, Inc., New York, 1983.*

Kenyatta, Jomo; *Facing Mt. Kenya,* Vintage Books, New York, 1962.*

Kochman, Thomas; *Black and White—Styles in Conflict,* University of Chicago Press, Chicago, 1981.

Kwitny, Jonathan; *Endless Enemies: The Making of an Unfriendly World,* Congden & Weed, New York, 1984.

Lasky, Victor; *Jimmy Carter: The Man & The Myth,* Richard Marek Publishers, Inc., New York, 1979.*

Mamdami, Mahmood; *Imperialism and Fascism in Uganda,* African World Press, Trenton, N.J., 1984.*

Meyer, Marvin W.; *The Secret Teachings of Jesus,* Vintage Books, New York, 1986.

Mysteries of the Ancient World, Special Publications Division, National Geographic Society, Washington, D.C., 1979.

Orwell, George; *1984,* New American Library, New York; Originally published in 1949.*

Parrinder, E.G.; *African Traditional Religion,* Hutchinson's University Library, London, 1st edition 1954, 2nd revised edition 1962.*

The People's Press Puerto Rico Project, *PUERTO RICO—The Flame of Resistance,* The People's Press, San Francisco, 1977.*

The Random House College Dictionary, Revised Edition, Jess Stein: Editor-in-Chief, Random House, Inc., New York, 1982.*

Sagan, Carl; *Broca's Brain,* Ballantine Books, New York, 1980.

Stewart, Desmond; *The Pyramids and the Sphinx,* Newsweek Book Division, New York, 1971.*

Terkel, Studs; *"The Good War"—An Oral History of World War Two,* Pantheon Books, New York, 1984.*

Terry, Wallace; *Bloods, An Oral History Of The Vietnam War By Black Veterans,* Random House, Inc., New York, 1984.*

Velikovsky, Immanuel; *Ages in Chaos,* Doubleday & Co., Inc., New York, 1952.*

Velikovsky, Immanuel; *Oedipus and Ahknaton,* Pocket Books, New York, 1960.*

Velikovsky, Immanuel; *Earth in Upheaval,* Pocket Books, New York, 1977, originally published in 1955.*

Velikovsky, Immanuel; *Worlds in Collision,* Pocket Books, New York, 1977, originally published in 1950.*

Velikovsky Reconsidered, The Editors of Pensée, Doubleday & Co., Inc., Garden City, New York, 1976.

Wallechinsky, David and Wallace, Irving; *The People's Almanac,* Doubleday & Co., Inc., New York, 1975.*

Wallechinsky, David and Wallace, Irving; *The People's Almanac #2,* Bantam Books, Inc., New York, 1978.*

Wallechinsky, David; Wallace, Irving; Wallace, Amy and Wallace, Sylvia; *The Book of Lists #2,* Bantam Books, Inc., New York, 1980.*

Weston, George M.; *The Progress of Slavery in the United States,* published by the author, Washington, 1857.*

Williams, Chancellor; *The Destruction of Black Civilization: Great Issues of a Race from 4500 B.C. to 2000 A.D.,* Third World Press, Chicago, 1976.*

Wilson, Ian; *Jesus: The Evidence,* Harper & Row, New York, 1984.*

X, Malcolm; *The Autobiography of Malcolm X,* as told to Alex Haley, Ballantine Books, New York, 1973.

Yette, Samuel F.; *The Choice: The Issue of Black Survival in America,* Cottage Books, Silver Spring, Md., 1971.*

Yadin, Yigael; *The Art of Warfare in Biblical Lands,* Volume One, International Publishing Co., Ltd., Jerusalem, 1963.

Zinn, Howard; *A People's History of the United States,* Perennial Library, New York, 1980.*

Reports:

Report of the National Advisory Commission on Civil Disorders (The Kerner Commission), Washington, D.C., U.S.G.P.O., 1968.*

Periodicals:

The City Paper, Washington, D.C.*

Commentary, New York.*

The Daily Princetonian, Princeton, N.J.*

Newsweek, New York.*

The New York Times, New York.*

Playboy, Chicago.*

Science, Washington, D.C.*

Time, New York.*

U.S. News & World Report, Washington, D.C.*

The Wall Street Journal, Princeton, N.J.*

The Washington Post, Washington, D.C.*

INDEX

210